The Brain
and the Mind

Grange BOOKS

This edition published in 2005 by Grange Books
an imprint of Grange Books Plc
The Grange
Kingsnorth Industrial Estate
Hoo, Near Rochester
Kent ME3 9ND
www.Grangebooks.co.uk

ISBN: 1-84013-802-5

Printed in China

Editorial and design:
The Brown Reference Group plc
8 Chapel Place
Rivington Street
London
EC2A 3DQ
UK
www.brownreference.com

FOR THE BROWN REFERENCE GROUP PLC
Editors: Windsor Chorlton, Karen Frazer, Leon Gray,
Simon Hall, Marcus Hardy, Jim Martin, Shirin Patel,
Frank Ritter, Henry Russell, Gillian Sutton, Susan Watt
Indexer: Kay Ollerenshaw
Picture Researcher: Helen Simm
Illustrators: Darren Awuah, Dax Fullbrook, Mark Walker
Designers: Reg Cox, Mike Leaman, Sarah Williams
Design Manager: Lynne Ross
Managing Editor: Bridget Giles
Production Director: Alastair Gourlay
Editorial Director: Lindsey Lowe

CONTRIBUTORS

Consultant:
Arvid Kappas, PhD
Senior Lecturer,
Department of Psychology,
University of Hull, UK

Authors:
Guy R. Lefrançois, PhD
Honorary Professor, Department
of Educational Psychology,
University of Alberta, Canada
Perception

Guido H. E. Gendolla, PhD
Senior Lecturer, Department of Psychology,
University of Erlangen, Germany
Emotion and Motivation

Ian Hocking, PhD
School of Psychology,
University of Exeter, UK
Artificial Minds

Vincent Reid
Developmental Neuroscientist,
Center for Brain and Cognitive Development,
School of Psychology, Birkbeck College,
University of London, UK
*History of the Brain &
Biology of the Brain*

Fiona Starr, PhD
Clinical Psychologist,
Insititute of Social Science Research,
University of Middlesex, UK
Consciousness

C. Mark Wessinger, PhD
Assistant Professor,
Department of Psychology,
Gettysburg College, PA
The Mind

Contents

About This Set

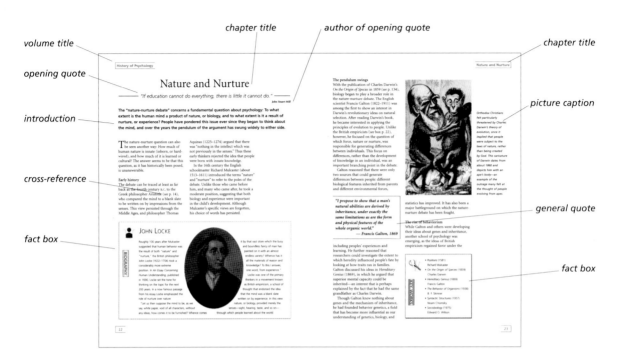

volume title

opening quote

introduction

cross-reference

fact box

chapter title

author of opening quote

chapter title

picture caption

general quote

fact box

These pages explain how to use the *Psychology* encyclopedia. There are six volumes in the set, each one illustrated with color photographs and specially commissioned artworks. Each volume has its own contents list at the beginning and a glossary at the back explaining important terms. More information, such as websites and related reference works, are listed in the Resources section, also found at the back of each volume.

To find articles on a particular subject, look for it in the set index at the back of each volume. Once you have started to read a relevant chapter, cross-references within that chapter and in the connections box at the end of the chapter will guide you to other related pages and chapters elsewhere in the set.

Every chapter has several color-coded fact boxes featuring information related to the subject discussed. They fall into distinct groups, which are described in more detail in the box opposite (p. 5).

The diagram above shows the typical elements found within a chapter in this set. The various types of fact box are explained more fully in the box shown opposite.

THE SIX VOLUMES

History of psychology (Volume One) takes a look at psychology's development throughout history. It starts in ancient Greece when concepts of "mind" existed only as a topic of philosophical debate, looks at the subject's development into a separate field of scientific research, then follows its division into various schools of thought. It also explores the effects of scientific developments, discusses recent approaches, and considers the effects of new research in nonwestern cultures.

The brain and the mind (Volume Two) analyzes the relationship between the mind and the brain and looks at how the brain works in detail. The history of neuroscience is followed by a study of the physiology of the brain and how this relates to functions such as thinking. Chapters tackle the concept of the mind as an intangible and invisible entity, the nature of consciousness, and how our perceptual systems work to interpret the sensations we feel. In a chapter entitled Artificial Minds the volume explores whether or not machines will ever be able to think as humans do.

Thinking and knowing (Volume Three) looks at how the brain processes, stores, and retrieves information. It covers cognitive processes that we share with animals, such as associative learning, and those that are exclusive to people, such as language processing.

Developmental psychology (Volume Four) focuses on changes in psychological development from birth, throughout childhood, and into old age. It covers theories of social and intellectual development, particularly those of Jean Piaget and Lev Vygotsky. It also covers social and emotional development and how they can be improved and nurtured.

Social psychology (Volume Five) studies people as unique individuals and as social animals. It analyzes the notions of personality and intelligence as well as considering how people relate to and communicate with each other and society, and the social groups that they form.

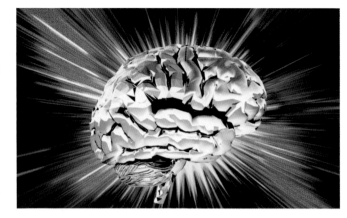

Psychologists using a variety of approaches work in different fields (developmental, social, or abnormal, for example), but all study the brain, trying to figure out how it functions and how it influences people's behavior, thoughts, and emotions.

Abnormal psychology (Volume Six) asks what is abnormality? It shows how the number and types of abnormalities recognized as mental disorders have changed over time and examines specific disorders and their causes. It also looks at diagnosis of disorders and treatments, which can be psychological (talking cures) or physical (drugs and surgery). The social issues associated with abnormality and how society deals with people who have mental disorders are also explored.

KEY DATES
Lists some of the important events in the history of the topic discussed.

KEY POINTS
Summarizes some of the key points made in the chapter.

KEY TERMS
Provides concise definitions of terms that appear in the chapter.

KEY WORKS
Lists key books and papers published by researchers in the field.

FOCUS ON
Takes a closer look at either a related topic or an aspect of the topic discussed.

EXPERIMENT
Takes a closer look at experimental work carried out by researchers in the field.

CASE STUDY
Discusses in-depth studies of particular individuals carried out by researchers.

BIOGRAPHY
Provides historical information about key figures mentioned in the chapter.

PSYCHOLOGY & SOCIETY
Takes a look at the interesting effects within society of the psychological theories discussed.

CONNECTIONS
Lists other chapters in the set containing information related to the topic discussed.

The History of the Brain

—————— *"The brain is an organ of minor importance."* ——————

Aristotle

Historical records suggest that ancient civilizations such as the Egyptians, Greeks, and Romans did not recognize the importance of the brain. It was not until the European Renaissance that the brain was examined in detail, and scientists advanced new theories about what it did. Many conflicting and controversial claims were made about the brain in the 19th century. It was only in the latter part of the 20th century that scientists formalized their understanding of how the brain works. This new branch of psychology is called neuropsychology.

When did humankind first become aware of the significance of the brain? All the information we have about prehistoric cultures comes from fossilized human remains and artifacts. More than 100 years ago archaeologists and paleontologists excavated human skulls dating back to the Stone Age. The skulls showed clear indications of primitive surgery—holes drilled in the upper forehead into the frontal lobes of the brain. This evidence was surprising. Up until the discovery surgery was thought to be a relatively modern practice. No one can be sure why these operations, known as trephinations, were done. Some scientists suggest they were attempts to relieve mental disorders. Others believe that trephinations were performed on men who had sustained serious head injuries in battle. Bone fragments forced inside the skull as a result of a heavy blow may have pressed against the brain tissue, causing severe behavioral changes. The only way inside the skull would be to drill a hole through it. Researchers have also noted that prehistoric peoples suffered chronic infestations of dog tapeworm in the brain. Trephination may have been performed to remove the tapeworm larvae, which affected behavior by pressing on the brain. Yet another theory suggests that the operation was an attempt to remove harmful spirits from the body: the holes was bored to let the evil spirits out.

Ancient Egyptians embalm a corpse. They believed this process would keep the person's life-force alive. A death mask (center left) was made of the face, and some internal organs were preserved, but the brain was discarded as it was believed to be of little significance.

Whatever the reason for these early operations, it is clear that many patients survived. More than half of the skulls show signs of healing over several years, although this does not indicate that the surgery cured the mystery conditions. Examples of such skulls have been found throughout the world, from the Americas and Europe to North Africa and Russia.

Egyptian understanding

It is clear from descriptions of existing papyruses that the ancient Egyptians did not understand the significance of the brain. An important ritual in ancient Egyptian culture reflects this fact. When a person died, the ancient Egyptians embalmed the body and preserved certain internal organs in preparation for the

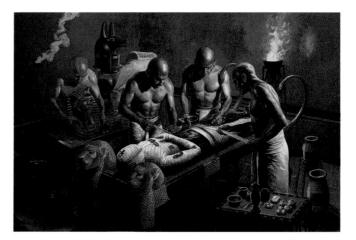

journey into the afterlife. Organs such as the heart and lungs were removed and preserved in jars in the tomb or placed back inside the corpse once it had been prepared for embalming. In ancient Egyptian culture the heart held special significance—this organ embodied memory, thought, and wisdom, as well as emotions such as bravery and love. It is well documented that the embalmers removed the brain through the nose and discarded it, suggesting that the ancient Egyptians did not think it was important.

But the ancient Egyptians did have a limited knowledge of the structure of the brain. The first documented use of the term *neuro* appears in the Edwin Smith Surgical Papyrus, which was found in 1862 in Luxor, Egypt, by the American Egyptologist Edwin Smith. The Surgical

> *"Deafness as well as aphasia are recognized in fractures of the temporal region."*
> (Surgical Papyrus)
> — G. Horax, 1952

Papyrus dates from about 1700 B.C. and was possibly written by the Egyptian physician Imhotep, who had been studying texts dating from 3000 B.C. It contains accounts of 48 surgical cases, some of which include discussion of the structure of the brain as well as a wider description of the central nervous system.

The majority of patients described in the Surgical Papyrus sustained accidents during construction work. There are also some cases in which head wounds appear to have been caused by weapons such as clubs and spears. One case describes a patient with a gaping wound in the head. The surgeon clearly describes the linings, or meninges, that protect the brain. He also describes the cerebrospinal fluid, which protects the delicate brain tissues and spinal cord. It is not clear whether surgeons of the time understood the function of these anatomical features.

KEY POINTS

- Fossil evidence suggests that prehistoric people performed surgery to the skull. The fossilized skulls also show signs of healing over several years, indicating that many people survived these primitive operations.
- The writings of Hippocrates, and later Galen, started the debate on the nature and functions of the brain.
- Advancing from anatomical discoveries of the European Renaissance, Thomas Willis published his *Cerebri Anatome* in 1664. For more than 300 years Willis's work remained a basic text on the brain and spinal cord.
- The 19th-century phrenology of Franz Josef Gall, though itself discredited, suggested that different mental functions might be localized in specific parts of the brain.
- Mapping of functions of the human cortex, such as control of body movements and memory, began in the late 19th century with the work of Eduard Hitzig and John Hughlings Jackson, and later in the 20th century with the work of Wilder Penfield.
- In 1859 Charles Darwin published his theory of evolution in which he suggested that the human brain was the result of a gradual and increasingly successful adaptation to change.
- When the early hominids first stood up and walked on two feet, their hands were freed for manipulation of objects and the eventual use of tools. This opened up vast possibilities for the evolution of the brain.
- People have basic instincts and rudimentary sensory systems in common with many less-intelligent vertebrates. This suggests that all organisms share a common brain ancestry.
- The human cortex is deeply folded. Only apes, dolphins, and whales have similar folding. All these species seem to possess a theory of mind—the understanding that other individuals have different perceptions, likes, and dislikes.
- Some scientists think that the human brain has ceased to evolve, but the increase in the size of newborns' heads over the last 200 years may indicate that this is not the case.

Greek and Roman advances

We have to move forward to the time of ancient Greece and the Roman Empire, over a thousand years later, to find the first true discussion on the nature and functions of the brain. Ancient Greek concepts of the brain depended on the school of thought to which different thinkers belonged. Aristotle (384–322 B.C.), the Greek philosopher, did not mention a role for the brain. Like the ancient Egyptians, he believed the heart to be the seat of all mental processes (*see* Vol. 1, pp. 10–15). Long before

Aristotle was born, however, the Greek physician Hippocrates (c.460–c.377 B.C.), the so-called father of medicine, clearly described the relationship between the brain and epilepsy in his writings.

At the height of the Roman Empire the Greek physician and philosopher Galen (A.D. 129–c.199) produced a vast amount of literature on medicine and medical practices of the time. Observation was the key to Galen's method, and his techniques continue to underlie modern scientific method. Galen's discussion of the function of individual organs was vital in the formation of modern thinking on how internal organs relate to each other and are positioned in the body. Galen was also interested in the brain, theorizing that its function was related to the sense of smell. While he was correct in making this single association, Galen's theory illustrates how extremely limited the understanding of brain function was at that time. Yet Galen's legacy had a profound effect on later historical periods. Indeed, Galen's mixture of medicine and philosophy remained a primary text for medical practitioners until the early 19th century.

The head is the soul

The Maori colonized the islands that make up New Zealand from about A.D. 850 and established a flourishing civilization throughout the country. The Maoris preserved the heads of their enemies by drying them. Their aim was to emphasize tattoo marks and facial

A Maori warrior's head from the Pacific islands of New Zealand. The Maori clearly understood that the head was vital to the functioning of the body, as the retaining of only the head and the discarding of the rest of the body illustrates.

features. Some of the preserved heads, known as *mokomokai,* were used for trade. While the Maoris did not attach special significance to the brain itself, this form of headhunting does indicate that the head was very important.

The Middle Ages

The Middle Ages were an era of bloody conflict. Many surgeons developed their skill on the battlefield—the so-called "school of surgery." Although warfare presented a vast array of different injuries, there was relatively little advancement of the concepts of the ancient Greeks and Romans until the start of the Renaissance.

The Renaissance

The Renaissance was a time in European history that began in Italy at about the start of the 15th century. It was a period of intense intellectual questioning in all areas of scientific thought. Physicians applied new techniques to the healing arts, and the brain did not escape close examination. The Italian Leonardo da Vinci (1452–1519), for example, created wax casts of the four ventricles (cavities containing cerebrospinal fluid) in the brain to determine their volume and to monitor changes in the brain after death.

Despite da Vinci's examinations, it was not until 1543, with the publication of the book *On the Workings of the Human Body* by the Belgian anatomist Andreas Vesalius (1514–1564), that Galen's concepts of the brain were challenged. Vesalius had been a follower of Galen's ideas. He lectured on Galen's laws to his students at Padua, Italy,

THE HISTORY OF NEUROANATOMICAL DIRECTIONS

During the Renaissance many different schools of anatomy in England, France, Germany, and Italy were involved in a period of intense research. Each country thought that the language used in relation to anatomical structures should be its own—Italians wanted Italian names for their discoveries, while the English, French, and Germans also wanted to use their own languages.

In 1585 the school of the Italian physician Costanzo Varolio (1543–1575) suggested that locations within the nervous system should be described in terms of their relation to the spinal cord. This system of naming parts of the nervous system was dubbed "neuroanatomical directions." Varolio asserted that all the different parts of the nervous system should be assigned Latin names, not the language of the person who discovered them, and that they be consistent with other medical texts, which were usually written in Latin. Varolio thought that new discoveries should be named by the physician who made the discovery, and that the same person should be the first to define the anatomical structure.

Since there were not enough cadavers (human corpses) for students to examine, many dissections were performed on other vertebrates. So the terminology of neuroanatomical directions evolved to apply to all vertebrates—from mammals and amphibians to birds, reptiles, and fish. Eventually a consensus formed on the terminology to be used for neuroanatomical directions. A vertebrate's front end, with the nose or beak, was called the anterior, or rostral, location. The tail end of the vertebrate was termed the posterior, or caudal, part. The back was referred to as the dorsal surface, while the front and chest were called the ventral surface. The top of the head was the superior surface, while the bottom of the head was the inferior surface.

Throughout the 16th and 17th centuries, building on the work of Varolio, many anatomists concentrated on studying the brain as a separate organ. The different schools of anatomy soon realized that different parts of the brain itself also had to be named consistently. More neuroanatomical directions were soon needed for this particular organ. The school of the English physician Thomas Willis (1621–1675) coined the definitions of medial, meaning closer to the midline, and lateral, meaning away from the midline, to describe the area near the longitudinal fissure—the dividing line between the hemispheres, or halves, of the brain.

The same neuroanatomical directions are still used to denote specific locations in the nervous system. It was only when the terms were accepted by all the rival schools that each could build on the others' research.

---

performing dissections for his pupils. The dissections culminated in four anatomical charts that would influence the study of anatomy for more than 200 years after his death. Through his studies Vesalius began to question Galen's established ideas. He went on to suggest that Galen had in fact dissected apes rather than humans to arrive at his conclusions on human anatomy all those centuries ago.

Renaissance achievements

Vesalius's revolutionary approaches to the study of the brain inspired many scientists to produce new, fascinating, and unexpected results. In 1573 the Italian physician Costanzo Varolio (1543–1575) became the first person to dissect the brain in its entirety, starting at the brain stem. (The brain stem contains nerve fibers connecting the two hemispheres of the cerebrum to the spinal cord and controls subconscious activities such as breathing, the sleep/wakefulness cycle, and heart rate.) In 1583 the German physician Felix Platter (1536–1614) dissected the human eye and realized that the eye only gathered light, dispelling the assumption that it also interpreted the information. Three years later the Italian physician Arcangelo Piccolomini (1525–1586) distinguished between two types of matter in the brain—the gray cortex and white matter. In 1587 the Italian physician Giulio Cesare Aranzi (1530–1589) clarified the nature of the brain's ventricles and identified the hippocampus deep within the brain.

Other scientific breakthroughs combined with these advances in neuroanatomy (the study of the structure of the nervous system). Perhaps most important was the invention of the compound microscope (with two interacting lenses) in 1595 by the Dutch eyeglass-maker Zacharias Janssen (1580–1638). Janssen's microscope was capable of magnifying images up to ten times. Although a simple device, Janssen's microscope triggered the development of more complex instruments that would eventually be able to focus on the microscopic world of the cell.

Mind and matter

In 1623 the Italian scientist Galileo Galilei (1564–1642) proposed that science should only be concerned with "primary qualities"—those of the external world that could be measured or weighed. Galileo suggested that "secondary qualities," such as emotion, meaning, and value, did not fall into the realms of science. The French philosopher René Descartes (1596–1650) supported Galileo's idea and went further by naming the primary quality "matter" (relating to physical substance) and the secondary quality "mind" (relating to thinking substance). Throughout most of the 17th century this distinction meant that scientists concentrated their studies on the brain as a physical quantity. The formal science of neuroanatomy was born.

Systematic anatomy

Neuroanatomy owes more to Thomas Willis (1621–1675) than to any other person. Born in England, Willis intended to become a minister for the

Zacharias Janssen's compound microscope. At the time of its discovery scientists did not realize that the brain is made up of millions of tiny cells. Janssen's microscope eventually would lead to the development of extremely powerful instruments capable of viewing the microscopic world.

Anglican church and started to study for a degree in theology at Christ's College, Oxford. Willis abandoned his studies, although not his faith, at the beginning of the English Civil War (1642–1645). He embarked on a degree in medicine and served as a physician in the army of King Charles I. Battlefield injuries and numerous fatalities provided Willis many opportunities to observe at first hand the human body in great detail.

The culmination of Willis's observations was the celebrated book *Cerebri Anatome* (*Anatomy of the Brain*), which he published in 1664. Still a basic text on the anatomy of the central nervous system (brain and spinal cord), the book embraced the concept of blood circulation that the English physician William Harvey (1578–1657) had published in 1628. One of his legacies is that a part of the brain—a collection of arteries at the base of the brain called the circle of Willis (*see* diagram at right)—still bears his name. Willis understood that the circle was the interconnection of the major vessels supplying blood to the brain. Willis was the first person to use the phrase "reflex action" when referring to an involuntary response to a stimulus. Amazingly, he also challenged Galileo and Descartes's theory of mind and matter by suggesting that cognitive functions, such as memory and vision, were located in specific places in the brain. But Willis's main ambition was to prove to a skeptical medical profession that pharmacology (the study of drugs) could be based on anatomical observations. He only partially succeeded, but his contribution to neuroanatomy is nevertheless extraordinary.

Phrenology

The German physician Franz Joseph Gall (1758–1828) was also a proponent of Willis's idea that specific regions of brain tissue direct specific activities. Gall provoked controversy when he suggested that a person's abilities could be defined by measuring the contours of his or her head. He believed that bumps on the head

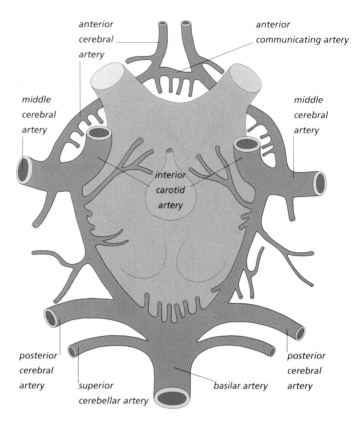

could be "read" to reveal the structure of the underlying cortex—the outer layer of the brain. Gall published the so-called "science" of phrenology in 1808. He compiled "evidence" for his claims by suggesting that heads of prison convicts were enlarged in certain areas, linking the bumps with immoral or deviant behavior. All the while, Gall drew up complex maps of the skull and sought endorsement from the medical and scientific communities. While many condemned Gall's work, his ideas became popular, and phrenology was practiced for more than 100 years (*see* Vol. 1, pp. 30–39).

The brain and behavior

Phrenology would have been dismissed rather more quickly had it not been for the stimulating effect it had on the debate about localization of brain functions. As knowledge of the relationship between the brain and behavior increased,

The circle of Willis—a collection of arteries at the base of the brain—was described by Thomas Willis in 1664. Scientists and the medical profession still call this area the circle of Willis in recognition of Thomas Willis's remarkable achievements in the field of neuroscience.

Labels in diagram: anterior cerebral artery; anterior communicating artery; middle cerebral artery; middle cerebral artery; interior carotid artery; posterior cerebral artery; posterior cerebral artery; superior cerebellar artery; basilar artery researchers tried to link everything from emotional states to personality with specific areas in the brain.

A major advance in the study of the physical workings of the brain came in 1791. The Italian scientist Luigi Galvani (1737–1798) showed that electricity existed within living things. Galvani demonstrated muscular contractions in frogs' legs by using electrical currents. From his observations Galvani asserted that nerve cells in the brain acted as a control center for the movement using electrical current. Unfortunately, Galvani did not have the technology at hand to measure the tiny electrical currents involved—they were later measured in 1850 by the German physiologist Emil Du Bois-Reymond (1818–1896).

The German physiologist Eduard Hitzig (1838–1907) was the first person to attempt stimulation of a living brain with an electrical current. In 1860 he was a field surgeon in a military hospital, which gave him access to many patients who had had parts of their brains exposed by severe head injuries. He discovered that a small amount of current applied to the occipital lobes at the back of the head made his patients' eyes move to the left or the right. In 1870 Hitzig and his colleague Gustav Fritsch (1839–1927) stimulated the brains of live dogs and found that an electric current applied to the surface of the cortex made the dogs move specific body parts. They concluded that only specific parts of the brain could control specific movements of the body.

Neuroscience did not always require experimentation of that type. Simply observing people's behavior could lead to great discoveries about the organization of the human brain. The British neurologist John Hughlings Jackson (1835–1911)

AN OBSESSION WITH THE BRAIN

FOCUS ON

The German-born mathematician and physicist Albert Einstein (1879–1955) bequeathed his brain to science. After his death researchers measured his brain in every possible way—from its weight to the relative size of specific parts—to measure his genius and to analyze the relationship between brain features and intelligence. Some startling claims were made, for example, that a large pair of temporal lobes reveals a high intelligence.

While Einstein was unquestionably an intelligent man, he was not talented in every respect. For example, he was known to have a poor sense of direction. So what could be made of his brain? Probably very little because brain anatomy, while related to general intelligence, is not the same as general intelligence. The measurements of Einstein's brain revealed next to nothing about his intelligence and personality. If he were still alive, modern technology, such as fMRI (see Vol. 1, pp. 96–103) could tell us much about how his brain worked. Researchers still publish papers about Einstein's brain, but it is clear to neuroscientists that without a precise understanding of how brain areas function and connect, anatomical knowledge is of limited use in understanding how the brain works.

Albert Einstein's brain has evoked endless debate as neuroscientists have tried to link brain dimensions with intelligence. Neuroscience has been much more successful than anatomy in discovering how the brain works.

noticed that the epileptic seizures of his wife followed a set pattern. The seizure would begin in one of her hands, move to the wrist, shoulder, and then to her face. Finally, it would affect the leg on the same side of her body as the affected hand. Then the seizure would stop. Jackson came to believe that the seizures were caused by electric discharges in the brain. Further, the discharges started at one location within the brain and radiated outward, affecting other parts of the brain as they went. That suggested to Jackson that the brain is divided into parts, with each part related to a part of the body. Since the pattern of his wife's seizures never changed, Jackson theorized that the brain must be organized in a set pattern. These assumptions, formulated in 1865, were all correct. It would take another 75 years before the scientific investigation of the Canadian neurologist Wilder Graves Penfield (1891–1976) would prove them to be so.

Popular disquiet

While scientists such as Hitzig and Fritsch believed that artificial stimulation of the human brain yielded valuable information about neuroanatomy that was otherwise unobtainable, society as a whole has long been uncomfortable with unraveling the the secrets of the brain.

In the novel *Frankenstein, or the Modern Prometheus,* published in 1818 by the English novelist Mary Wollstonecraft Shelley (1797–1851), the scientist Dr. Frankenstein creates a creature from the head and body parts recovered from dead people, bringing it to life with an electric current. Scientists in the 19th century believed reanimation of dead tissue to be a possibility, and Shelley referred to some of the most advanced concepts in medicine when creating her story. The story expressed Shelley's fears that scientific inquiry could destroy the essence of human personality and individuality, and that science was progressing too quickly for important ethical counterbalances to be discussed. Nevertheless, the quest for

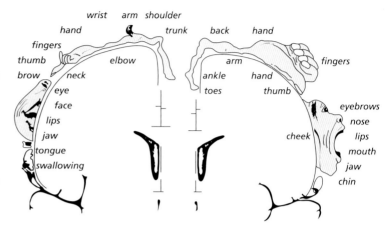

new knowledge meant that research of this kind continued unabated throughout the 19th and 20th centuries.

Mapping the cortex

Building on the avalanche of scientific research concerning the organization of the brain, Wilder Graves Penfield made several discoveries about the nature of the cortex (the outer layer of the brain) in the 1950s. Penfield treated patients with severe epilepsy, and many reported that they felt a strange "aura" before having a seizure. Penfield was aware of John Hughlings Jackson's work and realized that the feeling could be related to the exact areas in which the epilepsy originated. He thought that if he could find that part of the patient's brain, then he could remove or destroy it and stop the epilepsy.

Penfield's map shows the specific areas of the brain that are involved with the body's sense of touch. The areas of the body are enlarged in proportion to the amount of touch-related information that they convey to the brain.

> *"The human brain is not a previously programmed calculator. It is a living, growing, changing organ."*
> *— Wilder Penfield, 1959*

Penfield anesthetized his patients but kept them conscious while he opened their skulls and attempted to find the origin of their epilepsy. Unexpectedly, stimulation of specific parts of the cortex led to specific associations for the patients. For example, if Penfield stimulated areas in the temporal lobes, he could provoke the memories of his patients. These memories were clearer than those recalled by usual means or were of events that had been forgotten. If Penfield stimulated the same area at different times, the same memory would be evoked. Penfield had discovered a physical basis for memory.

Possibly the most important legacy Penfield left for neuroscience was his detailed map of the parts of the cortex that are involved with the body's sense of touch (*see* diagram p. 13). Penfield located the areas of nerves within the cortex that are activated by touch sensations in the skin of different parts of the body. Much more touch-related information is received from the face, lips, hands, and fingers than from other parts of the body. That is due to the presence of much higher concentrations of sensory receptors in the skin of these particular body parts. Areas such as the arms, torso, and legs have relatively few receptors. Penfield found that dense concentrations of receptors were connected to relatively large areas of cortex, while body areas

with fewer receptors were served by smaller areas of cortex. He represented his findings by a drawing in which the size of each body part is determined by the density of receptors and the amount of cortex devoted to it. The face and hands are thus vastly out of proportion to the abdomen and limbs. Penfield discovered that everyone's control centers for touch in the cortex are in the same place.

Evolution and the brain

Many philosophers and scientists have tried to understand why the human brain, in particular, has developed skills that far outstrip the brains of all other species while having so much in common with the behaviors of other animals. When the English naturalist Charles Darwin (1809–1882) published his famous work *On the Origin of Species* in 1859, he presented the world with new and convincing answers to these questions.

The heart of Darwin's theory is that all living things evolved from a few common ancestors by a mechanism called natural selection. According to this theory, some

WHEN LOBOTOMIES WERE COMMONPLACE

FOCUS ON

At one time many patients underwent lobotomies—operations in which connections between the frontal lobes and the rest of the brain are severed. Widely used in the 1940s and 1950s, lobotomies are now performed only as a last resort in the treatment of severe, chronic depression. In the 1940s surgeons claimed a high success rate for prefrontal lobotomy operations in reducing aggressive behavior in violent patients. With the introduction of therapeutic drugs in the late 1950s, however, this practice was largely abandoned. It is now accepted that patients never recovered normal mental capacity, some died prematurely, and most are now in psychiatric care. Another popular technique at that time

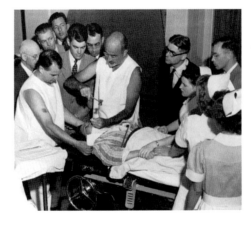

Neurologist Dr. Walter Freeman performs a lobotomy in 1949. This operation involves inserting an instrument like an ice pick under the eyelid of the patient to cut connections in the front part of the brain.

was electroconvulsive therapy (ECT), in which an electric current is applied to the brain. Again, the introduction of drug therapy has mainly replaced the use of ECT.

in response to environmental factors, such as radiation, which alter the DNA in genes. They can also occur when DNA is replicated during cell division.

Most mutations produce unfavorable characteristics, but some help organisms adapt better to their environment. Natural selection sorts out the good from the bad to ensure that beneficial mutations are passed on to subsequent generations.

Human evolution

How does Darwin's theory fit in with the evolution of human beings? Scientists studying the human fossil record, called anthropologists, believe that humans share a common ancestor with apes such as chimpanzees and gorillas. To support this theory, anthropologists point out that the fossilized remains of ancient humanlike beings and apes reveal many similarities.

The ancestors of modern humans probably began evolving separately from the ancestors of apes between 10 million and 5 million years ago. This period marks the beginning of the development of the hominids—a group consisting of modern people and early humanlike ancestors. Most anthropologists agree that environmental change was a very important factor in initiating the course of human evolution.

The oldest known hominids—the australopithecines, or australopiths for short—first appeared in Africa around 4 million years ago and died out somewhere between 2 million and 1 million years ago. The fossilized remains of australopith skulls suggest that the surface area of the cortex was large, although the brain was only one-third the size of our own.

The next step in human evolution came around 2.4 million years ago, again only in Africa, with the appearance of hominids from the genus *Homo*. The link between the australopiths and the earliest example, *Homo habilis,* has yet to be discovered, but fossil evidence indicates that *Homo habilis* had a larger brain and cortex surface area than the australopiths. They were the first hominids to make and use tools.

organisms are better able to adapt to their environment and overcome pressures such as starvation, predation, and disease. These individuals are more likely to live longer and leave a greater number of offspring than other members of their species. The parents pass on the advantage to their offspring, and so the proportion of better-adapted individuals increases from one generation to the next.

Darwin supported his theory with evidence from many scientific fields, through personal observations of living species, and through examination of fossil remains. But Darwin did not understand how the advantageous traits were passed down through the generations. This gap was filled by the Austrian monk Gregor Mendel who, in 1865, proposed that traits are inherited on pairs of special molecules of inheritance—later called genes. The rediscovery of Mendel's work in 1900 led to the current understanding of the mechanisms and principles of genetics.

The genetic factor

One of the most important features of Darwinian evolution is the role of mutation. Mutations produce random variations in the genetic makeup of an organism. They often occur when sperm and egg combine to form an embryo during fertilization. Mutations also occur

The Galápagos Islands, where Charles Darwin observed and collected specimens of birds and tortoises that resembled species found on nearby continents. The observations he made led to the development of his theory of evolution by natural selection.

Homo erectus appears to have evolved from *Homo habilis* around 1.9 million years ago, again with a slightly larger brain and cortex surface area and an ability to light fires. *Homo erectus* was a successful species. Fossil evidence indicates that *Homo erectus* spread from Africa to colonize Asia and Europe.

Early forms of *Homo sapiens,* the direct ancestor of modern human beings, first appeared about 500,000 years ago. *Homo sapiens* had an even larger brain capacity than *Homo erectus.* The appearance of the Neanderthals (around 200,000 years ago), with a skull almost double the size of *Homo erectus* and similar in capacity to that of modern human beings, has caused much controversy among anthropologists. Some believe that the Neanderthals were in fact the same species as *Homo sapiens*— the ancestors of modern humans. Others suggest that the Neanderthals evolved separately from *Homo sapiens* and died out when groups of *Homo sapiens* spread north from Africa and challenged the Neanderthals for their territories.

Whatever the true identity of our early *Homo sapiens* ancestors, anthropologists can be sure that the first modern humans, *Homo sapiens sapiens,* first appeared around 120,000 years ago. Around 80,000 years later that same species developed Cro-Magnon culture. Tools became more sophisticated, primitive cave artwork appeared, and agriculture set the stage for modern civilization.

Increasing intelligence
It is often easier to think of the evolution of the brain as the gradual development of increasing intelligence. Highly evolved vertebrates, such as humans, have highly evolved brains and are more intelligent than vertebrates like fish, reptiles, and birds. But how do we compare the intelligence of animals that represent different stages in evolution?

Until relatively recently, scientists only concerned themselves with brain size— the volume or weight of the brain—as a measure of intelligence. Of course, there is no relationship, since that would mean an elephant, whose brain weighs nearly five times as much as a human brain, would be five times more intelligent. Scientists then explored intelligence as a measure of brain mass in relation to body mass. The brain-to-body-mass ratios indicated that

---

ARE HEAD TRANSPLANTS POSSIBLE?

FOCUS ON

In the 1950s the Soviet scientist Vladimir Demikhov created several two-headed dogs in which the transplanted head was kept alive by connection to the host's blood circulation. In 1970 the neurosurgeon Robert J. White transplanted the head of a rhesus monkey onto the decapitated body of another individual, after which the monkey regained consciousness, ate, and followed the movements of laboratory staff with its eyes. According to White, doctors already have the knowledge needed to transplant a human head, although he believes that transplantation of the brain alone is much more difficult.

In theory the body of any healthy person who suffers fatal head wounds and is pronounced brain dead could be used for the operation. Many surgeons operate daily on the human neck and have the skill to sever and reconnect the blood vessels of the head and its new body rapidly enough to keep both alive. The surgeons would join the vertebrae (neck bones) of the head and body using metal plates. Drugs would suppress the immune system in a bid to prevent it from rejecting the new body (as has occurred in the case of recent transplants of limbs and hands, as well as organs such as the kidney and liver). But at present there is one major unresolved problem. Once severed, the nerves of the spinal cord do not regrow—even within a single organism. Without an intact spinal cord the head could not control the body.

Even without control of the body, the operation could still prolong the lives of people paralyzed from the neck downward, who often die prematurely. With body control, thanks to some future breakthrough in spinal nerve science, paralyzed people might yet live normally. These possibilities do, however, raise important ethical questions.

small birds were the most intelligent animals, while humans ranked alongside mice as a close second. Again, this relationship does not hold, so the scientists reexamined their thinking. As they gained a better understanding of the structure of the brain, scientists noted fairly marked anatomical differences between different organisms. It soon became clear that these differences provided some measure of the intelligence of the organism.

Brain anatomy and intelligence

The area of the brain known as the brain stem appears to have changed very little from early in the evolutionary development of all mammals. The brain stems of the rat and the cat, for example, are very similar to the human brain stem. Even reptiles, which developed much earlier than mammals, have a similar brain stem, with the same major nerve pathways. Brain-stem activities are crucial for survival. They include the regulation of breathing, heartbeat, and blood-sugar levels. These activities are considered to be reflex, or subconscious, actions.

Paul MacLean (pp. 103–104) suggested that the human brain was not simply one brain, but three brains that had evolved in succession, one atop the other, during the course of evolution. At the base is the hindbrain, or "reptile brain," so-called

A Neanderthal skull. The brain size of a Neanderthal was about the same as the size of a modern human relative to his or her body mass. Whether Neanderthals form the evolutionary link between Homo erectus *and modern humans is still a matter of controversy.*

because it contains all the structures needed for a reptile to survive. The reptile brain consists of a small clump of cells atop the spine, to which the cerebellum—a clump of brain cells that control movement—is attached.

Around the reptile brain is the second-level brain—the forebrain or "old-mammalian brain." The forebrain contains structures that are developed in mammals but not very well developed in reptiles. Collectively known as the limbic system, these structures—the thalamus, amygdala, hippocampus, and hypothalamus—increase the range of mammalian behavior but are still largely concerned with basic functions such as reproduction and self-preservation. They also include some emotions. The "new mammalian brain" contains the most recently evolved parts of the mammalian nervous system, including the outer layer of the brain—the cerebral neocortex, or just cortex for short.

The cortex

The cortex is almost entirely exclusive to mammals. While all mammals may have areas of cortex in their brains, there is a great deal of variation between species in how much the cortex is folded into sulci (fissures) and gyri (ridges). A species that has very little or no cortical folding is known as a lissencephalic (meaning "smooth brain") species. Lissencephalic species include rats, mice, and some types

Size does not matter. Larger animals generally have bigger brains than smaller animals, but that does not mean they are more intelligent.

The relative size of the brain in a human, a chimpanzee, a monkey, a cat, a rabbit, a frog, and a bird. Even if it is measured relative to the mass of the animal's body, the size of the brain does not prove to be an accurate way of determining general intelligence. Scientists now think that the degree of folding in the cerebral cortex is a better measure of intelligence.

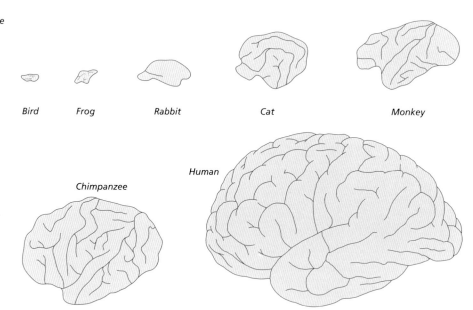

Bird   Frog   Rabbit   Cat   Monkey

Chimpanzee   Human

of monkey. Fissures and ridges greatly increase the total surface area of a cortex. Many scientists now think that a greater degree of folding in a species corresponds to an increased level of intelligence.

Superimposed systems
During the evolution of the human brain new systems developed while old systems were still in use. Consequently the brain possesses more than one system to process information from certain senses. For example, the visual system in the brain consists of the magnocellular and the parvocellular systems. While the parvocellular system analyzes the identities of objects in the visual field, the magnocellular system is more concerned with color, spatial relationships between objects, detection of movement, and other perceptions. The two systems work together to produce sight.

Psychologists believe that the parvocellular system is far older than the magnocellular system—the reptile brain also has a parvocellular system. Where the human brain has two systems that perform the same task, the newer system always completes the task more efficiently than the older one. The old system is used less and less unless the new system suffers an accident, when the old system acts as a backup. In one way this is not a beneficial change because damage to a person's cortex (*see* pp. 20–39) can result in a severe loss in the person's ability to process information. The tendency to move functions to newer structures in the brain is called encephalization.

The end of evolution?
Some scientists now argue that human evolution has reached its pinnacle. Although natural selection ensures that the environment helps shape evolutionary change, modern humans have altered the environment artificially to fulfill, in evolutionary terms, short-term ambitions. Other scientists argue that the future of human evolution depends on the brain developing an increased capacity to store and use knowledge. Scientists support this theory by noting that head sizes of newborn babies have increased over the last 200 years. This bears out the idea that the human brain is continuing to evolve. Indeed, doctors suggest that in 100 years' time women may only be able to give birth by Cesarean section due to the increases in newborn head size.

EXPERIMENT

THE THEORY OF MIND—UNIQUELY HUMAN?

Fossil evidence and DNA analysis suggests that humans and nonhuman primates, such as chimpanzees and gorillas, share a common ancestor. However, many psychologists argue that people are the only species with a theory of mind—human individuals understand that other individuals do not necessarily want or need the same things that they themselves do. Researchers have studied nonhuman primates, dolphins, and even pigeons to assess whether they have a theory of mind, but the results of these studies are inconclusive. Some appear to support the notion that primates do have a theory of mind, while others seem to rule it out completely.

Recent research led by Brian Hare suggests that chimpanzees have at least some degree of a theory of mind. Chimpanzees compete for food, but they are also animals with a hierarchical social structure. So a dominant chimpanzee always eats first, followed by the subordinate members of its group. Hare placed two chimps in two cages separated by a central cage in which he placed food. The subordinate chimpanzee could see all the food, but some of the food was hidden from the dominant chimpanzee. Changing the chimps' sightlines by moving the cages around, Hare discovered that the subordinate chimp would take any food that the dominant chimp could not see, as long as it could not be seen doing it. The subordinate chimp's behavior showed its awareness that the dominant chimp would want the food and indeed had its usual right to it. At the same time, it demonstrated an awareness of the other chimp's mind. Not only did the chimpanzee use its awareness of what the other chimpanzee could do, it also used the information to plan future decisions.

Do chimpanzees have a theory of mind? Recent research indicates that they do. Unlike humans, however, they only possess some features of a theory of mind. These findings enable the researchers to refine their theories about the evolutionary development of the human brain.

Hare's team suggested that theory of mind is a graded phenomenon—while people have a complete theory of mind, primates have it only to a certain degree. What does this finding indicate for the human brain? Chimpanzees are very closely related to humans at an evolutionary level. DNA analysis has also shown that chimpanzees share more than 99 percent of the same genes as people. Researchers are constantly modifying their models of the evolutionary development of the brain to accept or reject the results of research with our evolutionary cousins. Current researchers believe that the complex, high-level ways in which our brains process and use knowledge—by forming intentions, for example—had already evolved before people began to gather in groups and form societies. If so, some of the areas of the brain associated with behaviors that make us uniquely human must be at least 100,000 years old.

CONNECTIONS

Biology of the Brain

— *"The human brain is the most complicated organization of matter we know."* —

Isaac Asimov

The brain is an amazing organ. It holds our memories, dreams, fears, hopes, and every thought we have, both conscious and unconscious. Through the nervous system it controls activities of the body that we are not even aware are happening, as well as those we are aware of. Yet the brain is an organ much like the others that help us function, although far more complex. It can be understood anatomically, its regions named, its parts exposed, and its cells analyzed.

The brain cannot be understood without considering the whole nervous system, of which the brain is but one part—the most important part. All animals, including people, have a nervous system, though complexity varies from one type of animal to the next.

The human nervous system is the most complex of all. It has two major divisions: The first is the central nervous system (CNS), which is made up of the brain and spinal cord. The brain is the control center of the nervous system. It interprets and stores information gathered from the senses and uses it to control the body. The CNS is covered in more detail later in this chapter (*see* pp. 23–29).

PERIPHERAL NERVOUS SYSTEM

The second division of the nervous system is the peripheral nervous system (PNS). The PNS sends information to and receives commands from the CNS. It comprises the spinal and cranial nerves, which connect the CNS to the rest of the body. Almost all of the nerves in the peripheral nervous system are spinal nerves, and they interact with the brain via the spinal cord. The cranial nerves (*see* box p. 21) are an important exception to this rule because they interact directly with the brain. Apart from the vagus nerve, cranial nerves are largely concerned with the head, back, and shoulders. They connect the brain to the eyes, ears, and

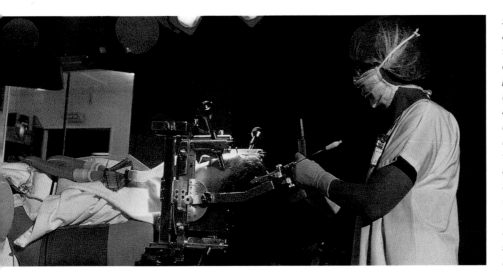

Surgeons operate on a patient suffering from Parkinson's disease. They are placing electrodes inside the skull in an attempt to control and monitor the disease. Modern surgical techniques are based on a well-developed understanding of the brain and how it works, but there is far more that scientists still do not know about the brain.

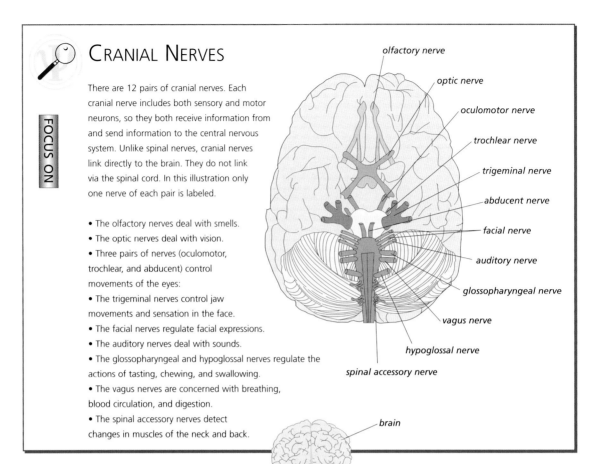

CRANIAL NERVES

There are 12 pairs of cranial nerves. Each cranial nerve includes both sensory and motor neurons, so they both receive information from and send information to the central nervous system. Unlike spinal nerves, cranial nerves link directly to the brain. They do not link via the spinal cord. In this illustration only one nerve of each pair is labeled.

- The olfactory nerves deal with smells.
- The optic nerves deal with vision.
- Three pairs of nerves (oculomotor, trochlear, and abducent) control movements of the eyes:
- The trigeminal nerves control jaw movements and sensation in the face.
- The facial nerves regulate facial expressions.
- The auditory nerves deal with sounds.
- The glossopharyngeal and hypoglossal nerves regulate the actions of tasting, chewing, and swallowing.
- The vagus nerves are concerned with breathing, blood circulation, and digestion.
- The spinal accessory nerves detect changes in muscles of the neck and back.

olfactory nerve
optic nerve
oculomotor nerve
trochlear nerve
trigeminal nerve
abducent nerve
facial nerve
auditory nerve
glossopharyngeal nerve
vagus nerve
hypoglossal nerve
spinal accessory nerve

other parts of the head; spinal nerves connect with the spinal cord and link the CNS to the rest of the body, including the internal organs, skin, and muscles.

Autonomic and somatic systems

The PNS is itself divided into two parts, the autonomic nervous system and the somatic nervous system. The autonomic nervous system controls the automatic (unconscious or involuntary) internal body functions, such as saliva production, widening of pupils in the eyes, breathing, heartbeat, and digestion. The somatic nervous system controls the skeletal muscles, which are attached to the skeleton and govern voluntary (deliberate or conscious) movements of the body.

Two kinds of neurons (nerve cells) send information in both the autonomic and the somatic nervous systems.

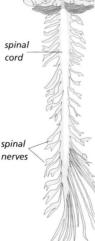

brain

spinal cord

spinal nerves

There are 31 pairs of spinal nerves. They link to the spinal cord through spaces between vertebrae.

Afferent, or sensory, neurons carry information from the internal organs or from receptors in the eyes, ears, nose, tongue, and skin toward the CNS. Efferent, or motor, neurons carry information in the opposite direction, from the CNS to the internal organs in the autonomic system and from the CNS to muscles in the somatic system. Neurons are covered in more detail later in this chapter (*see* pp. 29–35).

Sympathetic and parasympathetic

The autonomic nervous system can be divided into two systems: the sympathetic and parasympathetic systems, both of which conduct nerve impulses from the CNS to the body's internal organs. Their function is to produce a balanced response in the body when sudden changes in energy are needed. If a person has to run,

DIVISIONS OF THE NERVOUS SYSTEM

NERVOUS SYSTEM

- The nervous system is divided into the central nervous system and the peripheral nervous system.

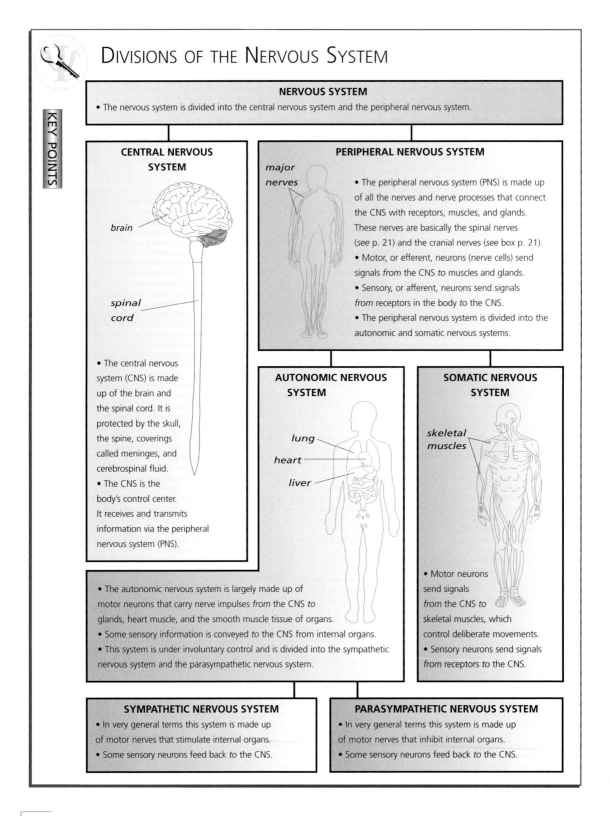

CENTRAL NERVOUS SYSTEM

brain

spinal cord

- The central nervous system (CNS) is made up of the brain and the spinal cord. It is protected by the skull, the spine, coverings called meninges, and cerebrospinal fluid.
- The CNS is the body's control center. It receives and transmits information via the peripheral nervous system (PNS).

PERIPHERAL NERVOUS SYSTEM

major nerves

- The peripheral nervous system (PNS) is made up of all the nerves and nerve processes that connect the CNS with receptors, muscles, and glands. These nerves are basically the spinal nerves (see p. 21) and the cranial nerves (see box p. 21).
- Motor, or efferent, neurons (nerve cells) send signals from the CNS to muscles and glands.
- Sensory, or afferent, neurons send signals from receptors in the body to the CNS.
- The peripheral nervous system is divided into the autonomic and somatic nervous systems.

AUTONOMIC NERVOUS SYSTEM

lung

heart

liver

- The autonomic nervous system is largely made up of motor neurons that carry nerve impulses from the CNS to glands, heart muscle, and the smooth muscle tissue of organs.
- Some sensory information is conveyed to the CNS from internal organs.
- This system is under involuntary control and is divided into the sympathetic nervous system and the parasympathetic nervous system.

SOMATIC NERVOUS SYSTEM

skeletal muscles

- Motor neurons send signals from the CNS to skeletal muscles, which control deliberate movements.
- Sensory neurons send signals from receptors to the CNS.

SYMPATHETIC NERVOUS SYSTEM

- In very general terms this system is made up of motor nerves that stimulate internal organs.
- Some sensory neurons feed back to the CNS.

PARASYMPATHETIC NERVOUS SYSTEM

- In very general terms this system is made up of motor nerves that inhibit internal organs.
- Some sensory neurons feed back to the CNS.

the heart and lungs are stimulated, and the activity of the digestive system is reduced. To achieve this, there is some feedback of sensory information via afferent nerves, but these two systems are largely efferent.

Together the sympathetic and parasympathetic nerves control how much energy each organ in the body should have and when each should have it. Levels of nerve activity in each of the two systems and the interaction between them decide the outcome for each organ. In very general terms sympathetic nerves stimulate activity, while parasympathetic nerves reduce activity. The sympathetic system causes the organs of the body to expend more energy; the parasympathetic system causes them to conserve energy. The fight-or-flight response (*see* pp. 86–109), a reaction that occurs when someone is frightened, is a function of the sympathetic nervous system.

CENTRAL NERVOUS SYSTEM

The spinal cord is a length of nerve tissue about 18 inches (45cm) long that runs from the hindbrain (*see* p. 25) to the pelvis (hipbone); it is protected by the vertebrae (interconnecting bones) of the spine, or backbone. A cross section of the spinal cord shows an **H**-shaped gray mass surrounded by white tissue. The gray matter contains a high density of nerve cell bodies that connect directly to neurons joining the spinal cord from elsewhere in the body. The white matter consists of neurons that send information up and down the spinal cord.

A layer of myelin, a fatty substance, covers the white matter and gives it its distinctive color. During the early development of a human fetus the bones of the spine grow around the spinal cord and protect the delicate nerve tissue in a thick bone shell. Violent accidents such as car crashes can break the protective bone and sever the spinal cord. When that occurs, the parts of the body below the damage have no way of communicating with the brain and are immediately

paralyzed. The cut nerve cells of a severed spinal cord cannot knit back together, so the paralysis is complete and, sadly, permanent.

The meninges

The spinal cord and the brain are protected by three membranes, or linings, called meninges. The outer membrane is a hard-wearing and tough covering called the dura mater, which is Latin for "hard mother." Some people have suffered damage to their skull that has left the dura mater intact; amazingly, they have suffered no trauma to the brain. Inside the dura mater is the arachnoid mater, so named because it resembles a spiderweb. The membrane has a spongy consistency and protects the brain in the same way as a fender protects a car from impact. Below the arachnoid membrane is an area termed the subarachnoid space, which houses blood vessels. Sticking to the surface of the nervous tissues of the brain

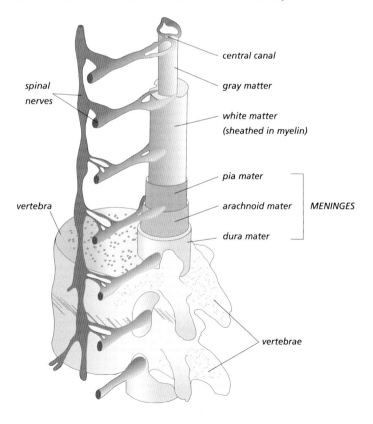

A section of the spinal cord, showing the cord itself (white and gray matter), surrounded by the three linings, or meninges, and contained within the bones, or vertebrae, of the spinal column. Spinal nerves link the cord to the rest of the body.

central canal

gray matter

white matter (sheathed in myelin)

spinal nerves

pia mater

arachnoid mater

dura mater

MENINGES

vertebra

vertebrae

skull

dura mater

venous sinus

arachnoid mater

brain

pia mater

MENINGES

cerebellum

vertebrae

central canal

spinal cord

Left: Diagram of a skull and brain sliced in half, showing the ventricles (chambers). Cerebrospinal fluid is produced by the linings (1) of all the ventricles. The fluid flows from the lateral ventricles (2) to the third (3) and fourth (4) ventricles. From the fourth ventricle the fluid flows up the rear of the brain (5) along the subarachnoid space. Fluid flows down the spinal cord along the central canal and the rear subarachnoid space (6). The fluid flows up the front of the spinal cord (7). After circulating, the fluid is reabsorbed into the blood via projections of the arachnoid mater (8) that connect to a blood vessel called the venous sinus.

and spinal cord is the delicate pia mater, which means "pious mother" in Latin. This layer provides a cushion against damage.

Cerebrospinal fluid

The brain and spinal cord are also protected by a liquid called cerebrospinal fluid. This crystal-clear fluid fills the subarachnoid space of the brain and spinal cord, and the hollow core, or central canal, of the spinal cord, So, both spinal cord and brain are virtually suspended in this fluid. This cushions them from impacts caused by movements of the body.

Cerebrospinal fluid is produced in four interconnecting chambers, called ventricles, inside the brain (*see* above). The fluid flows through the two lateral ventricles and the third ventricle, which lies in the cerebrum, and into the fourth ventricle, which is located in the brain stem. From there it moves both upward into the subarachnoid space and downward into the central canal and outer sheath of the spinal cord. Finally, the fluid drains into the jugular veins in the neck. If the flow of cerebrospinal fluid is blocked, the fluid builds up and makes the ventricles in the brain expand. That causes a disorder called hydrocephalus,

which means "water-headed." To remedy the condition, surgeons insert a mechanical shunt into a ventricle. The shunt drains in one direction only and allows the excess fluid to flow out.

BRAIN DIVISIONS

The brain has three distinct regions: the hindbrain, the midbrain, and the forebrain. Anatomists divide them into five parts, each of which owes its existence to an evolutionary advance from other animals. Each division has its own function, and each is vital for everyday functioning.

Hindbrain 1: the myelencephalon

The region of the hindbrain called the myelencephalon is also known as the medulla, short for medulla oblongata (*see* artwork right). The myelencephalon transmits information from other parts of the brain to the spinal cord, from where it travels to the rest of the body. Within the myelencephalon, and the pons (*see* top artwork, p. 25), too, is a structure named the reticular formation, so called because of its netlike appearance (*reticulum* means "small net" in Latin). The reticular formation is heavily involved in almost all of our autonomic nervous system activities, including our sleeping and respiratory (breathing) reflexes.

myelencephalon

Above: The myelencephalon (or medulla; a part of the hindbrain) houses the parts of the reticular formation that lie outside the pons.

However, it also has a role in cognitive (information-processing) activities such as the focusing of attention and the direction of movement.

Hindbrain 2: the metencephalon

The metencephalon (*see* artwork top right) is the second half of the hindbrain. It is divided into two main parts: the pons and the cerebellum.

The pons is a bulge on the surface of the brain stem that houses that part of the reticular formation not contained in the myelencephalon, or medulla (*see* page 24). Some cranial nerves exit the pons.

The cerebellum The second part of the metencephalon is the cerebellum, which means "small brain." It is a large structure at the back of the brain stem. Its appearance, a bit like that of a cauliflower or broccoli, clearly distinguishes it from the rest of the brain. Its main function is related to motor activity (muscle control), and it is vital to the sensorimotor system—the interaction of sense receptors and muscular responses. People with damaged cerebellums suffer from a lack of orientation and balance, and may have difficulty in understanding how their body relates to the space that it occupies.

Midbrain: the mesencephalon

Unlike the hindbrain and the forebrain, the midbrain, or mesencephalon (*see* artwork center right), has no divisions. It is covered by a layer of tissue called the tectum. On the roof of the midbrain the tectum forms two pairs of lumps called the inferior colliculi and the superior colliculi. The inferior colliculi are involved in processing information from the ears, while the superior colliculi are involved in processing information from the eyes. The midbrain also contains the cerebral aqueduct, which connects the third and the fourth ventricles. The cerebral aqueduct is surrounded by the periaqueductal gray, which has a pain-reducing role similar to that of opiate drugs. Also within the

cerebellum
pons

Above: The metencephalon (part of the hindbrain) is made of the pons and the cerebellum.

mesencephalon

Above: Along with the myelencephalon (medulla) and pons, the mesencephalon forms the brain stem.

thalamus

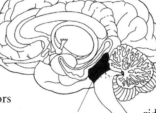

Above: The forebrain includes the thalamus and the hypothalamus. The latter lies below the former on the floor of the third ventricle.

midbrain are areas called the substantia nigra and the red nucleus, which are vital to the sensorimotor system.

Forebrain 1: The diencephalon

The diencephalon and the telencephalon are the two parts of the forebrain. The diencephalon (*see* artwork bottom left) includes the thalamus and the hypothalamus.

The thalamus sits on the top of the brain stem and is shaped into two lobes, each of which rests on a side of the third ventricle. The two lobes are connected by the massa intermedia, a band of gray tissue that crosses the third ventricle. Some people do not have a massa intermedia, but scientists think that the brains of these people have adapted to compensate. The ability of the brain to adapt in such ways is termed neural plasticity.

The thalamus is often regarded as a relay station between the senses and the cortex. The cortex is the outer layer of the brain and has many ridges and grooves, more correctly called gyri and sulci. The thalamus processes raw data and sends the information to the correct areas of the cortex. Information from the eyes is processed by the lateral geniculate nuclei, while the medial geniculate nuclei work on information from the ears. The ventral geniculate nuclei deal with information sent from all parts of body by nerve receptors of the somatosensory system. Further projections from the thalamus connect with other areas of the brain, some of them unrelated to sensory processing.

The hypothalamus is a much smaller structure than the thalamus. It plays a vital part in many behaviors and activities of the body, including emotional states, and influences some of them by controlling the release of hormones from the pituitary gland, which is directly connected to the hypothalamus. The pituitary gland is sometimes called the master gland because its function is to compel other glands to release hormones. The pituitary gland is very important for sexual functions; among other things, it triggers the menstrual period in women.

The optic chiasm is an important part of the diencephalon. It is where optic nerves (from the eyes) join together. From the optic chiasm the nerves run into the brain as the optic tract. The optic chiasm forms an **X** since some nerves cross from each of the eyes to parts of the brain on the opposite side of the head. The left visual field (range of vision) from both eyes is sent to the right side of the brain, while information from the right visual field is sent to the left side of the brain. Other structures of note in the diencephalon are the two mamilliary bodies—they are parts of the hypothalamus responsible for some actions of the pituitary gland.

telencephalon

Left: The most important part of the forebrain is the telencephalon, which is made up of the two cerebral hemispheres and the cortex.

much information is received, processed, and stored, and where voluntary movements are initiated. Functions such as learning, memory, language comprehension, and problem solving are all housed in the telencephalon. The most complex anatomical structures in the human body reside in the telencephalon.

CEREBRAL CORTEX

The cortex is a wrinkly layer of tissue that covers the outside of the cerebral hemispheres. The wrinkles increase the amount of cortex that can fit within the skull. The large wrinkles are known as fissures, while smaller wrinkles, or grooves, are referred to as sulci. Gyri are the ridges between the wrinkles. Fissures appear in all human brains in the same places, but there is much variation between people in the size and shape of their sulci. The longitudinal fissure divides the two hemispheres of the brain. Bundles of nerve cells called commissures provide the only means of communication between the hemispheres; the largest commissure is the corpus callosum. Each hemisphere has a lateral fissure, and the central fissure increases the size of the cortex. The precentral gyrus (*see* p. 27) contains detailed information on the layout of the body and is related to motor (muscle-activating) activities. The postcentral gyrus (*see* p. 27) is largely related to the body's sensory receptor system. Anatomists use the fissures to define the four main lobes of each cerebral hemisphere. They are, in order from the closest to the face to the farthest back, the frontal lobe, the temporal lobe, the parietal lobe, and the occipital lobe.

Right: The two hemispheres of the human brain are cross-wired in many ways. This diagram shows how optic nerves cross to form the X-shaped optic chiasm. The corpus callosum is a thick bundle of nerve tissue that links the two hemispheres.

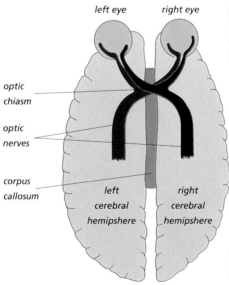

left eye   right eye

optic chiasm

optic nerves

corpus callosum

left cerebral hemisphere   right cerebral hemisphere

 Nerves that collect data from the right field of vision.

 Nerves that collect data from the left field of vision.

Forebrain 2: The telencephalon
The telencephalon (*see* artwork top) makes up the largest part of the human brain. It includes the two cerebral hemispheres and their outer layer, or cortex. It is the area of the brain where

The frontal lobes

The two frontal lobes lie just behind the face, end at the central sulcus, and include the precentral gyrus. In evolutionary terms the frontal lobes are the most recent addition to the human brain and contain areas involved in people's most complex cognitive functions and behaviors. Damage to the frontal lobes produces "executive function disorders" in which the person cannot plan actions, becomes distracted, and can lose the ability to restrain impulses, a condition known as disinhibition. One important part of the left frontal lobe, termed Broca's area, is related to the production of speech.

The parietal lobes

A parietal lobe lies between the central sulcus and the occipital lobe of each cerebral hemisphere. The postcentral gyrus is located in the parietal lobe. The parietal lobes process spatial information in advanced ways, such as the creation of mental images and the recognition of people's faces.

The parietal lobes also have some relationship with the proprioceptive system, which senses movement in the body's tissues. Damage to this area can produce a condition known as unilateral neglect, in which a person ignores stimuli from one side of space. Affected people do not attend to things on one side of the body, and they may apply makeup to only one side of the face or comb the hair on only one side of their head.

The occipital lobes

An occipital lobe lies at the rear of each cerebral hemisphere. The main function of the occipital area is to process visual information. The optic nerve ends in this area, and the occipital lobes sort the information it carries into color, shape, and the identity of individual objects. Damage to the occipital area impairs vision, with results varying from blindness to seeing the world as a series of photographs rather than as moving images.

PARTS OF THE BRAIN

KEY POINTS

- The brain can be divided into the forebrain, the hindbrain, and the midbrain.
- **The hindbrain** comprises the myelencephalon (medulla, or medulla oblongata) and the metencephalon.
- The metencephalon is made up of the pons and the cerebellum. The cerebellum coordinates motor activities, allowing smooth and precise movements.
- The reticular formation lies within the pons (of the metencephalon) and the myelencephalon. It is largely concerned with functions of the autonomic nervous system—those activities not under conscious control.
- **The midbrain** is the mesencephalon. It processes information from the ears and eyes, and has a role in pain control.
- **The brain stem** is made of the midbrain and the hindbrain. It is largely responsible for regulating automatic (unconscious) functions, such as heartbeat, respiration, blood pressure, digestion, and some reflex actions.
- **The forebrain** comprises the telencephalon and the diencephalon. The diencephalon has two parts: the thalamus and the hypothalamus.
- The thalamus relays information from the senses to the cortex.
- The hypothalamus has overall control of the body's automatic processes and controls the release of hormones. It is an important part of the limbic system (see pp.102–104).
- The largest part of the brain, the telencephalon, is made up of the cerebral cortex and the cerebral hemispheres—the two halves into which the telencephalon is divided.
- The cerebral cortex, or cortex, is the heavily folded outer layer of the brain. It is responsible for conscious thought, initiates deliberate movements, and interprets information from the senses. The cortex is divided into the frontal, parietal, occipital, and temporal lobes.

precentral gyrus (motor cortex)

postcentral gyrus (sensory cortex)

central sulcus

1

2

3

4

Left: diagram showing the four main lobes of the brain:

1. Frontal lobe
2. Parietal lobe
3. Temporal lobe
4. Occipital lobe

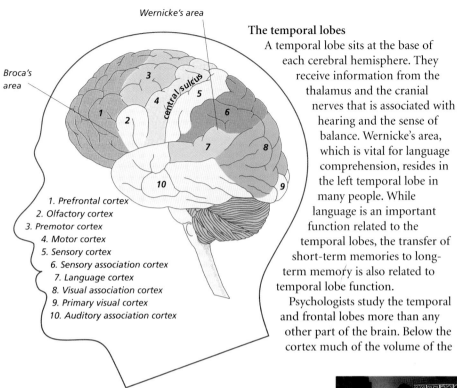

Wernicke's area

Broca's area

central sulcus

1. Prefrontal cortex
2. Olfactory cortex
3. Premotor cortex
4. Motor cortex
5. Sensory cortex
6. Sensory association cortex
7. Language cortex
8. Visual association cortex
9. Primary visual cortex
10. Auditory association cortex

The temporal lobes

A temporal lobe sits at the base of each cerebral hemisphere. They receive information from the thalamus and the cranial nerves that is associated with hearing and the sense of balance. Wernicke's area, which is vital for language comprehension, resides in the left temporal lobe in many people. While language is an important function related to the temporal lobes, the transfer of short-term memories to long-term memory is also related to temporal lobe function.

Psychologists study the temporal and frontal lobes more than any other part of the brain. Below the cortex much of the volume of the

Left: The main functions of different parts of the cortex. The regions labeled 1–4 are part of the frontal lobes. Regions 5 to 8 are parts of the parietal lobes; 9 is the occipital lobe; and 10 is part of the temporal lobe. The motor cortex and the sensory cortex are also known as the precentral gyrus and the postcentral gyrus for their positions on either side of the central sulcus.

Neurosurgeons examining brain scans. Technological advances have enabled doctors to identify more accurately than ever before the exact parts of the brain in which certain functions occur or fail to occur.

BRAIN DAMAGE

FOCUS ON

Much of what we know in modern cognitive neuroscience (the study of how the brain processes information) has come to us from clinical neuropsychology, an area of study concerned with people who have suffered brain damage after severe head injuries or diseases, such as tumors. The damage to the brain, referred to as trauma, may occur only in the area of an injury, or it may affect all the brain, as do the plaques and tangles of nerves caused by Alzheimer's disease (*see* Vol. 6, pp. 20–67).

Some unfortunate accidents have helped neuroscientists understand how the brain works. One of the most famous patients of the 19th century was Phineas Gage, who survived having a rod driven through part of his brain (*see* Vol. 1, pp. 90–95); another example is the case of someone identified only as H. M., who suffered from amnesia after brain surgery for epilepsy (*see* Vol. 1, pp. 96–103).

The role of a clinical neuropsychologist is to assess the brain-damaged person's cognitive (information-processing) capacity, using a variety of nonverbal, literary, and arithmetical tests. The patient's performance is compared

to results from people of the same age and educational level who have no brain damage. If differences are found in specific cognitive skills, such as reading ability, then the neuropsychologist can determine which areas of the brain have been damaged and suggest rehabilitation techniques. Brain-imaging techniques, which have improved dramatically in the last 50 years (*see* box p. 29, and Vol. 1, pp. 96–103) are also used. These techniques, such as fMRI and CT and PET scanning, provide information on brain processes and activity.

LOOKING AT THE LIVING BRAIN

EXPERIMENT

Modern technology has allowed researchers to investigate the brain without having to resort to procedures that require surgery. Neuro- (brain-) imaging techniques vary across three dimensions, with some performing better than others in one dimension but not as well in the others. Each dimension is vitally important to our understanding of how the brain works.

First, researchers get anatomical images of the brain by using computed tomography (CT scanning) and magnetic resonance imaging (MRI). These technologies provide the best images of brain tissues. Second, functional images of the brain demonstrate how the brain is used by specific cognitive processes. The most widely used functional technique is a variation on the MRI system known as functional MRI (fMRI). Another functional technique is positron emission tomography (PET), a technique that shows how cells use glucose (sugar) from the bloodstream. The third type of neuroimaging system provides a very poor anatomical representation of the brain but has a faster resolution than the other systems. It is used to record changes that result from cognitive processes. For example,

electroencephalography (EEG) or magneto-encephalography (MEG) can measure changes every millisecond (see Vol. 1, pp. 96–103); fMRI can measure changes in the brain only every five seconds.

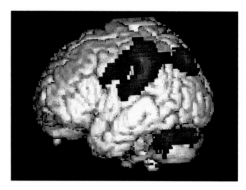

This fMRI image of the brain shows activation of the parietal (top) lobe and cerebellum. The person was engaged in spatial activities at the time of testing; they are governed primarily by the parietal lobes.

---

cerebral hemispheres is taken up by nerve connections between regions of the cortex. This area is loosely termed the limbic system (*see* pp. 104–106). Its function is to motivate and link areas of the diencephalon and the telencephalon. Behaviors such as eating, fighting, escaping, and sexual arousal are all

> *"The highest activities of consciousness have their origins in physical occurrences of the brain."*
> —*Somerset Maugham, 1938*

regulated by the limbic system. The basal ganglia, a part of the limbic system, consist of nerve cells that seem to be related to voluntary motor actions. Parkinson's disease, a brain disorder that is characterized by motor problems such

as rigidity and tremors, appears to be the result of nerve cell damage in areas of the basal ganglia.

CELLS OF THE NERVOUS SYSTEM

There are many different types of cells in the human body. They are all specialized for a specific task, whether that is lining the stomach or communicating with other parts of the body. Cells of the nervous system are also specialized into different types, with each type having its own function. In the human nervous system there are two main types of cells: neurons and glial cells.

Neurons

Neurons (nerve cells) may communicate with each other on an individual basis or as networked collections of millions or billions. Outside the central nervous system (CNS) nerve cells band together to form cablelike nerves that link the brain

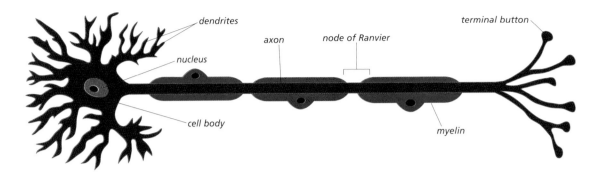

to the rest of the body via the spinal cord. Neurons are classified by function into three main types: motor neurons, sensory neurons, and interneurons.

Motor neurons carry messages from the CNS to muscles and glands. Motor neurons trigger movements, deliberate or otherwise, and other activities such as the release of hormones. A typical neuron of the motor type looks like a tree, with a root system, a trunk, and a system of branches. The "roots" are referred to as dendrites (from the Greek *dendron*, meaning "tree"). At the center of the "root system" lies the soma, or cell body, of the neuron. Inside the soma is the nucleus, which is the cell's control center and is where genetic (inherited) material is stored. Other important components of the soma include the mitochondria, which produce energy for the cell to feed on, and ribosomes, where proteins are synthesized. The "trunk" of the neuron is called the axon, and it can be short or long depending on the type of cell.

The axon is covered by the fatty substance called myelin. The myelin sheath insulates the axon and speeds up the transmission of electricity from one neuron to another. Myelin does not cover all the axon, however. There are tiny gaps between sections of the sheath where there are no myelin cells; these gaps are known as the nodes of Ranvier. The "branches" of the axon are at the opposite end from the dendrites, and each branch ends in a terminal button. The buttons connect with nearby neurons across a

Above: The main parts of a motor neuron. The nucleus is the cell's control center. The axon is the longest extension of the cell body. The axons of thousands of neurons make up the cablelike nerves of the peripheral nervous system. Dendrites are shorter extensions of the cell body. All extensions of a neuron's body, axons and dendrites, are called processes.

Above: The cell body of a neuron, as in most other types of cells, contains miniorgans called organelles. This mitochondrion (plural: mitochondria) is one such organelle. It produces molecules of ATP (adenosine triphosphate), which the cell breaks down to release energy.

junction called the synapse (*see* p. 37), and each root and branch of the neuron is linked via synapses to the dendrites of many other neurons or to other tissues.

Sensory neurons send nerve impulses from the eyes, ears, nose, tongue, and receptors in the body, organs, and skin to the CNS. Individual sensory neurons belong to certain sensory systems and do not report changes detected by other sensory systems. Some can detect only heat, others pressure, for example. Sensory neurons differ from motor neurons in that axons extend away from the cell body in two directions, and their dendrites extend from the end of one axon rather than surround the cell body

Interneurons exist only in the CNS. A single interneuron connects many nerve cells to many other neurons, and often the cells it transmits to are also interneurons. Interneurons often lack an axon, consisting only of a soma with dendrites and terminal buttons.

Cortical neurons The cortex contains two types of neurons that do not exist in other parts of the nervous system. Pyramidal cells are named for the pyramid-shaped cell body. When an electroencephalograph (EEG) is used to record data from the human brain, the electrical activity it detects is probably produced primarily by pyramidal cells. That is because pyramidal cells are oriented in a specific way to the surface of the scalp, where the EEG recording electrodes are placed. Stellate, or star-shaped, cells are the other major form of cell in the cortex.

PAIN TRAVELS A SEPARATE HIGHWAY

Pain has long been a confusing topic for psychologists. The term is ambiguous because it refers to many different sensations, including feelings of extreme heat or cold, fatigue in joints produced by standing in the same position for too long, or the suffering caused by a broken limb. Pain exists only in the brain, a fact illustrated by "phantom" limb pain, in which pain may still be felt from a hand or foot that has been amputated. Pain alerts us to the threat or site of tissue damage, and it varies according to its cause. A sharp pain makes us withdraw instantly from its source, such as a hot pot; throbbing pain reminds us to protect a recent injury; unrelieved, intense pain warns of the life-threatening damage caused by some cancers.

By the 1950s scientists could detect pain-related activity in single neurons as well as in networks of neurons. In 1959 the psychologist Willem Noordenbos suggested a theory to account for the detection of pain-related activity in a neuron. He argued that cells in the central nervous system (CNS) do not communicate with only one other cell but operate in networks. If one cell in a network is aggravated, then the other cells also become slightly aggravated—there is a carryover effect. Noordenbos's theory—in which one pain area produces the sensation over the entire body—subsequently became known as the multisynaptic afferent system.

Researchers Ronald Melzack and Patrick Wall proposed the most commonly accepted theory of pain in 1965.

Called the pain gate control theory, it suggested that there are two types of nerve transmissions in the spinal cord. A "gate" in the spinal cord remains closed when normal nerve impulses are conducted through the spinal cord. But if pain signals act on the CNS in significant amounts, then the gate will open and conduct the pain to other parts of the CNS. Building on Melzack and Wall's ideas, other researchers suggested that if the transmission of normal nerve activity were made to be of a high frequency, then the pain gate could not open to send pain signals to the rest of the CNS. This revelation produced the transcutaneous electrical nerve stimulation (TENS) machine, which is commonly used for pain relief during childbirth. The machine operator places electrodes against the skin of the woman in labor and sends small amounts of electrical current through the electrode. The resulting tingling sensation on the skin can be successful in keeping closed the gates in the spinal cord and blocking the form of nerve stimulation that creates the sensation of pain.

Pain researchers have noted that a person's state of mind can greatly influence his or her perception of pain. If a person is highly involved in an emotional activity (even watching a "horror" movie is adequate), toleration of pain can increase substantially. Engaging in sexual activity can increase a man's pain threshold by more than nine times, suggesting that the pain gate may close spontaneously at certain times.

Glial cells

In addition to neurons the CNS contains glia, or glial cells. Glia comes from the Greek for "sticky glue." Glia support the neurons in their functions, and there are ten times as many glial cells in the CNS as there are neurons. Glia are essential for the formation of myelin sheaths around axons. Glia also clean neurons by flushing out old material, and they take the place of any neurons that die. One of their more important tasks is to supply the neurons with nutrients, and consequently many glial cells interact with nutrient-carrying blood cells. Star-shaped astrocytes are the largest known type of glial cell and may be involved in preventing harmful material from entering the brain via the blood. Radial glia guide neurons during the formation of the brain.

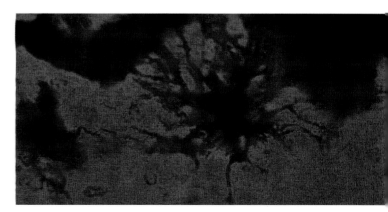

A star-shaped astrocyte, a type of glial cell, in the CNS.

Neuronal layers of the cortex

The cortex has six "laminae," or layers, of cells that have specialized contact with each other. Each layer has different types of cells and interconnections. Scientists have numbered the layers from I (one), which is closest to the surface of the brain, to VI (six), which is the deepest layer. Pyramidal cells occur in layers II (two), III (three), and V (five), while stellate cells occur in layers II to VI.

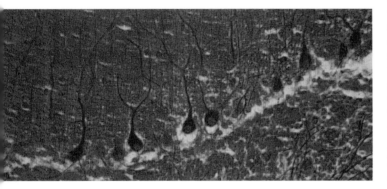

These Purkinje cells are located in the cortex (outer layer) of the cerebellum. They are named for French anatomist Jan Purkinje (1787–1869), who discovered them. Purkinje cells are large neurons with branching extensions.

The interconnections between different layers are still not fully understood, but stellate cells in layer IV (four) appear to process information received from the senses, since layer IV is the one in which projections from the thalamus end. Layer V pyramidal cells send impulses related to muscle activities out of the cortex to the

> *"[The brain is] an enchanted loom where millions of flashing shuttles weave a dissolving pattern, always a meaningful pattern though never an abiding one."*
> —Sir Charles Sherrington, 1906

spinal cord. The thickness of each of the laminae varies depending on the area of the brain they cover. For example, areas of the brain concerned with the senses have a thicker layer IV, while areas concerned with control of muscle and gland activity have a thicker layer V.

THE NERVE IMPULSE

To perform their varied and complex tasks, neurons have to communicate with each other. That involves two processes: electrically, via the nerve impulse (or action potential), and chemically using neurotransmitters.

The synapse (*see* p. 37) is vital to communication between cells; it is the junction at which neurons communicate with each other as well as with muscles and glands. A synapse includes a synaptic cleft, or gap between the communicating cells; it also includes the parts of the cells immediately on either side of the synaptic cleft—for example, the terminal button sending the signal and the part of the dendrite receiving the impulse. The nerve impulse travels from the cell body, down the axon and to the terminal buttons. Once there, it crosses the synaptic cleft using neurotransmitters. Neurotransmitters are covered in more detail later in this chapter (*see* pp. 35–39).

PUMPING AND DIFFUSING

FOCUS ON

Substances such as sodium and potassium ions pass through the cell membrane into the cell in two ways: diffusion and active transportation. Substances diffuse (spread out) within a solution until their concentration is the same in all parts of the solution. During a nerve impulse sodium channels open up in the cell membrane, for instance, and sodium ions quickly rush in to equalize the sodium ion content on both sides of the membrane. Diffusion is called passive transportation since the cell does not provide energy for the transportation of the ions—it simply lets them in and out.

In active transportation the cell takes an active role. The cell moves ions with the aid of small molecular "pumps" powered by tiny chemical power supplies. Active transportation is vital to maintain an unequal distribution of ions in the extracellular and intracellular liquids. Without it diffusion would ultimately result in an even distribution of ions, so no nerve impulses could be generated. One important pump is the sodium-potassium pump, which transports sodium and potassium ions in opposite directions across the cell membrane.

If you put a sugar cube in a cup of coffee, the cube dissolves, and the particles diffuse until the drink is sweet throughout.

Bags of chemicals in solution

All cells, neurons included, are like bags of chemicals in solution (dissolved in fluid). The cell membrane encloses the cell and its contents, and it controls the flow of substances between the outside and the inside of the cell (see box p. 32). The solution inside the membrane is known as intracellular fluid. Outside and between all the cells of the brain is the extracellular space, which is filled with extracellular fluid. Many vital chemicals are dissolved in these fluids. Of most importance are the concentrations of ions of sodium and potassium. Ions are atoms (tiny particles of matter) that have either a positive or a negative electrical charge. Sodium and potassium ions both have positive charges.

Resting potential

When the cell is not activated by a stimulus, the membrane stays in what is called its resting state (or resting potential). In the resting state there is a greater concentration of potassium ions on the inside of the cell than on the outside, and a greater concentration of sodium ions on the outside than the inside. The nerve cell constantly pumps sodium ions (Na^+) out of the cell and potassium ions (K^+) into the cell. Both trickle back (or diffuse; see box p. 32) across the cell membrane, but at different rates. In the resting state potassium ions can diffuse across the cell membrane with more ease than sodium ions. The result is a greater concentration of positive ions on the outside of the cell than on the inside. There are still more potassium ions on the inside than the outside of the cell, but the unequal distribution of positive ions as a whole gives the inside of the cell a very small negative charge.

Action potential

A nerve impulse, or action potential, occurs when a neuron is stimulated to fire by neurotransmitters. Channels in the stimulated section of the membrane open up, and sodium ions flood into the cell. That gives that section of the interior a

In its resting state (1) a neuron has a slight negative charge on the inside of the cell. During a nerve impulse sodium ions (Na+) flood into the cell (2), reversing the polarity (charge). This depolarization, the charge, travels along the cell. Meanwhile, potassium ions flood out of the cell, repolarizing the cell (making the interior negative again) (3).

sudden positive charge. This is called depolarization since the charge (polarity) is reversed. As the difference in charge between the inside and the outside of the cell is reduced, potassium channels open up briefly. They allow potassium ions to flood out of the cell, so the interior is once again negative. This is called repolarization (since the charge reverts to normal). By this time, however, the incoming sodium ions have triggered more sodium channels to open up in adjacent parts of the cell membrane. So, more sodium ions flood in farther along the membrane, temporarily reversing the charge in that region. In turn, potassium channels open, the ions flood out, and the section of membrane returns to its normal polarity. In this way the charge travels down the cell body and axon as a wave of depolarization followed by repolarization until it reaches the terminal buttons.

1 Resting stage

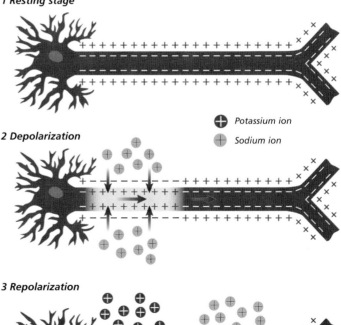

2 Depolarization

⊕ Potassium ion
⊕ Sodium ion

3 Repolarization

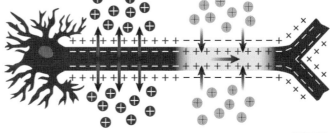

Inhibition

After a nerve impulse has passed, no further impulses can occur until the neuron has returned to its resting state. During repolarization the cell returns to a negative value a little higher than it was before the action potential occurred. The slight increase in the negative charge keeps the cell from repeatedly producing action potentials and is known as an inhibition or relative refractory period. (However, if the neuron is heavily stimulated, perhaps by a sensor detecting a major change, the inhibition period may not occur.) When the sodium channels close totally, there is no possibility of a new action potential. This is known as an absolute refractory period and can last for up to two milliseconds. One millisecond after the refractory period there is a flow of potassium ions inward into the cell, and it returns to the resting state once again.

THE SEARCH FOR NEW CONNECTIONS

The 1990s were declared "the decade of the brain" by president George Bush because many discoveries were made during that time. One belief that was challenged during the 1990s was that neurons are not capable of growth. Researchers had accepted that once a neuron is formed, which occurs by the eighteenth week of pregnancy, no further changes to the neuron or the neural network can take place. They argued that nerve cells do not regenerate to repair damage caused by head injuries or any other harmful environmental effects, such as disease. But in 1996 Swedish researchers showed that tiny amounts of neurons formed after birth in mice, and the neurons migrated to damaged areas to regenerate them. That remarkable discovery prompted researchers to reexamine the human central nervous system and determine whether it has any regenerative effects similar to those seen in mice. Researchers into nervous tissue regeneration are trying to find alternatives to the use of laboratory animals.

In the early 1990s cognitive neuroscientist Vilayanur Ramachandran discovered that the human brain reorganizes itself far more than anyone suspected. People who had lost limbs in car accidents reported to him that they could still feel their missing limbs. While this had been recognized since the American Civil War (1861–1865), Ramachandran realized that he could solve the mystery of what was happening with a very simple test. When he brushed his patients' faces with a cotton ball, they reported, to his surprise, that he was touching their "phantom" limb. Even more interestingly, Ramachandran found that he could map the whole missing hand, finger by finger, on the face of his patients. Ramachandran had noted that the part of the cortex that controls the hand lies close to the part that controls the face. After his patients lost their limbs, the flow of information from them to the brain had ceased. The section of cortex controlling the face had taken over the areas that previously controlled the hand and were using them to process their information. The discovery suggested that some neural connections had been reactivated after years of disuse, or that neural growth in the adult human nervous system, previously thought never to occur, had taken place.

Research is ongoing into ways that the human body can be coaxed to regenerate damage to the central nervous system. Potential benefits are great for people with major damage to the spine, like movie star Christopher Reeves (right), who was crippled in a horse-riding accident.

Local potentials

A neuron's dendrites receive thousands of signals at the same time. Each stimulus can result in a local reversal of polarity (charge) but may not cause an action potential. The difference between the charge of the inside and the outside of the cell is called a local potential. When many local potentials occur simultaneously, their charges can be combined in what is called a spatial sum, with the result that one polarity may be more powerful than the other. A positive spatial charge results in an action potential. Charges can cancel each other to make the net charge zero.

Continuous activation

Motor and sensory neurons remain inactive unless stimulated by other neurons into firing a nerve impulse. Yet many other neurons in the central nervous system (CNS) produce action potentials continuously. Other CNS neurons produce action potentials at regular intervals, an activity called oscillation. A further group of CNS neurons produces action potentials at irregular intervals. The human brain is so complex that it is almost impossible to say where in the CNS the electrical activity of these neurons originates. Researchers suggest that many cells spontaneously activate themselves without being provoked by other cells to produce an action potential. The presence of such cells in the brain allows transmission of two forms of information rather than only one—spontaneously activating neurons can increase or decrease their activation, while neurons that do not activate unless stimulated can only increase activity.

NEUROTRANSMITTERS

Once a nerve impulse has reached the firing cell's terminal buttons, it has to get the message across the synapse (the junction between two communicating cells). Chemicals called neurotransmitters are used to do this. Also, not all neurons communicate with nerve impulses along their axons. Motor neurons and sensory

KEY POINTS

- Cells of the nervous system include neurons and glial cells.
- Glial cells help neurons perform their tasks.
- Sensory (or afferent) neurons send signals *from* receptors in the body *toward* the central nervous system (CNS)
- Motor (or efferent) neurons send signals *from* the CNS *toward* muscles and glands.
- Interneurons link neurons together.
- The main parts of a neuron are the dendrites, branchlike extensions that receive signals, the cell body, and the axon (or trunk), which sends out signals via its terminal buttons.
- Neurons communicate with each other using nerve impulses and neurotransmitters.
- The nerve impulse (or action potential) is a wave of bioelectricity that travels from dendrite to terminal button.
- Neurotransmitters allow cells to communicate across synapses. The synapse is the junction between two neurons. It includes the presynaptic membrane, a synaptic cleft (gap), and a postsynaptic membrane.
- Many legal and illegal drugs work by affecting the performance of neurotransmitters.

neurons do, but neurons in some parts of the brain, including the areas related to learning, memory, planning, and perception, do not have axons and do not communicate with nerve impulses. They use neurotransmitters instead.

Release, uptake, and reuptake

Inside the terminal buttons of a neuron are tiny vesicles (fluid-filled sacs) that contain neurotransmitters and miniorgans called cisternas. The cisternas make neurotransmitters from chemicals inside the cell. When a nerve impulse reaches the membrane of a terminal button (the presynaptic membrane), it causes some of the vesicles to fuse with the cell wall and spill molecules of neurotransmitter into the synaptic cleft. This method of release is called exocytosis (*see* right).

Two things can happen to the neurotransmitters in the synaptic cleft. Some diffuse to the other side of the synapse and attach to receptors (special binding sites) in a nearby part of the membrane of the next neuron (called the postsynaptic membrane). This is termed uptake. Alternatively, the neurotransmitter

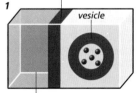

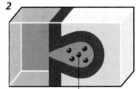

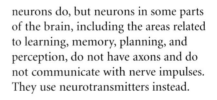

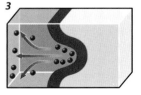

*Exocytosis: A vesicle of neurotransmitters fuses with the cell membrane (**1–2**). The neurotransmitters are released into the synaptic cleft (**3**).*

THE EFFECTS OF DRUGS

Drugs affect communication between neurons in one of two ways. A drug that in some way promotes the activity of a neurotransmitter is called an agonist of that neurotransmitter. A drug that reduces the activity of a particular neurotransmitter at the synapse is termed an antagonist of that neurotransmitter.

Drugs can interrupt neurotransmitter production in a variety of ways. An agonist drug may increase production of the enzymes from which the neurotransmitter is formed. It may also destroy enzymes that break up the neurotransmitter while it is still in the cytoplasm. Some agonist drugs can block reuptake of the neurotransmitter by the terminal button, so more of it reaches and affects the postsynaptic membrane.

An example of an agonistic drug is MDMA (methylenodioxymethamphetamine), the illegal drug also known as ecstasy. MDMA is an amphetamine, which are stimulating drugs that heighten awareness and intensify feelings of pleasure. MDMA stimulates the brain and increases the amount of the neurotransmitter serotonin that is released into the synaptic clefts. It also inhibits the reuptake of serotonin by the axon terminals that release it. Recent research has indicated that ecstasy causes the release of serotonin regardless of calcium levels, which implies that the neurotransmitter is released regardless of the number of nerve impulses that the neuron has produced. As with other stimulants, this increases the heart rate and blood pressure and causes the mind to become hyperalert.

Antagonistic drugs can affect the same mechanisms of neurotransmitter production, but with different results. An antagonistic drug can block neurotransmitter formation by destroying the enzymes necessary to create the neurotransmitter. It may make vesicles burst and discharge the neurotransmitters into the axon, where they are destroyed by enzymes. The drug may also block the release of a neurotransmitter into the synapse by clogging the sites of release. Finally, some antagonistic drugs work by acting as a false neurotransmitter. They bind to the postsynaptic receptors of the real neurotransmitter and block its entry into the postsynaptic neuron.

Hallucinogenic drugs, such as LSD (lysergic acid diethylamide; also called "acid"), closely resemble neurotransmitters in their chemical composition. LSD blocks serotonin receptors in the presynaptic membrane, causing them to slow the reuptake of serotonin from the synapse. At the same time, serotonin receptors in the postsynaptic membrane become overstimulated, resulting in a flood of sensory information that the brain perceives as hallucinations. LSD permanently seals some of the presynaptic receptors with its own synthesized chemical structure, which may explain why people who take LSD sometimes experience hallucinogenic effects days after they first use the drug, in what are called "flashbacks." Serotonin is involved in the patterns of sleeping and waking. One theory suggests that LSD activates dreaming while the person is still conscious. Other theories exist, but none has been proved.

Many of the drugs taken at raves such as this affect the performance of neurotransmitters. Research has shown that one use of any recreational drug can cause permanent damage to the brain's cognitive abilities. Furthermore, every year thousands of people die from drug overdoses.

may drift in the cleft only to be taken up by the same neuron that discharged it in the first place. This is termed reuptake.

Types of neurotransmitters

There are four main classes of known neurotransmitters. At least as many again must exist since the brain performs functions that cannot be explained by only those neurotransmitters already known.

As well as large-molecule transmitters, or neuropeptides, there are three groups of small-molecule transmitters:
• the amino acid neurotransmitters;
• monoamine neurotransmitters; and
• acetlycholine.
In the 1980s researchers discovered that dissolved molecules of the gas nitric oxide function as neurotransmitters, creating a new, fifth, class, the gaseous transmitters.

Small-molecule neurotransmitters

Small-molecule neurotransmitters are stored inside vesicles made from parts of the presynaptic membrane or other parts of the terminal button that have broken away from the neuron. The vesicles lie close to areas of the presynaptic membrane that have high numbers of calcium channels. Triggered by a nerve impulse, the calcium channels open, and the synaptic vesicles merge with the presynaptic membrane, releasing neurotransmitters through the channels into the synaptic cleft (this is exocytosis).

Small-molecule neurotransmitters bind to receptor molecules in nearby parts of the postsynaptic membrane of the adjoining neuron (the postsynaptic cell). One of three events then takes place:
• The molecule may open a channel for a particular chemical and its ions.
• The molecule may close a channel, denying the ion access to the cell.
• The molecule may cause a chain of chemical reactions inside the postsynaptic cell. That occurs when neurotransmitters bind to the postsynaptic cell and form new molecules with chemicals inside the cell. Those newly formed molecules are called second messengers.

Small-molecule neurotransmitters have a very short life. They are broken down by enzymes in the synaptic fluid or in the postsynaptic cell, or they are received back by the presynaptic button and recycled.

Amino acid neurotransmitters play a major role in most rapid changes in the synapses between neurons that lie close together. Amino acids are the building blocks of proteins. There are four types: aspartate, glutamate, glycine, and gamma-aminobutyruc acid (GABA). The first three are made from food proteins, while GABA is synthesized from glutamate, which triggers neurons to fire nerve impulses. GABA prevents nerve impulses. Other amino acid neurotransmitters include more than 20 large-molecule peptides that act as endorphins (natural painkillers) in the brain. They sometimes occur as hormones elsewhere in the body.

Monoamine neurotransmitters are produced from a single (mono) amino acid. The effects of monoamines are usually more widely spread than those of amino acid neurotransmitters, and their chemical structure is generally slightly larger. Dense collections of monoamine

> *"[Synaptic transmission] must constitute links in an extremely complicated nerve net in which, within limits, everything synapses more or less with everything else."*
> **—Willem Noordenbos, 1959**

neurotransmitters exist in the brain stem, where the cell bodies of many neurons are located. The neurons release monoamine from as many different sites as possible. There are four main monoamine types: dopamine, epinephrine (or adrenaline), norepinephrine, and serotonin.

Dopamine, epinephrine, and norepinephrine are produced from the dietary enzyme tyrosine. Enzymes from

nerve impulse

terminal button (presynaptic membrane)

vesicle

neurotransmitter

reuptake

synaptic cleft

receptor

postsynaptic membrane

When a nerve impulse reaches the terminal button of a neuron, vesicles containing neurotransmitters fuse with the cell wall and release their contents into the synaptic cleft (gap between two communicating cells). The neurotransmitters bind to receptor sites on the postsynaptic membrane (of the nearby cell). Some are reabsorbed by the same cell that released them. This is termed reuptake.

dopamine-releasing neurons act on tyrosine to produce l-dopa, then other enzymes create dopamine from the l-dopa. Dopamine is involved in movement, attention, and learning. Lack of dopamine-releasing neurons causes Parkinson's disease (see Vol. 6, pp. 20–67), which results in tremors, rigidity of limbs, and problems with balance. The disease is treated with synthetic l-dopa, but the drug works for only a limited period, after which the signs associated with Parkinson's disease recur. Excess dopamine has been linked to schizophrenia (see Vol. 6, pp. 20–67), in which reality cannot be distinguished from delusion. Dopamine is used to make norepinephrine and epinephrine, which are involved in the regulation of alertness and the ability to respond rapidly to a threat.

Serotonin plays a part in sleep and arousal, sensitivity to pain, and the control of appetite and mood. It is created from the chemical tryptophan, which is itself a product of the breakdown of dietary proteins. A lack of serotonin has been linked to schizophrenic behaviors.

Acetylcholine is produced from choline in the diet. This neurotransmitter is important at junctions between muscle cells and motor neurons, and makes muscles contract. It also occurs at synapses in the autonomic nervous system and is involved in memory function. Acetylcholine is deactivated in the synaptic cleft by another chemical from the same family, which breaks acetylcholine down into two smaller chemical compounds. They are taken up by the terminal button, and their components are recycled.

Neuropeptides

One important group of large-molecule neurotransmitters is the neuropeptides (or peptides), which consist of chains of amino acid molecules. Neuropeptides were identified as a class of transmitter in 1975. Neuropeptide vesicles are darker in appearance and larger than small-molecule vesicles, and they can reside anywhere in the terminal button.

Neuropeptides are not only released from the terminal button but can also be released from the sides of an axon, so they have a more wide-reaching effect than many other neurotransmitters operating in the nervous system.

Many neuropeptides occur as hormones in other parts of the body. Those peptides are released by the endocrine gland, but recently they were discovered in various concentrations in nerve tissue. It appears that some peptides are produced by neurons primarily to use as neurotransmitters. This information proved to many researchers that neuropeptides are a new class of neurotransmitter rather than a hormone.

Peptides and exocytosis

The exocytosis of peptides is controlled by calcium ions, but in a different way than the exocytosis of small-molecule transmitters. A nerve cell releases peptides gradually in response to the general level of calcium ions in the cell, which may be raised due to an increase in the rate of nerve impulses passing through the cell. Released peptides have a much more wide-reaching effect than small-molecule neurotransmitters, which act only locally. Peptides travel through the extracellular fluid into the brain's ventricles and the bloodstream. Peptides can bind to cells that are in entirely different nerve systems from the releasing cell and can travel over the entire brain to find a suitable binding site—in mice they have been traced from the occipital lobes to the frontal lobes. When a peptide eventually binds to a neuronal membrane, it causes a gradual change in the neuron that is triggered by second messengers (molecules formed by the peptide from chemicals in the cell membrane). Peptides make changes in neurons that are long-lasting, in contrast to the momentary effects produced by small-molecule neurotransmitters.

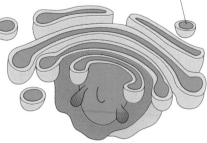

rough ER

ribosomes

Endoplasmic reticulum (or "ER" above) and the Golgi apparatus (below) are among the vital miniorgans that all cells need to function. Inside neurons these two structures are involved in the production of neuropeptides. ER is a network of fluid-filled tubes. Tiny granular organelles called ribosomes stud the surface of rough ER. Ribosomes make neuropeptides from chemicals in the cell. The neurotransmitters are packaged into vesicles by the Golgi apparatus. The vesicles travel to sites of release along tiny tubes called microtubules.

vesicle breaks away from Golgi apparatus

PROZAC

EXPERIMENT

The antidepressant drug Prozac (fluoxetine) first went on sale in the United States in 1987. It was one of the first drugs to be designed in the laboratory, rather than stumbled on by chance during drug testing.

Research had indicated that low levels of serotonin are associated with sleeplessness and irritation, and that depression is relieved by maintaining normal serotonin levels. Prozac is a selective serotonin reuptake inhibitor (SSRI)—it decreases reuptake by the presynaptic cell of a specific type of serotonin from the synapse. Levels of serotonin in the synaptic cleft therefore remain high. Reuptake of serotonin is performed by molecular pumps in the presynaptic membrane, and Prozac finds them and blocks them with its own molecules. Prozac also inhibits enzyme activity that breaks down serotonin in the synaptic cleft. Prozac is prescribed for a variety of reasons, not least because it may be more effective than other SSRIs in the short term. Prozac can be started at a higher level of dosage because it is not as toxic as other antidepressant drugs.

Prozac was tested in double-blind trials. In this rigorous testing procedure individuals are given either a genuine drug or a placebo (a dummy drug), and their reactions are recorded. Neither the test administrators nor the subjects are told who has the real drug and who has the placebo in case the information influences the outcome of the trial. Drugs like Prozac, the products of highly focused investigation followed by rigorous scientific testing, could change the shape of the pharmaceutical industry during the next few decades.

Neurotransmitter functions

The differences between the two types of neurotransmitters suggest that they have different roles in the nervous system. Peptide neurotransmitters seem to act as neuromodulators: They either increase or decrease the sensitivity of a large number of neurons to the effects of small-molecule neurotransmitters. Some researchers have suggested that neuromodulators influence our behavior by regulating the emotional and motivational effectiveness of neurotransmitters in the brain. Small-molecule neurotransmitters appear to send short-lived messages to nearby postsynaptic receptors that act either to excite or inhibit formation of nerve impulses in the neuron.

A neurotransmitter can only excite or inhibit electrical activity in a neuron when it binds to the right type of receptor on the postsynaptic membrane. A transmitter deposited in the synapse will not be accepted by the postsynaptic membrane of the nearest dendrite if it has no receptors for that type of neurotransmitter. Some transmitters function as small-molecule transmitters at certain receptors but as neuromodulators at other receptors.

By chance, the mineral element lithium was found to have a beneficial effect on people who suffer from bipolar 1 disorder, which is also called manic depression (*see* Vol. 6, pp. 20–67). The drug was originally designed to help investigate the urine of psychotic patients. Bipolar 1 disorder causes swings of mood from mania to severe depression, and lithium helps reduce the frequency and severity of the mood swings. It is particularly effective against the manic phases of the disorder. The chemical reactions produced by lithium in the brain are still not entirely clear. It is assumed that the mineral's chemical structure binds to serotonin pathways and acts as a blocking agent for reuptake of the transmitter. Lithium, like many drugs currently available, has its origins in trial and error, rather than deliberate manufacture based on an understanding of how the brain works.

Peptides have been traced from the occipital lobes to the frontal lobes in mice. Very little is known about the pathways they take in humans, though.

CONNECTIONS

- Neuropsychology: Volume 1, pp. 90–95
- Brain-imaging Techniques: Volume 1, pp. 96–103
- Mental Disorders: Volume 6, pp. 20–67

The Mind

Are mind and brain flipsides of the same coin?

The commonsense view of the relationship between the mind and the brain is generally accepted by most modern psychologists. Our perceptions of the world depend on the way in which physical stimuli operate on our bodies and, ultimately, generate thoughts, feelings, and consciousness. Conversely, our thoughts and desires clearly operate on our bodies and affect our actions. But this intimate relationship is the subject of much controversy. How can a physical object such as the brain operate on an intangible and invisible entity such as the mind?

Speculation about the nature of the mind and its relationship with the brain and body is as old as history itself. Before psychology developed into a distinct discipline in the late nineteenth century, the answers to these questions lay in the realms of philosophy. The Greek philosopher Plato (c.428–348 B.C.) was perhaps the first person to put forward a theory on the nature of the mind. Plato argued that the mind was a nonphysical entity. He used the Greek word *psyche,* meaning "soul," to describe this invisible substance. He believed that it was separate and distinct from the rest of the body—the physical substance. Plato went on to suggest that the mental and physical substances could exist separately since they had no natural connection. Philosophers call Plato's theory of mind-and-body separation "dualism."

"The soul must be a substance as the form of natural body potential with life, and [such] substance is an actuality. So the soul is an actuality of such as body."
—from **De Anima, Aristotle**

Aristotle (384–322 B.C.), another Greek philosopher, disagreed with Plato's theory of dualism. Aristotle thought that the mental substance (what Aristotle called "form") and physical substance (or "matter") were connected. Aristotle believed that every living thing was a combination of matter and form—each dependent on the other. Much later the ideas of Plato and Aristotle were taken up by the theologians and philosophers of a

Algebra is strictly logical. For example, if x + y = 15 and x = 2y, x is always 10, and y is always 5. But there are few certainties about this woman's mind.

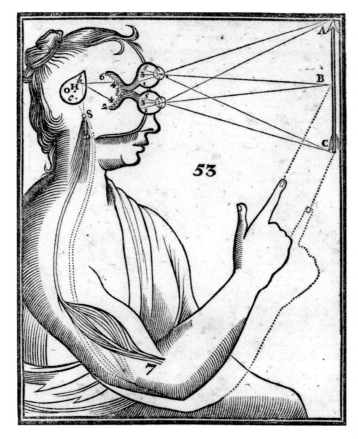

53

Consequently, Descartes decided to build a completely new system of philosophy based on his own firm foundations. Descartes decided to doubt everything—everything he had ever been taught and everything he could perceive in the world around him. Desperately, Descartes looked

> *"Intuition is the undoubting conception of a pure and attentive mind, which arises from the light of reason alone, and is more certain than deduction."*
> — *René Descartes, 1637*

for something that would be impossible to question. The revelation came when Descartes realized the one fact that he could not deny: The fact that he was doubting. Only one thing cannot be doubted—doubt itself. His discovery is summed up in the famous philosophical argument *"Cogito ergo sum"* ("I think, therefore I am").

Once Descartes felt safe that he existed, he felt he could also be sure that the world around him existed. Descartes then began to look for differences between himself and the natural world. Like his beloved mathematics, Descartes believed that the

period in history called the Scholastic era. In addition the Scholastic philosophers believed that our ability to form ideas was a gift given by God. The Christian philosopher St. Augustine (A.D. 354–430) named this gift illumination: "As the eyes have need of the light of the Sun in order to see sensible objects, so the intellect needs the light of God to know the world of intelligible beings." The Scholastic belief of the nature of the mind continued to be popular well into the Middle Ages.

The Cartesian model

The most explicit statement of mind-and-body dualism was made by the French mathematician and philosopher René Descartes (1596–1650). The certainty of mathematics appealed to Descartes, but he was opposed to the doubts created in the philosophies of his predecessors from ancient Greece and the Scholastic era.

A diagram depicting René Descartes's theory of vision from the Treatise on Man (1686). Descartes tried to synthesize philosophy and mathematics or, as he put it, "bridge the gulf between the domain of natural science and the soul." He believed that mental operations could be represented by abstract symbols "in the same system as the perceptual states that produced them" and used symbols from algebra to explain his theory of mental representation.

KEY POINTS

- The relationship between the mind and brain activity is unclear.
- Some people say that we can never understand the link between mind and brain, others that it is futile to try to find out.
- Scientists are committed to explore the mysteries of the mind, but they are divided about how best to proceed.
- Introspection now plays a less important role in trying to understand the mind.
- Scientific measurement has replaced self-examination as the basis of psychological research.

natural world was shaped by physical laws. But he could not apply the same rules to his mind. So, like Plato, Descartes believed in dualism. He believed that the mind, or "mental substance," was distinct from the body, or "material substance."

Descartes's view of dualism, called substance dualism, differs slightly from Plato's ideas. Although Descartes held that the mind and body were separate and distinct, they were not entirely unrelated. Descartes believed that mind and body could interact, forming a "union" that resulted in a human being.

Descartes's philosophy raised an important question: How do two such disparate things such as the mind and body interact? Descartes believed that the mind and the body made contact at the pineal gland in the center of the brain. Undoubtedly, people experience things, such as a rise in temperature or a bright light, that elicit responses, such as perspiration or shutting the eyes. Descartes's theory did not go on to explain the mechanisms by which mind and body made this type of contact. This "mind-body problem" opened up one of the most important and controversial debates in the history of philosophy.

Perspectives post-Descartes

Descartes's work prompted many philosophers to attempt to solve the mind-body problem. Unlike most of his contemporaries, who attacked the mind-body problem in terms of alternative philosophies, the English empiricist philosopher John Locke (1632–1704) moved the debate into the psychological realm of experience. Locke did not think that the physical or the mental was really fundamental. The reality was somewhere neutral in between them. In a work entitled *Essay Concerning Human Understanding* Locke described the mind as a *tabula rasa* (from the Latin words meaning "blank slate"). Locke argued that all people gained knowledge through experience (*see* Vol. 1, pp. 22–29). According to Locke, sensory experience,

or sensation, provided one kind of experience. The other, which Locke called reflection, was the mind's combination and comparison of various sensory impressions. Locke concluded that people do not have direct knowledge of the physical world, only of the sensations or reflections produced by them.

Locke went on to argue that while we cannot prove that the material world exists, our senses give us evidence affording all the certainty that we need. Locke's position was, however, essentially dualist: Mind and body remain distinct. Moreover, Locke regarded it as in

> "If men are for a long time accustomed only to one sort or method of thoughts, their minds grow stiff in it."
> — John Locke, 1690

principle impossible for humans to have any understanding of the relation between mind and body. All the perceptions of one's own body, as of the rest of the physical world, are ideas in the mind.

The other great empiricist philosopher, the Scotsman David Hume (1711–1776), much admired the scientific method of the English scientist Sir Isaac Newton (1643–1727). In his *Philosophical Essays Concerning Human Understanding* (1748) Hume developed a theory of knowledge based on scientific principles. Like Locke, Hume thought that the mind does not create ideas but forms them from the senses. Hume went on to define knowledge as either "relations of matter" or "matters of fact." Ideas are simply related meanings, for example, that movement consists of the relationship between space and time. Matters of fact must be accepted for what they are, for example, that grass is green and that fire is hot.

Hume was troubled by the concept of causality (the cause and effect in any relationship). He believed that the knowledge of the relationship between

THE EVOLUTION OF A SCIENCE

Psychology first arrived as a fully fledged science in 1879, when Wilhelm Wundt (1832–1920) (*see* Vol. 1, pp. 30–39) set up a laboratory in Leipzig, Germany, that was designed to explore systematically the operation of perception. This earliest school of psychology has become known as structuralism because it tried to identify and define the building blocks of mental structures such as the formation of concepts, planning, and thinking. Structuralists believed that they were the basis of consciousness. Wundt claimed to have objectively identified the two main components of consciousness: sensations (hearing, smell, taste, touch, and vision) and feelings (such as anger, fear, and love). One problem with these findings was that the primary research technique used to reach these conclusions was introspection. The word literally means "looking within." It requires people to think about what they think and do, and to report their findings. For example, subjects might be given several pieces of information to memorize or a problem to solve; they are then asked to describe what went through their minds while they were performing these tasks. The results are interesting as far as they go, but there are limitations. Naturally, people will report only those processes of which they are aware—anything unconscious will be beyond their purview. In addition, any description of what happened, no matter how detailed or accurate, is not a description of how it happened. Moreover, the results of such experiments produce subjective results based on the personal experience of the subject. Science relies on objectivity. Thus theories based on introspection fell out of fashion.

The study of mental processes and consciousness was promoted by several other movements, including functionalism and Gestalt psychology. The functionalists (*see* Vol. 1, pp. 40–45) tried to investigate how mental processes helped us function in and adapt to our environment. This approach was influenced by the British naturalist Charles Darwin (1809–1882) and his theories of natural selection. The emphasis on Darwinism and its link between humans and animals gave rise to the notion that human psychology is related to the psychology of animals. This suggested that the observation of animals could provide clues to human behavior.

Gestalt psychologists (*see* Vol. 1, pp. 46–51) sought to understand how the whole of consciousness arises from individual component perceptions. Scientists such as Max

Wilhelm Wundt was the first person to bring the methodology of the natural sciences to the study of the mind. He is thus widely regarded as the founder of experimental psychology.

Wertheimer (1880–1943) believed that many of our thoughts come from what we perceive and the natural tendency of our brains to structure the information. They developed more than a hundred perceptual laws, or principles, that describe how brains organize and make sense of the world around us. The Gestalt approach can be summarized by the statement: "The whole is more than the sum of its parts."

However, these theories were superseded by behaviorism (*see* Vol. 1, pp. 74–89), a new movement in psychology that started in the United States in the early 20th century. Behaviorists took issue with other movements in psychology that were concentrating on understanding mental processes. Behaviorists regarded theories of mental processes as unclear and woolly, and rejected the idea that psychology should focus on the study of the psyche and other unseen phenomena. Instead, they contended that psychology should study only directly observable behaviors.

Behaviorism remained the dominant approach to psychology until the 1950s, which marked the beginning of the cognitive revolution (*see* Vol. 1, pp. 104–117). This new movement was inspired mainly by the development of computers, machines that could solve mental problems without outwardly observable behavior. Thus the computer came to represent a model for human mental processes as they might be if they were not complicated by other factors such as emotions. This paved the way for the development of cognitive neuroscience, the interdisciplinary study of connections between the brain and the mind.

matters of fact, such as a fire (cause) being hot (effect), result from an internal association of the two ideas "fire" and "hot." The knowledge of causality comes from the accumulation of subjective experiences. Not only do we think of the fire being hot, we expect and believe it to be hot. The implication of this idea is that cause-and-effect relationships are based on subjectivity. Scientists try to be objective, but since they rely on observing causal relationships, science itself is based on subjectivity. So there can be no rational, scientific theory of how we accumulate knowledge.

Kant's Copernican Revolution

In the eighteenth century the German philosopher Immanuel Kant (1724–1804) attempted to combine the theories of the empiricists Locke and Hume with those of Descartes and other rationalist philosophers. Unlike the empiricists, who state that all knowledge is based on the accumulation of sensory experiences, rationalists believe that knowledge can be gained just by thinking and reasoning. Kant agreed that knowledge depended on all these qualities.

The problem of knowledge, as Kant viewed it, was how to link sensory experiences with innate knowledge, that is, knowledge we all have from birth. His starting point was to distinguish between analytic and synthetic judgments. Analytic judgments are ones in which the truth of such a judgment can be known by analyzing the subject. A synthetic judgment is one in which the truth of a statement cannot be known through analyzing the subject.

Kant also distinguished two ways in which humans can accumulate knowledge. Something is known a priori if it cannot be derived from or tested by any sensory experiences. Something is known a posteriori if it can be derived from or tested by experience. Philosophers before Kant believed that analytic judgments were a priori and that synthetic judgments were a posteriori. Analytic a priori judgments

were always true—but true only about the meaning and relations of words, not about the world. On the other hand, synthetic a posteriori judgments were about the world—but based on probability. This infers that we could have no certain knowledge about experience. Kant did not agree. He believed that experience provides the content (the synthetic element), and the mind provides the structure (the a priori element) that determines the way in which the content will be understood.

Kant called the innate contribution of the mind a "category" and listed four different categories by which the contents of experience are ordered. The categories are quantity (how much of something),

> *"That all our knowledge begins with experience there can be no doubt."*
> —Immanuel Kant, 1781

quality (the types of things), relation (how things interact), and modality (what things can be). We apply them to our everyday experiences to make sense of the world. For example, space is a structure in the mind that relates objects to one another. The innate contribution of the mind gives meaning to our experiences. The mind is not shaped by the world of experience, rather the world of experience is shaped by the patterns set by the mind.

Whether things really are the way they appear to us is something we can never know because all our knowledge is prestructured by the mind. This is the basis for Kant's famous distinction between the unknowable noumenon ("thing-in-itself") and the phenomenon ("thing-as-it-appears"). Kant called his theory the "Copernican Revolution" of philosophy. Just as the Polish scientist Nicolaus Copernicus (1473–1543) reversed the way scientists viewed the relationship between the Earth and the Sun, so Kant reversed the way that philosophers viewed the relationship between the world of experience and the world of the mind.

A science of mind

The study of the mind remained the province of philosophical debate until the end of the nineteenth century. Then three major developments laid the foundations for the scientific study of the mind.

The first was made by the German philosopher and psychologist Franz Brentano (1838–1917). In 1874 Brentano published his *Psychology from an Empirical Standpoint*, in which he tried to establish a systematic study of psychology that would form the basis of a science of the mind. Brentano revived the Scholastic philosophical theory of intentionality. The concept of intentionality enables philosophers to deal with the problems of dualism by relating what appears in the mind to the real object. Some dualist philosophers think that an experienced and remembered object, such as someone's impression of a flower, can exist in our consciousness even though the real flower exists outside the mind. Brentano's theory of intentionality avoided the question of whether consciousness exists—it is certain that we see a flower when we look at one. We direct our consciousness onto the flower and recognize it. The word "intentionality" comes from the Latin *intendo*, meaning "to aim at or point toward." The only problems Brentano faced were how the flower comes to have a meaning for our consciousness and how our mind relates to the flower.

The second breakthrough was the establishment of psychology as a distinct scientific discipline in the 19th century. The German physiologist and

William James—one of the early pioneers of psychology. Before he began teaching psychology at Harvard University in 1875 there was no formal recognition of the subject as a scientific discipline. James developed his new science over the next 10 years. The culmination of his work was one of the most influential texts in the history of modern psychology— Principles of Psychology. *Five years before the book was published, however, James shifted attention to philosophy and religion—subjects that continued to interest James until his death in 1910.*

psychologist Wilhelm Wundt (*see* box p. 43) opened the first psychology laboratory at the University of Leipzig, Germany, in 1879. Wundt and his colleagues were trying to study the mind using a process called "introspection"—a method in which people observe and analyze their own thoughts, feelings, and mental images. The subjects recorded their introspections under controlled conditions, and Wundt used the same physical surroundings and the same stimuli for each experiment. Even though philosophers had spent thousands of years trying to understand the mind, that was the first time the methods of science were applied to the study of mental processes.

The last major breakthrough in the development of a science of the mind was made by the American philosopher and psychologist William James (1842–1910). James published his *Principles of Psychology* in 1890—a monumental work in two huge volumes. *Principles of Psychology* assimilated mental science into a purely biological discipline and treated thinking and knowledge as tools in the struggle to survive. At the same time, James made the fullest use of principles of psychophysics—the study of the effect of physical processes on the mental processes of an organism.

Seeds of doubt

Within a few decades the experimental methods of Wundt became overshadowed by the behaviorist approach. According to behaviorists such as the American psychologist John Broadus Watson (1878–1958), psychologists could learn more about the workings of the mind by studying the relationship between

FOCUS ON

COGNITIVE NEUROSCIENCE—BIRTH OF A NEW FIELD

By the late 1970s neuroscientists had learned a great deal about how the brain is organized, and how it functions during the perception of simple stimuli. While cognitive psychologists characterized mental operations in terms of information processing, neurologists established links between areas of the brain that had been damaged and certain behavioral deficits. Meanwhile, computer scientists were busy trying to develop models that would imitate various human mental processes. A new mission was clearly required to help these disciplines work together toward their common goal. The breakthrough came in the back of a taxicab shared by the American psychologists George A. Miller and Michael Gazzaniga on their way to a dinner at the Algonquin Hotel in New York City. The meeting was being held for scientists from Rockefeller and Cornell universities who were joining forces to study the connection between the brain and the mind, a subject in need of a name. Out of the taxi ride came the term *cognitive neuroscience,* which quickly took hold. Cognitive neuroscience is now viewed as a mainstream psychological discipline that is on the leading edge of exploring how the mind works.

This successful merger of multiple disciplines with neuroscience has encouraged other subdisciplines within psychology to come into the fold. There is the emerging field of developmental neuroscience, which is the combination of developmental psychology and neuroscience, as championed by Helen Neville at the University of Oregon. There is also perceptual neuroscience, which is the combination of perceptual psychology and neuroscience; one of its leading proponents is Robert Savoy of the Rowland Institute, Cambridge, Massachusetts. And there is social neuroscience, the combination of social psychology and neuroscience, a field led by John Cacioppo at the University of Chicago. Developmental, perceptual, and social psychology were once considered incompatible with neuroscientific explanations. Similarly, cognitive psychology viewed the brain as a black box and considered that it was not important to know how the brain was involved in cognitive processes. Now all these disciplines have adopted a multilevel approach that actively seeks to incorporate the biology of the brain into their attempts to understand human nature. Professor Neville, for example, considers language development in conjunction with brain development. Professor Savoy looks at visual perception in conjunction with brain processes, primarily using functional magnetic resonance imaging (fMRI). Professor Cacioppo uses biological techniques when researching the psychology of human social interactions.

observable stimuli and the consequent behavioral responses. Extreme versions of behaviorism even went as far as to completely deny the existence of the mind. Most behaviorists thought that introspection was fundamentally flawed as a method of analysis. If people report their experiences after the introspection, they rely on memory, which experiments have shown to be inaccurate on occasion. Second, people find it difficult to observe any topic other than their own conscious experiences. They do not have access to the inner workings of mental processes, such as recognition, and so cannot be expected to account for them. Last, the lynchpin of science is objectivity. Introspection yields subjective results—opinionated thoughts as opposed to unbiased, objective information. Thus

the new science of the mind was no more a science than the philosophical discussions of previous centuries.

Cognitive science

The behaviorist approach dominated psychology throughout the first half of the twentieth century. Then, in the 1950s a new field of study called cognitive science revolutionized psychology.

Cognitive science developed from quite disparate fields of study. In 1956 a study published by the American psychologist George A. Miller (born 1920) showed that the capacity of human thought is limited. Miller suggested that most people can store only seven plus or minus two pieces of information in short-term memory and demonstrated a way of improving the capacity of short-term memory by storing chunks of information. Miller's study went some way to explain the mechanisms by which the mind stores information in the form of coded, mental representations.

The second major influence on the cognitive science revolution was made by the American linguist Noam Chomsky (born 1928) (*see* Vol. 1, pp. 118–125). In 1959 he published a study that showed that language was much more complex than anyone had previously believed. Language could not be a learned habit, as behaviorists thought. Chomsky viewed language as a way to express ideas and said that these ideas are expressed according to mental grammar in the form of rules.

However, perhaps the most important driving force was the invention of the first computing machines in the late 1940s. Soon after, pioneers in cognitive science— the American computer scientists John McCarthy and Allen Newell, the American mathematician Marvin Minsky, and the American economist and psychologist Herbert A. Simon—found ways to characterize the human thought process by constructing computer models of the mind, as well as attempting to build computers with an artificial intelligence.

Neuroscience

As cognitive science brings about new understanding about the mind, so neuroscience (the study of the brain) brings new understanding about the workings of the brain. Like modern cognitive psychologists, neuroscientists base their observations on empirical research. For example, they insert electrodes into the brain to record the activity of individual neurons. The neuroscientist then tries to work out how the billions of connected neurons that form our brains produce such a complex set of cognitive abilities. In addition, a new breed of cognitive psychologists, called cognitive neuropsychologists, gather data by observing the abilities of people whose brains have been damaged. Damage to specific areas often results in the loss of a particular mental function.

Neuroscientists use noninvasive brain-imaging technologies, such as magnetic resonance imaging (MRI) and positron emission tomography (PET) scanning equipment, to record brain activity while people perform various mental tasks. The images produced by these scans have identified areas of the brain that are involved in specific tasks, such as mental imagery and language processing.

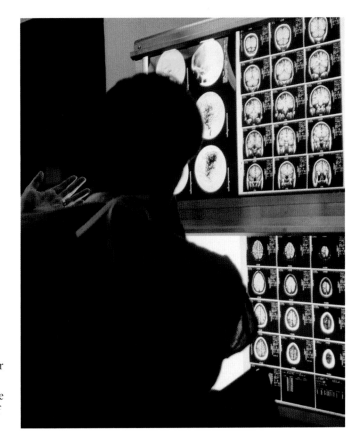

A NEW PHILOSOPHY

Very few modern philosophers perform experiments or construct computer models of the mind to formulate their theories. However, the relationship between philosophy and the new field of cognitive psychology remains a close one. The philosophy of mind does not have a distinct method—philosophers deal with general issues such as the relation of the mind and body and try to explain the concepts derived by cognitive scientists. In turn, the work of cognitive scientists can help improve philosophical approaches.

In light of the recent breakthroughs in neuroscience very few philosophers now subscribe to Descartes's dualist view. Philosophers argue that if all the matter in the world suddenly disappeared, it is hard to believe that some "vital force" such as the mind would remain. Therefore the mind must be viewed as some part of the

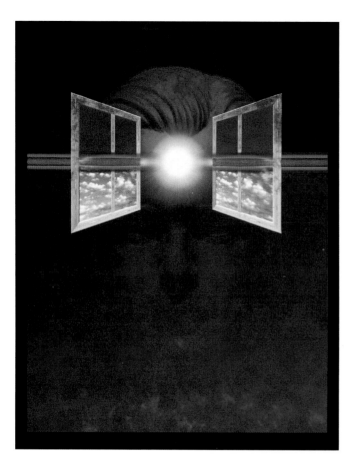

cells) in the brain. In addition, there is no reason to expect that the same neural process underlies a particular mental activity for every organism. So identity theory only allows for a single realization of a mental activity, for example, that every organism feels pain in the same way.

Functionalism

The criticisms leveled against identity theory have led to the development of another theory called functionalism. Functionalists believe that behavior is a result of a collection of mental processes and try to explain mental processes in terms of cause-and-effect relationships, which they call functions. Functionalists try to recognize the functions that produce certain behaviors and what those behaviors will be. They also allow for multiple meanings for different mental processes, so they do not think that behaviors can be pinpointed to specific areas of neural activity.

Eliminative materialism

In its most extreme view eliminative materialism, or eliminativism for short, advocates the elimination of psychological categories, such as attention and memory, in favor of a scientific explanation at the neurobiological level. This theory is known as reductionism and holds that neuroscience can provide an explanation for all mental events. So psychology can be reduced to neuroscience and eventually

physical world. Much of the recent philosophical debate aims to establish the laws that govern the mind. There are a number of theories that form a broad school of philosophy called materialism.

Identity theory

One of these theories, identity theory, or reductive materialism, is a simple idea. Proponents believe that mental states are identical, or related, to neural pathways in the brain. As more of these pathways are mapped, we may soon be able to denote mental processes like "desiring" with the activity of neurons in "Section 123abc" of a particular area of the brain.

Identity theory has failed to win over the hearts of most philosophers and psychologists. The main problem has been trying to match various mental activities to particular neurons (nerve

What lies behind the windows to the mind? This computer graphic is an illustrative analogy of the uncertainty of the relationship between mind and brain. One modern school of thought—the coevolutionary approach to the study of the mind advocated by Patricia Churchland—is bringing fascinating new insights into the nature and workings of the human mind and its relationship to the brain.

> *"Adopting the reductionist strategy means trying to explain the macro levels (psychological properties) in terms of micro levels (neural network properties)."*
> *— Patricia Churchland, 1995*

to chemistry and physics. Many proponents of this view believe that psychological categories such as memory are a useful way of describing mental events, but only if they are used as words.

The words do not apply to what is going on at the level of the neuron. For example, the idea of sleep has already been revised as research has revealed important brain differences in various stages of sleep.

Patricia Churchland, a philosopher at the University of California at San Diego, has developed this theory further. She believes that the mind should be investigated through multiple levels of research—molecular, cellular, functional, behavioral, systemwide, and brainwide— all at the same time. The advantage of what Churchland calls the coevolutionary approach to the study of the mind is that even though all the questions are concerned with understanding the relationship between the brain and the mind, they are all looking for different answers. Churchland believes that the results of each approach should be used to inform the others and thus improve our overall understanding of the mind.

Biological naturalism
John Searle (born 1932), professor of philosophy at the University of California at Berkeley, has expressed concerns about

> *"Above all, consciousness is a biological phenomenon . . . part of our ordinary biological history, along with digestion [and] growth."*
> —*John Searle, 1992*

the reductionist goal of discovering the neurobiological mechanisms underlying mental events. In a theory called biological naturalism Searle believes that mental processes can be explained by the behavior of some physical element in the brain, such as a neuron, but that these elements do not themselves individually perform these processes. For example, the brain is conscious, and consciousness is caused by neurons in the brain even though no single neuron is conscious. So studying the anatomy of the brain is not going to help further our understanding of the

mind. Searle suggests that psychologists should study the mind as far as possible on its own, using the same systematic observation and analysis that are employed in a chemistry or physics laboratory.

Daniel Dennett
No discussion of the philosophy of the mind would be complete without mentioning the American philosopher Daniel C. Dennett (born 1942), director of the Center for Cognitive Studies at Tufts University. Dennett is in favor of considering neuroscientific issues when trying to understand the mind. He has proposed that the latest machines already demonstrate mental abilities and that in the future they may well develop minds of their own. This is an extreme view of materialism. Instead of stating that the brain and mind are both biological phenomena, he says that a brain built out of computer hardware can also have a mind. He has written many books on this subject. In *Consciousness Explained* (1991) Dennett argues that consciousness cannot be a single brain function that takes place in a single location, but is rather an orchestrated combination of many continually changing brain functions.

John Searle, whose theory of biological naturalism has introduced a whole new approach to the study of the mind.

Backward referral hypothesis

Benjamin Libet, professor of physiology at the University of California, San Francisco, researched the mind-brain connection for nearly 30 years. In the 1990s, at the end of a controversial series of experiments he came to the conclusion that we are living in the past. Not very far in the past, only about half a second; but it takes that much time for us to become consciously aware of our perceptions. So by the time we become aware of stimuli and decide in our mind how to respond to them, our brain has often already initiated a possible response. These experiments formed the basis of his "backward referral hypothesis." Fortunately, backward referral is not so delayed that we act without thinking.

The light emitted by stars takes so long to reach Earth that we are seeing them not as they are now but as they used to be, often millions of years ago. This is analogous to the backward referral hypothesis of Benjamin Libet, which suggests that because of the time lapse between the receipt of a stimulus and its interpretation by our brains, we are living a fraction of a second in the past.

Awareness occurs so quickly that we have time to override any inappropriately triggered response. Libet believes that this ability to detect and correct instinctive misjudgments is the basis of free will.

The functions of the mind

When we consider the activities of the mind, it seems we need to consider a whole host of mental processes such as language, memory, and even consciousness itself. To begin with, let us look at how the brain takes in information from external stimuli so that we can interact with the world—in other words, the workings of sensation and perception.

How does the brain take information from the physical world and convert it into perceptions? How can we listen to a song on the radio, watch a football game on television, understand what a friend is saying to us on the phone—and, indeed, often perform more than one of these activities at the same time? When we consider the complexity of such processes, it is amazing that we can take up so much information. Fine hair filaments in our inner ears respond to changes in air pressure so we can hear. Light-sensitive cells at the back of our eyes respond to photons so we can see. Sensitive nerve endings in our fingertips respond to the feel of the keyboard as we type. Specific regions in the brain allow us to control our vocal cords so we can talk. Somehow we synthesize all this seemingly disparate information to form integrated perceptions, so that we can act, react, and survive in this data-saturated world.

We take these perceptual functions so much for granted that to understand how they work, it is useful to compare them with situations in which they have become a problem. Take the famous case of P. T., a man who, after sustaining brain damage, had particular difficulty in recognizing objects. That made his life difficult because as a farmer he had a large herd of cows and many acres to maintain.

The inner ear contains tiny hairs that respond to changes in air pressure. The nerve signals produced are then transferred to the brain and interpreted as sound by the hearer. The significance of the sound is interpreted by the mind.

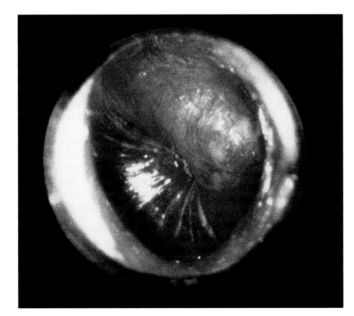

So he needed to know where he was and what was around him. Often he would be off on a remote part of his farm, working on a fence, then look up and not know where he was. Worse, when it came to milking time, he once found himself trying to milk a bull. Most troubling of all, P. T. no longer recognized the people around him. The woman who served him his breakfast every morning was a complete stranger. He had no trouble seeing her standing over the stove, frying his eggs and bacon. He could even describe her actions as she walked across the kitchen to bring him his plate. He simply failed to recognize her—until she spoke. On hearing her voice, the pieces of the puzzle would fall into to place, and he would suddenly realize that it was his wife.

> *"My aim is not to see patients as systems, but to picture a world . . . the landscapes of being in which these patients reside."*
> —*Oliver Sacks, 1973*

P. T. suffered from a condition known as visual agnosia. The British neurologist Oliver Sacks (born 1933) described a similar case in which a man could not tell the difference between his wife's face and his own hat until he heard her voice.

What these cases have in common is that both victims had normal vision. Opticians and ophthalmologists found that their eyes worked fine—the light that fell on the light-sensitive cells in the back of the eye was properly translated into nerve impulses and sent to the brain. But the brain could not make sense of it all. These were not disorders of sensation; they were disorders of perception. In visual agnosia the single stimulus of sight is insufficient to trigger recognition, but the combination of sight with other stimuli—sound, touch, smell, perhaps even taste—may enable sufferers to recognize previously unperceived wholes. Other agnosias—auditory (inability to recognize familiar sounds) and tactile (inability to recognize familiar objects through touch)—may be relieved by supplying the sufferer with visual information.

Attention and the mind

To act, react, and survive in the world, we need to know how to select and recognize what we perceive. The ability to do these things is known as "attention." The word

Oliver Sacks, author of The Man Who Mistook His Wife for a Hat (1985), a study of visual agnosia. Another of his books, Awakenings, *was made into a film starring Robert de Niro and Robin Williams.*

comes up in many contexts—we pay it; we give it; things come to it; we combine it with care; we may even seek it—but what exactly is it?

According to William James (*see* Vol. 1, pp. 30–39) in *Principles of Psychology*: "Everyone knows what attention is. It is the taking of the possession of the mind, in a clear and vivid form, of one out of what seem several simultaneously possible objects or trains of thought. Focalization, concentration of consciousness are of its essence. It implies withdrawal from some things in order to deal effectively with others, and it is a condition which has a real opposite in the confused, dazed, scatterbrain state."

What does this really mean? Certainly we can choose what to pay attention to. We have to, or we would be overwhelmed by information. The classic account of such voluntary aspects of attention is known as the "cocktail party effect" (*see* pp. 64–87). How is it that in the noisy, confusing environment of such a social occasion people can carry on individual conversations? We have probably all experienced some variation of this phenomenon—if not at a cocktail party, then perhaps in a library while studying. You may be concentrating on a particularly confusing text, reading it over and over again, trying to extract some meaning. Perhaps you are struggling because you are simultaneously aware of friends in a nearby alcove talking about the day's baseball game. You are torn between the two—part of you wants to work, but another part wants to know how your team did. So you must choose which input to respond to. You cannot follow both trains of thought.

Or can you? You may decide to tune out the baseball game discussion and concentrate on the text in front of you. After all, you can read about the game in the paper later. You have selectively chosen to attend to the text and ignore the baseball. But are you completely cut off from your friends' conversation? Research shows that you are not. You have merely decided not to select various pieces of information that have entered your brain through your ears. They are there all right, even though you have deliberately chosen not to access them. The classic example of this phenomenon is when people are able to hear their names in conversations to which they were paying no attention. The same principle would work in the baseball game example. Even though you are still working, if the other people suddenly start talking about the thing you particularly want to know—in this case the score—you will suddenly tune out of your text and in to their conversation.

Voluntary and reflexive attention

However, it should also be noted that we cannot always control our attention. The library baseball problem described above is an example of what is called voluntary attention. The other type of attention is reflexive attention—if we are working and the phone rings, we are immediately and involuntarily distracted from our work to listen to the sound. Reflexive and voluntary attention are related, and many psychologists think of them as parts of a continuum. By and large, you can choose what to pay attention to, but your attention may also be drawn automatically by significant events.

Thus it would appear that attention is a series of mental processes enabled by specific areas within the brain. We engage our attention when we decide or are drawn to attend to a particular incoming stimulus; when we want to stop paying attention or turn our attention to something else, we disengage. Clinical research has shown that the thalamus (an area in the center of the brain involved in relaying visual and auditory sensory information to the rest of the brain) is important for the so-called "engage function," and that the parietal lobe (an area at the top of the brain important for spatial processing) is involved in the disengage aspect. Meanwhile, the superior colliculus (a thumbnail-sized cluster of neurons in the brainstem important for

eye movements) is responsible for the moving of attention. Finally, overall control of attention is thought to be controlled by an area of the brain called the anterior cingulate. Located in the frontal lobe near the center of the brain just in front of and above the lateral ventricles, the anterior cingulate is an important gyrus (one of the convex folds on the surface of the brain, also called convolutions). Damage to any one of these areas can cause deficits in both voluntary and reflexive allocation of attention.

ADHD and autism

Brain damage is not the only source of attentional deficit. There are other conditions associated with attention deficits. Most notable are attention deficit

In 1967 Clara Claiborne Park published an account of the first eight years of the life of her daughter Elly (pictured below), who has autism. The book was the first "inside" story of an autistic child's development and life, and illustrated the absolute strangeness of the autistic mind.

THEORY OF MIND

The question of what makes us uniquely human has been hotly debated since the dawn of recorded history. What is it that sets us apart from other animals? Maybe it is because we can think about thinking, as well as think about what other people are thinking, and act on the conclusions reached. That is what is generally referred to as theory of mind (TOM). TOM includes the capacity for self-reflection, the ability to articulate understanding of one's own thoughts and knowledge together with some degree of insight into what others know and what they may be thinking.

Some investigations of the development of mind have been based on the idea that when children begin to have a capacity for deception (to tell lies), it is because they have begun to realize that not everyone knows what they know. In other words, they have made the discovery that sometimes they have unique knowledge that others do not have—maybe mommy didn't see them take the cookie from the cookie jar. (Unfortunately, what they may not yet realize is that mommy does see the crumbs around their mouths.)

This kind of development usually occurs between the ages of three and five years. If a child of about that age sees someone look in a box the contents of which are hidden from view, the child is able to figure out that the other person has knowledge that the child does not have. In younger children this mental capacity has not yet developed.

In many ways chimpanzees are very similar to humans—they are highly intelligent and can communicate with each other and with us. Fossil evidence and the analysis of human and chimp DNA suggest that we share a common ancestor with chimps. Physically, a chimp's brain is very similar to ours, too. So do chimps possess TOM? Recent evidence suggests that they do—at least to some degree. Deception has been observed in many chimp behaviors. For example, subordinate males have been known to attempt "sneaky" matings with females out of sight of

What is it that distinguishes humans from animals? Some people say that it is the power of speech; others say writing; a few believe that the one thing that makes us unique among living creatures is the capacity to tell lies.

the alpha (dominant) male. Similarly chimps have been known to make false alarm calls to scare the troop away from a tree laden with fruit so that they can eat it all themselves.

Many psychologists now think that TOM is graded. At the top end of the scale, humans possess a complete TOM. Lower down the scale primates such as chimps possess only certain features. Unfortunately, studies of other animals such as dolphins and even pigeons have proved inconclusive. So we must wait to find out whether it is TOM that makes us different from—and more intelligent than—all other animals.

hyperactivity disorder (ADHD) and autism. Autism derives from the Greek word *autos*, meaning "self." People with such a condition seem to live in a private, self-absorbed world. They have marked social attentional deficits—they may fail to attend to their mother's face or voice or to others calling their name. ADHD has several characteristic patterns—one in which children simply cannot pay attention, another in which they show hyperactivity and impulsivity, and a third that combines the symptoms of the other two. Although ADHD and autism are distinctly different disorders, both of which go well beyond attentional problems, both have been shown to correlate with underdeveloped or underactive frontal lobes. They are thought to be caused by underdeveloped or underactive anterior cingulate gyri. Interestingly, both autistics and ADHD sufferers show deficits in their theory of mind (*see* box on facing page).

MEMORY AND MIND

What happens after we selectively or reflexively attend to relevant information? We either relate it to previously acquired knowledge to recognize it, or we store it for later use. We remember millions of bits of information, some quite easily, others with difficulty. Why the big difference?

This question can be answered with reference to case studies of people with brain disorders who have deficits of memory. In the early 1950s the American neurosurgeon William Scoville of the Montreal Neurological Institute, Canada, developed a revolutionary surgical technique to cure epilepsy. Epilepsy is essentially caused by abnormal electrical activity in the brain. The condition can cause severe seizures, often resulting in

> "*Epilepsy is a local discharge-lesion of a few highly unstable cells of one half of the brain.*"
> —*John Hughlings Jackson, 1864*

loss of motor control and consciousness. Drug treatment is now used to control all except the most severe cases, but no such treatments were available to Scoville. To help alleviate the condition, he developed a surgical technique called bilateral resection of the medial temporal lobe. This operation involved removing large parts of the middle portion of the temporal lobe on both sides of the brain.

Scoville based this approach on work carried out in the late 19th century by the British neurologist John Hughlings Jackson (1835–1911). Jackson described

Before the advent of modern drug treatment the only hope of a cure for epilepsy was prayer. In this engraving victims go on pilgrimage to Luxembourg in Europe to pay homage at the shrine of St. Willibrord, the patron saint of sufferers.

A man with epilepsy is attached to an encephalogram machine that can measure the electrical activity in his brain. The graph readings thus obtained can now be used to identify a method of alleviating his symptoms.

the topographical organization of the human motor system and noted that the anatomy of the temporal lobes of many epileptic patients was unusual. Scoville's surgical operations were successful in alleviating the symptoms of epilepsy, but they had an unfortunate side effect. His patients came out of surgery without epilepsy but with severe and profound amnesia—they lacked the ability to remember past events. Further, the severity of their amnesia was directly proportional to the amount of the brain that had been removed—the larger the excision, the worse the memory loss.

The case of H. M.

The most famous case of this type was that of H. M., an epileptic in his twenties who was operated on by Scoville and then became the subject of a long-term study. The findings have contributed greatly to modern theories of amnesia, memory, the brain, and the mind.

Twenty months after surgery it was obvious that H. M. had a memory deficit. When a specialist interviewed him, then left the room only to return a few minutes later, H. M. could not recall having met him before. This was not an isolated incident and continued to recur for the next 40 years. H. M. could not seem to remember any new material. He had what is known as anterograde (forward-going) amnesia—in other words, he lacked the ability to form new memories of things that happened to him after the damage to his brain. Yet not all of his memory abilities were lost. H. M. could recall events that had happened to him before the operations (known as episodic memories), and he had retained some general knowledge (known as semantic memory). Nevertheless, he could not form new episodic or semantic memories. H. M. seemed to be living in the past. Or was he?

Some researchers refer to the combination of episodic and semantic memories as explicit memories because they are usually memories that we know we know. There is also another sort of memory, those that we don't know we know, which are known as implicit memories. They include memories of procedural skills (such as driving a car), conditioning (such as salivating on hearing a bell in expectation of food, in the manner of Pavlov's dogs), and priming (for example, recognizing the word "dog" more quickly when it is preceded by the word "cat" than when it is preceded by the word "car"). One winter H. M. fell on ice and broke his hip. As he recovered, he became quite adept at folding and unfolding his portable walker (a procedural memory), but he couldn't remember sustaining the injury that led to him needing it (which would have been an episodic memory). So H. M.'s implicit memory skills were relatively intact.

False-memory syndrome

This dissociation of explicit and implicit memories clearly demonstrates that memory is not a single, unitary system in the brain. We have memories with knowledge, and we have memories without knowledge. To complicate matters further, we also have "memories" that are false.

Every criminal prosecutor knows that an eyewitness account is among the most compelling evidence for establishing guilt in court. But can eyewitness testimony be trusted? In 1978 a study published by Elizabeth Loftus, a psychologist at the University of Washington, showed the difficulty of relying on eyewitness accounts. She showed her subjects color slides of an automobile accident and asked them what they saw in a later test session. Half of the people were shown slides containing a red stop sign where a pedestrian was hit; the other half were shown a red yield sign. When later answering questions about the signs, half received questions correctly referring to the sign, and half received misleading, incorrect questions. For example, they were asked, "When the car came to the red stop sign, did the driver stop?" This is an appropriate question for the stop sign group, but a misleading question for those who were originally shown the yield sign. In a subsequent recognition test many members of the misled yield sign group were adamant about having seen a stop sign. When questioned about a red stop sign, they altered their memory and believed they had seen a red stop sign. So it is not always the case that we can trust the evidence of our own minds.

Question: When is a stop sign not a stop sign? Answer: When you are asked misleading questions that lead you to doubt or deny the evidence of your own eyes.

The sad case of Phineas Gage

No discussion of the mind would be complete without mention of Phineas Gage. Gage was a railroad worker who helped build the Rutland and Burlington Railroad through the rocky terrain of the Green Mountains of Vermont in the mid-1880s. As foreman on the construction crew, he was responsible for setting the dynamite charges. This entailed drilling a hole in the rock bed, filling it with gunpowder, and placing a fuse on top. To ensure that the explosion blasted the rock, sand was poured into the hole and packed down using a large iron bar. This was an extremely important and delicate job, one that was entrusted only to the best and most experienced workers. But one day there was a problem.

Gage went to tamp the sand in place before it was poured into the hole, but while doing so, he caused a spark on the iron bar, which lit the fuse and set off the gunpowder charge. The iron bar was blown through the front of his head, ripping a hole in his lower cheek and the top of his skull. Gage literally lost half of his brain and figuratively lost half his mind. Remarkably, Gage survived. He even came through the accident conscious! He was rushed to a doctor, filled with disinfectants to diminish the chance of infection, and sewn up. Within two weeks Gage was back at work. He was no longer the man he had been, however. Before the accident Gage had been a model citizen—energetic, polite, and conscientious. Now he was lazy, rude, and reckless. He had been a clear thinker and shrewd manager of his affairs; after the accident he could not follow a coherent plan of action and constantly spoke of ill-conceived, untenable grand schemes. Not only was he no longer fit to be foreman, it soon became apparent that he was no longer employable at all. So he left the railroad and tried to make a life elsewhere. After roping horses in South America, laboring in California during the height of the gold rush, and working as a sideshow circus freak, Gage died.

A doctor examines a piece of human brain tissue to see if the person from which it was obtained died of Creutzfeldt-Jakob disease. This mind-affecting illness is passed from animals to humans.

Gage was buried with the tamping iron that had changed his personality. Several years later his body was exhumed, and the skull and tamping iron saved for posterity. In 1994 Antonio Damasio, his wife Hannah, and others used computer graphics and neural imaging techniques to plot the path of the steel rod as it passed through Gage's brain. He discovered that the motor regions of the frontal lobe remained intact, but that the ventromedial (front-middle) portions of the frontal lobe had been destroyed. The part of the frontal lobes responsible for speech and motor functions was apparently spared, so Damasio concluded that the changes in social behavior observed in Phineas Gage were due to this lesion. Damasio observed the same sort of change in other patients with similar lesions, causing a defect in decision making and the processing of emotion.

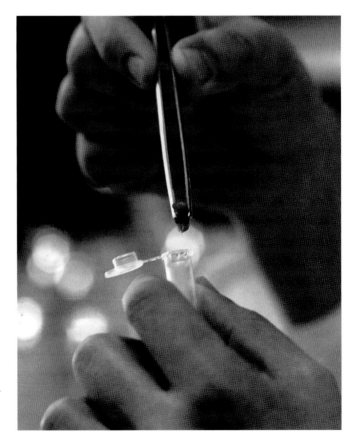

LOSING ONE'S MIND

In addition to the disorders of the mind that are now linked with certainty to various forms of brain damage there are several other diseases that affect the mind.

Dementia caused by CJD and BSE

Creutzfeldt-Jacob disease (CJD) is an organic brain syndrome caused by a viruslike organism that results in dementia (*see* Vol. 6, pp. 20–67), the rapid, progressive deterioration of mental processes such as perception, attention, memory, motor processes, and language. Dementia can seriously affect the sufferer's ability to carry out even simple daily tasks.

CJD is one of a group of diseases called spongiform encephalopathies because it usually produces microscopic holes in brain tissue, giving it a spongelike appearance. It is a rare disorder, occurring in no more than about one person in half a million throughout the world. However, the disease is fatal. Unfortunately, scientists are not sure exactly what causes it, or how it is contracted, and there is no known cure for the disease. It is known to

Ronald Reagan was president of the United States from 1981 to 1989. He retreated from public life after it was revealed that he was suffering from Alzheimer's disease.

be caused by a tiny protein particle called a prion (proteinaceous infectious particle) that many believe is transmitted through ingestion of infected animal tissue. This is the reason for the recent concern over bovine spongiform encephalopathy (BSE), also called mad-cow disease. BSE is thought to be transmitted from cow to cow when their feed contains recycled animal remains that were infected with BSE (that is, dead cows are ground up and added into animal feed as a protein source). Many scientists are concerned that BSE can infect humans if they eat tissue containing the infective agent, resulting in the human form CJD. A definitive diagnosis of CJD cannot be made until death, at which point the brain is examined under a microscope for a spongelike appearance in the brain tissue. CJD may take years to develop, so a person may be infected for some time without displaying any symptoms. There are also sheep, goat, deer, and pig versions of spongiform encephalopathy. The use of animal by-products as protein sources for animal feed has now generally been stopped. As a further measure, herds in which BSE occurs are destroyed to prevent the spread of CJD.

Dementia caused by Alzheimer's disease

A much more common disease that results in dementia is Alzheimer's disease. Like CJD, Alzheimer's is a degenerative disease of the brain from which there is no recovery. Slowly but surely, the disease damages many parts of the cerebral cortex and affects emotions, memory, language skills, reasoning, and motor processes. Again, scientists are not sure how the disease is caused. It is named after the German physician Dr. Alois Alzheimer (1864–1915), who in 1906 noticed amyloid plaques (abnormal clumps) and neurofibrillary tangles (bundles of neurons) in the brain tissue of a woman who had died of a previously unknown mental illness. Alzheimer's may now be diagnosed through brain scans and cognitive tests.

The mind of British novelist Iris Murdoch (1919–1999) was destroyed by Alzheimer's. In 2002 the story of her life and tragic demise was made into a film starring Kate Winslet and Judy Dench.

Alzheimer's begins with mild memory loss. Sufferers have trouble remembering recent events, activities, or the names of familiar people. These are all typical signs of aging and not in themselves necessarily anything to worry about. But in the case of Alzheimer's the symptoms progressively worsen. You may forget where you parked your car, then forget how to get to the store, then forget how to get home. This may be due to the progressive loss of the mental capacities essential to a healthy mind, such as thought and reason.

SUMMING UP

This chapter began with a warning that discussions of the nature and location of the mind often raise more questions than they answer. A quotation from Daniel Dennett in his book *Kinds of Minds* (1996) illustrates the problem:

"Can we ever really know what is going on in someone else's mind? Can a woman know what it is like to be a man? What

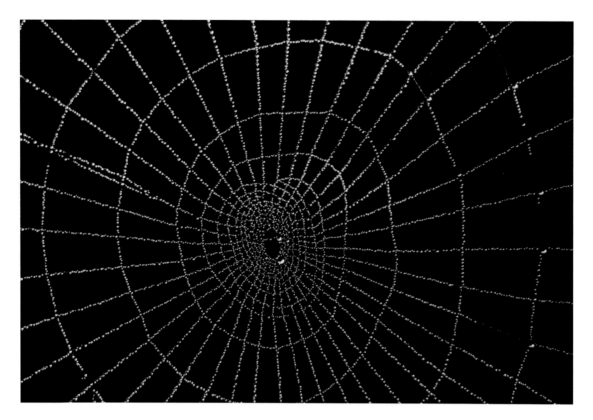

experiences does a baby have during childbirth? What experiences does a fetus have, if any, in its mother's womb? And what about non-human minds? What do horses think about? When a fish has a hook sticking through its lip, does it hurt the fish as much as it would hurt you? Can spiders think, or are they just robots, mindlessly spinning their elegant webs? For that matter, why couldn't a robot—if it were fancy enough—be conscious? Could it be that all animals, and even plants—and even bacteria—have minds?"

Most modern philosophers and neuroscientists agree that the mind is intrinsically linked to the brain. But if we look exclusively at mental operations, do we know any more about the brain-mind connection than when we started? Clearly, mental processes such as attention, memory, and language are brain-based. We have seen how people with brain damage have specific mental deficits. And we have learned about people who had more general brain problems, and how they had more general mental deficits. Certainly not all of these people can be described as having lost their minds, but it can easily be said that they have lost portions of their mind. So it seems reasonable to conclude that the brain is the basis for our mental capabilities and is therefore the basis for what we call the human mind.

Do spiders spin webs because they want to or simply because that is what they do? And how do we go about finding out?

CONNECTIONS

- Neuropsychology; Volume 1, pp. 90–95
- Cognitive Psychology: Volume 1, pp. 104–117

Perception

"Vision is the art of seeing the invisible."

Jonathan Swift

The smell of toast and coffee. The feel of cool grass beneath our bare feet. Bird song. The blue of the sky. We recognize these myriad colors and feelings, these sounds and smells because of our brain and its connections with our perceptual systems.

The world is filled with things that we can sense—that is, with forms of energy or structures that can be turned into sensation. Sensation is the activity of special organs—eyes, ears, nose, tongue, and other sensors—that respond to things like heat, cold, and pressure. Sensation alone would not be very meaningful without the brain, since it is nothing more than the transformation of physical stimuli, such as vibrations, light, and smelly molecules, into nerve impulses. It is

> *"Gibson felt that artificial laboratory situations had misled psychologists into conceptualizing perception as a physically passive, internal, cerebral event."*
> **—David Abram, 2002**

the brain's interpretation of those impulses that allows us to perceive the colors, shapes, sounds, and feelings of the world in which we live.

The experimental psychologist James J. Gibson (1904–1979) argued it is useful to consider sensation and perception together as making up our various perceptual systems. Those systems include not only the senses and the brain to which they are connected, but also different muscles and glands. For example, our visual system includes not only our eyes, with their light-sensitive cells, but also the networks of nerve cells that transmit visual impulses to the brain, the brain itself, and a variety of muscles that control

movements of the eye, head, and even the body. Gibson saw perception as innate and believed research in this area should be conducted in real-life situations.

Our senses

The ancient Greek philosopher Aristotle (384–322 B.C.) described the five human senses—hearing, smell, touch, taste, and vision—as the five windows through which our brains can perceive. Windows allow information in but do not analyze it. The senses are unlike ordinary windows in that they translate whatever is happening in the outside world, such as a shout or a drop in temperature, into electrical nerve impulses that the brain can interpret— those impulses allow the brain to perceive. Also unlike windows, our senses do not permit everything to pass through. Only a small fraction of all available stimulation results in nerve impulses that the brain can interpret. If that were not the case, we would be overwhelmed by our constant

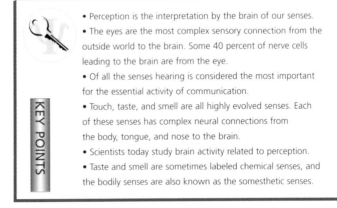

KEY POINTS
- Perception is the interpretation by the brain of our senses.
- The eyes are the most complex sensory connection from the outside world to the brain. Some 40 percent of nerve cells leading to the brain are from the eye.
- Of all the senses hearing is considered the most important for the essential activity of communication.
- Touch, taste, and smell are all highly evolved senses. Each of these senses has complex neural connections from the body, tongue, and nose to the brain.
- Scientists today study brain activity related to perception.
- Taste and smell are sometimes labeled chemical senses, and the bodily senses are also known as the somesthetic senses.

THE SENSES AND OUR PERCEPTUAL SYSTEMS

Psychologists use different terms when describing our perceptual systems. Some speak of the body senses, which are also known as the somesthetic senses. The somesthetic senses include the touch system, which enables us to sense pressure, pain, cold, and warmth. The bodily senses also include the systems that tell us about body position, movement, and the forces of gravity and acceleration, and those that allow us to balance. Gibson (see p. 62) called it the basic orienting system. Some psychologists also call taste and smell the savor system.

awareness of different sounds, sights, smells, tastes, and other sensations that surround us all the time. We notice only a few of those many potential signals—all the rest are ignored, just as we ignore the background noise of radio broadcasts.

In radio communication the difference between a signal and a noise is clear: The signal is the message; noise is static or perhaps other irrelevant messages that happen to be broadcast on the same frequency. Similarly, in our nervous systems the signal is nerve activity to which we are paying attention; everything else is noise. For example, while you read this page, the words are signals; the sounds of other people talking or the feeling of hunger in your stomach—they can be described as "noise."

Data-reduction systems

By filtering out noise, our brains save us from being overwhelmed. The senses take in information that the brain then filters, reducing the amount of data to which it must respond (see pp. 40–61). The role of the brain as a data-reduction system is well illustrated by the cocktail party phenomenon. Talking at a party, we might not be aware of the other conversations going on around us, but that can change in an instant. If someone within our range of hearing speaks our name or mentions a topic of interest to us, our attention might immediately shift. We tune in to what they are saying and suddenly hear snatches of the other conversation. What we perceive at any given time—that which is in

immediate conscious awareness—is the definition of attention. Attention and perception cannot easily be separated, even at the level of brain activity.

Signal thresholds

Our senses filter out many potential signals. Some of those, like the color of a policeman's shoes, are signals that are unlikely to draw anybody's attention. Others, like the weight of your glasses on your nose, are constant, and you adapt to them quickly. Still others, like the sound of a distant crow's wings, are below our hearing threshold. Early psychologists Gustav Fechner (1801–1887), Wilhelm Wundt (1832–1920), and Edward Bradford Titchener (1867–1927) were very interested in thresholds for stimulation (see Vol. 1, pp. 30-39). They asked questions such as: What is the minimum amount of light the human eye can detect? What is the softest sound the ear can perceive? What is the lightest touch the hand can feel?

To answer those questions, the researchers measured physical stimuli and their effects, laying the foundations of the science now known as psychophysics. At first, psychophysicists thought they could measure exactly the minimum amount of stimulation required for sensation. But they soon found that to be impossible. Some people are more sensitive than others, and an individual's threshold might vary from one day to the next. You can easily demonstrate how your own threshold varies. Take an alarm clock that ticks, place it at one end of your room, and walk just far enough away that you can no longer hear it. Now walk back very slowly until you reach the point at which you can again just hear it. That is your threshold for that stimulus. But if you stand still for a few seconds the sound may fade, or it may become louder. To find your threshold again, you will now have to lean forward or backward. Thresholds, Fechner concluded, are not fixed. Still, he reasoned, there is a point at which a stimulus will always be sensed and another at which it never will. Halfway between those two points, the threshold should be detected about 50 percent of the time. Fechner decided to call that point the absolute threshold. The table below gives some very approximate thresholds for each of the five senses.

The just-noticeable difference

Early psychophysicists wanted to know not only the least amount of stimulation that might be sensed, but also the least difference in stimulation that might be noticed. For example, even with your eyes closed, you could easily pick up two cats and say which is the heavier if one weighs 2 pounds (0.907kg) and the other weighs 4 pounds (1.814kg). But if the cats weigh 2 pounds 2 ounces (0.964kg) and 2 pounds 4 ounces (1.020kg), you probably could not tell which was heavier. The physiologist Ernst Weber (1798–1878) explained that the just-noticeable difference (JND) between two stimuli is a proportion rather than a constant amount. After studying a large number of people, he concluded that the JND for weight is about 1/53. That means that a weightlifter who normally lifts 200 pounds (90.7kg) would probably not notice an addition of 2 pounds (0.907kg), but would notice an addition of 5 pounds (2.3kg), which is more than 1/53rd of 200. One who lifts 300 pounds (136kg) would require an addition of 6 pounds (2.7kg) or more before noticing the difference. That is referred to as Weber's Law and included taste, brightness, and loudness as well as lifted weight. The tolerance levels for different stimuli can vary considerably from one person to another or from time to time for the same person.

Modern methods of research

In the study of sensation and perception the emphasis is no longer on the measurement of absolute thresholds and just-noticeable differences. Instead, modern scientists look at how the brain works to discover the relationship between nerve activity and perception. The study of how the nervous system works is termed neuroscience. This area of research is based on findings from studies of human behavior, animals, neurological patients, and of neurology and anatomy.

Perhaps the most important fact is that neuroscientists now have sophisticated instruments that allow them to detect and map brain activity in ways not possible only a few decades ago (see p. 78). They can measure activity in single nerve cells and often identify specific areas of the

---

FOCUS ON

THRESHOLDS FOR PERCEPTUAL SYSTEMS

These are stimuli that are just barely detectable by someone with average sensory sensitivity.

Perceptual system	Approximate minimum detectable stimulation
Visual	Candle flame at 30 miles (48km) on a clear and completely dark night.
Auditory	Watch ticking at 20 feet (6m) in an otherwise quiet room.
Taste	One teaspoon of sugar mixed with 2 gallons (7.5l) of pure water.
Smell	One drop of perfume in a six-room house.
Touch	The wing of a bee dropped on your cheek from a height of 1 inch (2.5cm).

brain that are involved when we respond to stimulation. Research reveals that there is an exceptionally close relationship between how we perceive and how we represent things in the brain. In a series of studies conducted by the psychologist Stephen Kosslyn and his associates at Harvard University participants are shown a map. On this map there are some clearly identifiable landmarks. Participants study the map, which is then removed. They are then asked to visualize the distance between two points on the map. Strikingly, the amount of time it takes them to do so is directly proportional to the actual distance between the two points. The farther apart the points are, the longer it takes participants to respond.

VISION

Our mental images are not flat representations; they are three-dimensional, with height, width, and depth. We can move them around mentally to examine them from different angles. According to Kosslyn, if you were asked whether frogs have lips and a short tail, you would look at your mental image of the frog from one end and then mentally rotate the image to look at the other end. If tails and lips were located at the same end of the frog, it would take you less time to answer the question. Not only is your image of the frog 3-D, but it might also have distinct features derived from some of your other senses. For example, your frog image might include something of the texture of the frog's skin, something of its croaking, something of the strength in its legs. In the same way, your image of a rose may smell so unusual that you have no words for it. Also, it might carry something of the sharpness of a rose's thorns. Although our mental images are not all visual, their visual components are among their most powerful aspects.

Your mental image of this red-eyed tree frog is three-dimensional and also includes some features such as the texture of its skin.

Human vision

More research has been conducted into people's vision and the visual system than any other perceptual systems. Our eyes are like an extension of our brains, pushed out toward the front of our heads along a stalk of nerve cells. That bundle of cells keeps our brain and eyes in constant contact. In fact, 40 percent of all the incoming nerve cells that connect our nervous system to the outside world come from the eyes.

> *"Our eyes are truly wondrous windows on the world. The last of our senses to evolve and the most sophisticated."*
> *—Ann Marie Seward Barry, 1997*

Color vision

The retina of each eye contains about seven million cones but almost 20 times as many rods. Those light-sensitive cells are packed extremely tightly in an area about the size of a small postage stamp that is as thin as tissue paper. Rods and cones are adapted for different functions. Rods are more sensitive to light than cones. In fact, they are so sensitive that they do

THE STRUCTURE OF THE EYE

The eye is a round organ jacketed in a tough, elastic coating known as the sclera. The sclera is the white of the eye as you look at it from the front (see diagram below). Each eyeball is housed in a bony socket and controlled by an intricate arrangement of muscles. Those muscles are able to rotate the eyes and change their direction, and they also keep the eyes in constant motion. Even when you look at something that is absolutely still, your eyes move constantly in tiny, jerky motions. These movements stop the image from fading.

At the very front of the eye the sclera bulges forward to form the cornea, which is like a transparent window. The cornea is isolated from the bloodstream, which is why corneal transplants are seldom rejected.

The cornea covers the iris, a colored disk with a hole in its center. The iris is what gives the eye its color. The opening in its center is the pupil, through which light enters the eye. The size of the pupil, which is controlled by the iris, determines how much light enters. As you can easily verify by standing in front of a mirror in a room where you can control light intensity, the pupils dilate (become larger) in dim light and constrict (become smaller) in bright light. Immediately behind the pupil is the lens, a transparent capsule held in place by the ciliary muscles. The ciliary muscles control the shape of the lens. The main function of the lens is to focus light so the image appears sharp on the light-sensitive cells at the back of the eye. A rounder lens focuses objects that are near; as the ciliary muscles elongate the lens, more distant objects come into focus.

At the back of the eyeball is an arrangement of light-sensitive cells and supporting nerve cells called the retina. The retina consists of three distinct layers. The first layer, farthest back from the front of the eye, is made up of light-sensitive cells known as rods and cones because of their shapes. These receptor cells send their messages indirectly to the brain through several other layers of cells. Next to the rods and cones, toward the front of the eye, is a layer of bipolar cells—with two main branches. One of those branches is connected to the rods and cones and is stimulated by the receptor cells; the other is connected to another layer of cells that lead directly to the optic nerve, the main nerve linking the eyes to the brain.

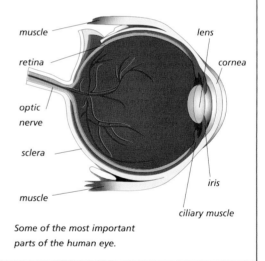

Some of the most important parts of the human eye.

not function well in normal light and are therefore used mainly for night vision. Cones, on the other hand, need good light to function. They allow us to see details and colors.

In spite of their different functions, rods and cones react to light in similar ways. Both contain light-absorbing molecules that change as they absorb light. For example, rods contain the dim-light receptor rhodopsin, a chemical so sensitive that a single photon can break down a rhodopsin molecule. As the rhodopsin breaks down, it initiates a nerve signal. If the rod is to continue to respond to light, components of the rhodopsin need to recombine. It is because recombination needs to take place in the dark that rods do not function well in the daytime.

The regeneration of rhodopsin dim-light receptors depends largely on vitamin A and certain proteins. Foods that are orange in color such as carrots and apricots are a rich source of vitamin A, so the old folk saying that you should eat carrots to enjoy good night vision is correct. Night blindness is common in areas where there is a shortage of foods containing vitamin A.

Theories of color vision

If you take all the colors of the rainbow and mix them, the result is white light. If you take only three of those colors—blue, green, and red—and combine them, the result is still white light. And if you combine pairs of those three colors, it is possible to generate all the colors that we can see (*see* p. 68).

The last of those facts is the basis for the trichromatic theory of color vision. This theory was first proposed by the physician Thomas Young (1773–1829) and was later revived and expanded by the physiologist Hermann Helmholtz (1821–1894). According to the Young-Helmholtz theory, it is possible to make all the colors we see simply by combining three different wavelengths—those of red, green, and blue—and the eye therefore needs only three kinds of color-sensitive cells. One kind would respond mainly to reds, one to greens, and the other to blues. Different levels of activity in each of those systems would lead us to perceive different colors. Evidence that Young and Helmholtz might be right was first found in studies of people who are color-blind, but it took more than 100 years. In the end science determined that

Carrots are a rich source of vitamin A, which helps people see in the dark.

there are in fact three types of cones in the human retina: one responds mainly to longer wavelengths (reds), another to waves of intermediate length (greens), and a third to shorter waves (blues).

Color blindness

If activity in three different types of cones is what allows us to see color, defects in one or more of those cone systems should

---

BEHEAD PEOPLE WITHOUT KILLING THEM

EXPERIMENT

There are no rods and cones in the area of the retina where the optic nerve joins the eyeball, resulting in a blind spot in our vision. You can demonstrate that by looking at the figure below. Hold the book 1 foot (30cm) or so in front of your face, close your right eye, and stare at the triangle on the right. Note how you can see the circle on the left even though you're staring at the triangle. Now move the book slowly back and forth.

When the image hits your blind spot, the circle will disappear completely. Repeat the procedure described above, but this time pay attention to how the line that runs through the triangle and the circle looks solid and continuous even after the circle has disappeared. That is an important illustration of how we see not only with our eyes but also with our brains. Because our brains expect the line to be continuous, we see it that way.

King Charles II of England, ruler from 1660 to 1685, would sometimes amuse himself by using his blind spot to "behead" various members of his court. All he had to do was close one eye, stare at some object off to the side, and move his head slowly until the head of the targeted person disappeared!

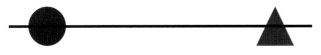

The blind spot is where the optic nerve leaves the eyeball, and there are no rods or cones. Follow the instructions above to demonstrate your blind spot.

have predictable consequences. For example, people with no functioning cone systems should see the world only in black, white, and shades of gray. And they should see poorly or not at all in daylight. That is in fact the case, although the condition is very rare. People with only one functioning cone system would be expected to see normally both by day and by night, but they would not be expected to distinguish different colors because they would see only different intensities of a single color. That condition, too, is rare, but does occur. People with two functioning cone systems would be expected to see many colors, but they would also be expected to confuse certain

Mixing lights is an additive process. If we mix all wavelengths (or just the three primary colors of red, blue, and green), the effect is like recombining them to yield white light. Mixing pigments (like mixing paints) is different from mixing colored lights.

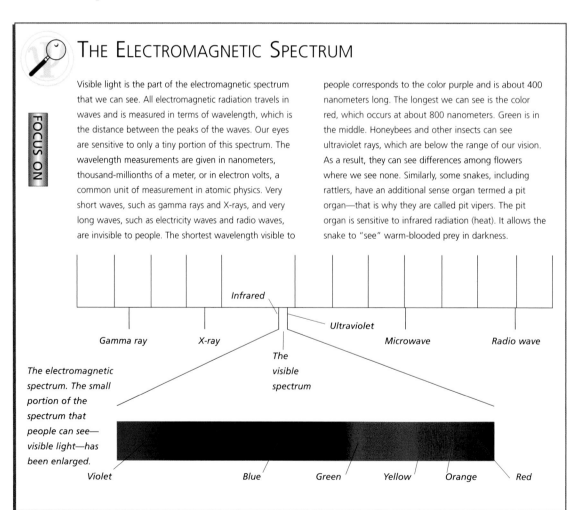

THE ELECTROMAGNETIC SPECTRUM

FOCUS ON

Visible light is the part of the electromagnetic spectrum that we can see. All electromagnetic radiation travels in waves and is measured in terms of wavelength, which is the distance between the peaks of the waves. Our eyes are sensitive to only a tiny portion of this spectrum. The wavelength measurements are given in nanometers, thousand-millionths of a meter, or in electron volts, a common unit of measurement in atomic physics. Very short waves, such as gamma rays and X-rays, and very long waves, such as electricity waves and radio waves, are invisible to people. The shortest wavelength visible to

people corresponds to the color purple and is about 400 nanometers long. The longest we can see is the color red, which occurs at about 800 nanometers. Green is in the middle. Honeybees and other insects can see ultraviolet rays, which are below the range of our vision. As a result, they can see differences among flowers where we see none. Similarly, some snakes, including rattlers, have an additional sense organ termed a pit organ—that is why they are called pit vipers. The pit organ is sensitive to infrared radiation (heat). It allows the snake to "see" warm-blooded prey in darkness.

Infrared

Ultraviolet

Gamma ray   X-ray   Microwave   Radio wave

The visible spectrum

The electromagnetic spectrum. The small portion of the spectrum that people can see— visible light—has been enlarged.

Violet   Blue   Green   Yellow   Orange   Red colors that others distinguish easily. In fact, about 10 percent of people have that condition, and 90 percent of them are men. The two colors most often confused are red and green; far less common is blue–yellow color blindness. In many cases the confusion is not total, and very bright colors can still be distinguished. It is partly for that reason, and partly because color is a subjective response, that many people who are color-blind are not aware of it.

Trichromatic theory does not explain everything about color vision. Almost 50 years after Helmholtz further developed Young's trichromatic theory, the neurologist Ewald Hering (1834–1918) pointed out that we do not seem to think in terms of "pure" colors, as might be expected on the basis of that theory. Instead, if you ask people to name pure colors, they will name the four primary colors: red, green, blue, and yellow. Those four colors represent two pairs of complementary or opposite colors: red is opposed to green, and blue is opposed to yellow. We cannot imagine a greenish red or a bluish yellow, just as there is no color such as blackish white. Accordingly, color vision is better explained by what Hering termed an opponent process system. That system consists of three separate channels corresponding to complementary pairs of colors: red–green, blue–yellow, and black–white (*see* box p. 71).

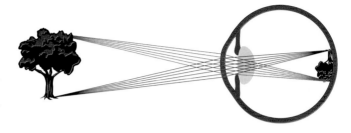

The eyes and the brain

The eyes react to light waves, translating them into nerve signals that travel to the brain. It is the brain that interprets the information and perceives color, form, texture, and movement. The connection between eye and brain is the optic nerve. Signals from the right half of each eye go to the left side of the brain—called the left hemisphere; signals from the left half of each eye go to the opposite hemisphere— the right side of the brain (*see* diagram p. 70). The main destination of visual signals is an area at the very back of the brain called the visual cortex, or the occipital lobe (*see* pp. 20–39). The image in the retina is upside down and smaller than the actual object (*see* diagram above). The visual cortex turns it upright and interprets it in order to make it look like the original object.

To examine the role of the brain in visual perception investigators placed see-through goggles on the eyes of

Light waves bounce off an object in different directions. Only some of them enter the eye, where they are brought together at a single point on the retina. The image on the retina is upside down and much smaller than the actual object. The visual cortex corrects the representation of the object.

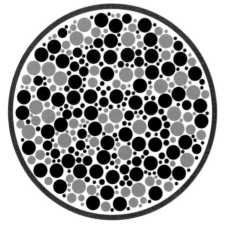

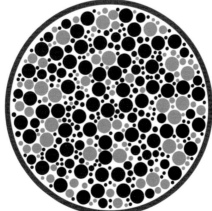

Two common tests for color blindness. If you are not color-blind, you will have little difficulty seeing the number 5 in the left-hand figure and the number 8 in the right-hand figure. People who are color blind will need a stronger contrast in colors before they are able to read the figures.

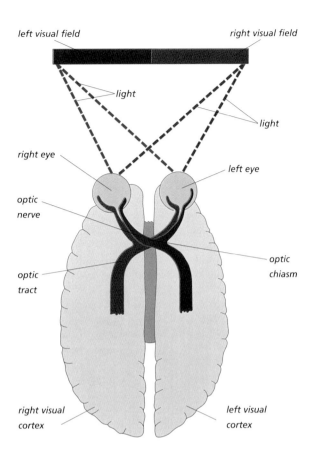

left visual field

right visual field

light

light

right eye

left eye

optic nerve

optic chiasm

optic tract

right visual cortex

left visual cortex

Feature detectors

Why do animals and people who are deprived of normal visual stimulation for a period after birth experience visual problems? Neurobiologists David Hubel and Thorsten Wiesel, who shared a Nobel Prize in 1981 for their discoveries about the role of the brain in vision, provide an answer. When they recorded the levels of

> *"Can the brain understand the brain? Can it understand the mind? Is it a giant computer, or some other kind of giant machine?"*
> — David Hubel, 1979

brain activity in animals that had been deprived of visual stimulation, they found that many cells in the visual cortex seemed to have stopped functioning.

In addition, there were far fewer connections between nerve cells in the visual cortex area of the brain. In one study the investigators reared cats with one eye sewn shut while the other one remained open. When they later removed the stitches so that both eyes could function, the visual cortex continued to respond only to the eye that had not been kept closed. In some of their studies Hubel and Wiesel were able to record activity in single cells of the visual cortex. That allowed them to determine the effect on the retina of very specific stimulation, and they discovered that certain brain cells in the visual cortex are activated by very precise kinds of stimulation. For example, some respond only to lines of a certain width, and others to very specific angles or clear-cut movements. Some respond to vertical lines, others to horizontal lines. And when those specialized cells, which are known as feature detectors, are not activated in the first weeks of life, many never function at all. Our perceptual systems depend on feature detectors to recognize everything in the world around us from furry cats to voices and people's faces.

chimpanzees at birth. The goggles allowed light to enter; however, the animals were unable to see shapes or patterns. Even after the goggles were removed, the chimpanzees required months before they could recognize objects or even guide their own movements in space. Most never achieved normal vision even after the goggles had been removed. Similarly, cats reared in the dark or blindfolded do not learn to see normally when the lights are later turned on or the blindfolds removed. People who are blind or deprived of light at an early age may have similar experiences (*see* box p. 71). Early brain development in relation to vision is impaired by this deprivation. It seems from these animal experiments and case studies on people that early visual stimulation is essential for the development of normal visual perception.

Images from the left visual field are transmitted to the right side of the brain, and images from the right visual field are transmitted to the left side of the brain. The visual cortex interprets and corrects them.

THE NEGATIVE AFTERIMAGE

EXPERIMENT

There is a simple demonstration you can perform that provides additional evidence of opponent processes in color vision (see p. 69). Take a few moments to follow the instructions beneath the figure to the right.

What you saw, if you have normal color vision, is a negative afterimage—an image in complementary colors. Since the flag you stared at is the exact opposite of the colors it should be, the afterimage should be colored appropriately. The best explanation is that the image of the flag activates certain cells but prevents activity in the opponent cells. When the image is removed, the previously inactive cells compensate by firing briefly. That gives rise to the perception of an image in complementary colors. It turns out that both Hering with the opponent process theory and Young-Helmholtz with the trichromatic theory (see p. 69) were correct. Trichromatic theory explains what happens in the cones of the retina, while opponent process theory explains

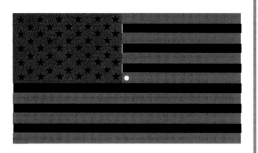

Stare at the center of the flag for half a minute or so, then shift your gaze to a blank sheet of paper. What you see is a negative afterimage.

what happens in a wider context in the rest of the eye, especially the bipolar cells (see box p. 66)—this means that if, for example, you are looking at a red object, the light waves bouncing off it would activate mainly the cones in the retina that respond to red, and your brain interprets the nerve signals from your eyes accordingly.

Recognizing faces and objects

By one rough estimate we recognize as many as 30,000 different objects. Some of those come in billions of different forms. The human face is a good example. As individuals we see only a very tiny fraction of this planet's six billion faces, yet we would have no difficulty in identifying any one of them as an example of a human face. More than that, we instantly recognize hundreds of faces of people we know. Yet the differences between those faces are often so subtle that we cannot put them into words. Unless there is something very remarkable about your face, like a recently broken nose, you might find it impossible to describe it so clearly that I could pick it out from

THE STORY OF S. B.

FOCUS ON

Richard Gregory, professor of neuropsychology at the University of Bristol, England, tells the story of S. B., a man who had been blind for the first 52 years of his life. During that time S. B. had adapted impressively. He rode confidently through his neighborhood on his bicycle with his hand on a friend's shoulder. He built things with tools in his own workshop, and he also spent much of his time trying to find out what the world would look like to someone with sight. Then, at the age of 52 S. B. had corneal transplants. When the bandages were removed, he could see for the first time. But what he saw was a blurred and indistinct world. Although he soon learned to

recognize familiar objects by sight, he developed little sense of perspective or depth and little understanding of speed or motion. So confused was he that he imagined he could easily lower himself to the ground from the window of his hospital room, not realizing it was more than 30 feet (9m) up! So uncertain was he of speed and distance that he became utterly terrified of crossing streets.

Like many individuals in similar circumstances, S. B. became increasingly depressed following his surgery, eventually choosing to spend long periods of time sitting alone at home in the dark. Some three years after the surgery S. B. died.

VISUAL AGNOSIAS

Given a pickle to look at, there are some people who cannot name it even though they have not forgotten the word "pickle." Although they cannot name it, they might accurately describe the pickle's shape and color, and might even be able to draw it. But if allowed to touch or taste the pickle rather than just look at it, they might immediately be able to name it. Such people are said to have an agnosia (an inability to recognize objects by one or more senses). Agnosia can result from brain damage or disease. One highly specific form of agnosia, prosopagnosia, involves only faces. People with that condition can name any familiar object they see; but although they easily recognize faces as being faces, they cannot say whose faces they are or even whether or not they are familiar faces. For example, one typical 52-year-old patient with prosopagnosia could easily recognize and name just about anything other than a face. He knew what a face was, but he could not recognize even his wife's face or the faces of his children. Yet, when people he knew spoke, he recognized them immediately and could name them without any trouble.

Studies of the brains of people with agnosias give information about the parts of the brain that might be involved in recognition and naming. Agnosias provide evidence that recognizing and producing a name for an object or a face involve different parts of the brain for different perceptual systems. And the fact that visual agnosia can be limited to faces suggests that a very specific area of the brain is devoted to identifying faces by sight. That might have been of some evolutionary

What you see when you first glance at the two rows above is a row of 3 letters followed by a row of 3 numbers. You are unlikely to notice that the B is not really a B, or that it is identical to the 13. What we see is partly what we expect to see.

significance for an animal as social as people. Using our feature detectors, we often identify objects and faces on the basis of their individual features. But visual perception is more than just the mechanical process of detecting features such as angles and lines, and putting them together. Look at the two rows above, for example. They both seem pretty straightforward: A,B,C and 14, 13, 15. Now look again more closely. Note how the B in the first row and the 13 in the second row are identical. Undoubtedly, something other than your detection of features is involved here; otherwise, you would have seen either a B or a 13 in both rows.

In one series of experiments American and Mexican participants looked at pairs of slides using an apparatus that presents a different slide to each eye simultaneously. Under those conditions participants always saw only one slide. One pair of slides consisted of a typical Mexican scene and a typical U.S. scene. Which slide would the participants see? U.S. participants typically saw American scenes; Mexican participants did so only rarely. That is additional evidence that experience and expectations affect our perceptions.

among photographs of a dozen other similar faces. So how do we recognize faces? There is no simple answer to this question. In fact, facial recognition is so complex that even sophisticated computers have difficulties. Programmers find it hard to formulate the rules that would enable computers to detect important features and recognize familiar combinations. Our perceptual systems seem to have such feature detectors. They

can identify several dozen important features for visual perception and even more sounds for auditory perception.

Gestalt principles

Recognizing complex forms such as faces—or, even more difficult, facial expressions—seems to require a level of abstraction and decision making that is not very easily explained. According to the Gestalt psychologists Max Wertheimer

(1880–1943), Kurt Koffka (1886 –1941), and Wolfgang Köhler (1887–1967), we perceive not individual features, but wholes. The foundation of Gestalt theory (*see* Vol. 1, pp. 46–51) is that the whole is greater than the sum of its parts—it is the melody that counts, not the individual notes that it is composed from. And it is the organization of parts that defines the trapezoid, the triangle, the square, and the automobile, not the sum of its lines, angles, and components. Our brains seem to be geared toward the best interpretation of the sensory information they receive. And the best interpretation often reflects other Gestalt principles such as closure, continuity, similarity, and proximity (*see* box below).

FOCUS ON

SOME GESTALT PRINCIPLES OF PERCEPTION

In Gestalt theory (*see* Vol. 1, pp. 46–51) a sense of wholeness is more important than the individual bits and pieces of perception and behavior. We do not always see exactly what is out there. But what we do see often conforms to certain principles.

Perceiving depth and motion: The images on our retinas are flat and 2-D, having only height and width. But that isn't at all the way we see things. We see a 3-D world—with depth or distance. Some of the cues we use for judging depth and distance depend on the fact that we have two eyes—they are binocular cues. Other cues require one eye only—they are termed monocular cues.

Cues for depth and distance: Binocular cues are possible because our two eyes are about 2.25 inches (5.5cm) apart. As a result, the images reflected on each retina at the same moment are not identical. The difference (disparity) is greater for objects that are closer and less for objects that are farther away. In addition, the closer an object, the more our eye muscles have to pull our eyes together (the greater is our eyeball convergence). Our brains use both disparity (or difference) and convergence (meeting) to calculate approximately how far away something is. In addition to those two binocular cues there are at least four different monocular cues that help us judge distance. One is apparent size; because we know that an elephant is big, when it appears small, we know it's far away. Another is interposition; when we see that some objects are in front of others, we know which are closer and which are farther. Similarly, our understanding of aerial perspective tells us that distant objects appear hazier and less distinct than closer objects. Finally, our awareness of linear perspective informs us that parallel lines tend to converge at a distance. We use convergence as a clue to distance (*see* box p. 74).

Closure: We tend to complete patterns. We see a triangle rather than three separate lines.

a x y m
a x y m
a x y m
a x y m
a x y m
a x y m
a x y m
a x y m
a x y m
a x y m

Similarity: We group similar things together. We see four columns of identical letters rather than ten rows of different letters. When we hear two melodies or two conversations, at the same time, we recognize that there are two distinct melodies or conversations. We don't hear just a jumble of sounds.

Continuity: We tend to perceive things as being continuous. If notes are missing in a melody, we fill them in. Even if someone omits sounds in their speech, we still hear entire words. We see a straight line running through a wavy line, not a series of adjoining semicircles.

zz zz zz zz zz

Proximity: We group things that are close together, seeing five pairs of letters rather than ten separate ones.

These four diagrams are examples of the Gestalt principles of perception and how our brains interpret information.

VISUAL ILLUSIONS

What we know and expect sometimes misleads us. Three common visual illusions are shown below. Each is based on perspective: The lines and angles create a geometric illusion. In the top-hat illusion the curved lines suggest distance, so the hat seems to be taller than its brim is wide. In the Ponzo illusion the converging lines seem to be different heights, with the vertical line nearest the converging end of the lines appearing longer. In the Müller-Lyer illusion the arrows make the line on the right seem longer than the one on the left.

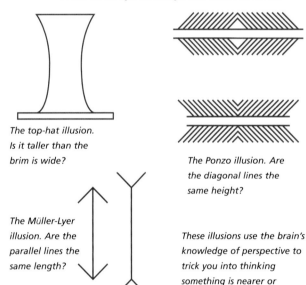

The top-hat illusion. Is it taller than the brim is wide?

The Ponzo illusion. Are the diagonal lines the same height?

The Müller-Lyer illusion. Are the parallel lines the same length?

These illusions use the brain's knowledge of perspective to trick you into thinking something is nearer or further away than it really is.

Perceiving motion

When an object moves across our field of vision, it creates a series of images on the retina, and we know it's moving. However, if you turn your head from left to right with your eyes open, you will have created a series of retinal images, but you won't see anything move. That's because your brain has compensated for your own movement. Similarly, if something moves by you and you move your head in perfect time with that object, there might not be a series of images created on your retina. But again, your brain compensates for your movement, and you know that the object has moved. Travel sickness is caused by the brain receiving confusing messages from the eye and inner ear. The conflict between the expected sensory stimuli and those perceived by the brain causes the brain to send out conflicting messages to the organs of the body. Not everything that appears to move really does so; sometimes our perception of movement is an illusion. Motion pictures, for example, are sequences of still pictures that are presented so rapidly they give the appearance of movement. Neon signs with lights that go on and off rapidly can create the same effect. There are lots of other illusions, such as those that are created by the brain's interpretation of perspective (*see* box left).

HEARING

Of all the senses, hearing is considered the most essential for spoken language and therefore the prevention of emotional isolation. Many animal species depend far more on hearing than on sight for their communication, orientation, and survival. Dolphins cannot rely on their vision in the sometimes murky waters of their environment, but they do not really need to; neither do bats. Both these species make sounds that bounce off the objects around them and return to their hearing in the form of echoes. Nerve signals from their hearing to their brains enable them to build images of their worlds from the

> " 'When I use a word,' Humpty Dumpty said in a rather scornful tone, 'it means just what I choose it to mean, neither more nor less.' "
> — Lewis Carroll, 1871

information they receive. Although we cannot know what mental representations they create from the echoes, their finely controlled movements indicate a spatial awareness at least as sophisticated as our own. To all intents and purposes they are able to "see" and are aware of the world around them. Although people's mental images are more visual than those of a bat or a dolphin, for those people who can hear, sound opens yet another window on the world for the brain.

The stimulus for sound

Sound is our perception of the effects of waves that are set off by vibrations. Sound waves involve the alternate compression and expansion of molecules—usually air molecules, but also molecules in liquids and solids. In fact, sound waves are misnamed because it is our perception of the waves that is the sound, not the waves themselves.

The creation and spread of sound waves are similar to what would happen if you threw a pebble into a calm pond. If you looked carefully, you would see how ripples start where the pebble enters the water and how they fan out in ever-widening circles. The ripples are created at a fixed rate—a number of them pass a certain point each second. That is their frequency. Frequency does not change as the waves fan out. Sound waves are very much like that. Frequency of sound waves is measured in Hertz (Hz) units. One Hz is one cycle, or one vibration, per second. The human ear is sensitive to frequencies between 16 and 20,000 Hz, provided they are loud enough. Sounds above those frequencies are supersonic; those below are subsonic. The lower the frequency, the lower the pitch (tone) we perceive.

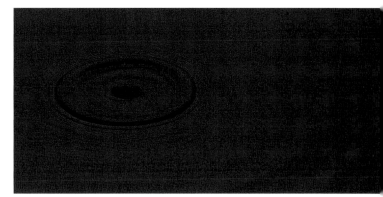

Dolphins emit signals that are up to 100,000 Hz and thus inaudible to humans. But some of their sounds are below 20,000 Hz; we can hear them.

Looking at the pond again, notice how the waves closest to where the pebble hit have higher peaks (greater amplitude) than more distant waves. Amplitude is the height of a wave. Amplitude decreases as distance increases until the waves stop altogether. In the case of sound, amplitude, or loudness, is measured in decibels. Zero decibels is the approximate lower threshold of our hearing. Very high intensities can be dangerous, especially with prolonged exposure. More than eight hours of exposure to sounds at 100 decibels can permanently damage hearing; sounds louder than 130 decibels present a risk of immediate damage. Rock bands often play at levels around 120 decibels.

Throwing a stone into water creates ripples spreading out over the calm sheet of water. This is similar to what happens when sound waves are created and spread. The waves in the center where the stone hit the water have a higher amplitude than those farther out. The greater the amplitude of a sound wave, the more noise it creates.

Dolphins live in an environment where they cannot always rely on their vision. Instead, they make very high-pitched sounds that bounce off objects (echo), enabling them to build up a picture of the world around them. They can also emit low-frequency sounds that are audible to people.

What would happen if you threw two pebbles into the pond? Waves would fan out from each pebble, crashing into each other and tumbling this way and that to create a network of little wavelets. Those wavelets could no longer be described in terms of frequency and amplitude alone because they would be too complex. Complexity is the third characteristic of sound waves. The sound waves that surround us are not usually pure sounds from one source; more often they are combinations of sounds. Our perception of the complexity of sound waves is what is known as timbre. It is that property of sound that enables us to distinguish between the voice of a parent and that of another person, for example.

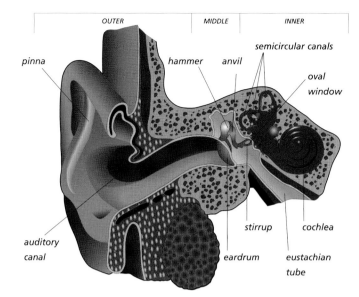

Structure of the ear

Trout and other fish have lines of pressure-sensitive cells on each side of their bodies (called the lateral line). Those cells enable them to detect vibrations and chemicals in the water, giving them underwater versions of the senses of smell and hearing. Similarly, some earless lizards and snakes sense vibrations through their bones, especially those of their jaws. But unlike these animals, people have ears.

The visible part of the human ear is the pinna in the outer ear, a piece of flesh that spirals like a question mark into either side of your head. The pinna, together with the short, wax-filled auditory canal, which conducts vibrations from the pinna to the eardrum, is part of the external ear (see diagram above).

The middle ear is a small, air-filled cavity containing three tiny bones (ossicles): the hammer (malleus) is connected directly to the eardrum at one end and to the anvil (incus) at the other. The anvil, in turn, connects with the stirrup (stapes). The stirrup fits over a small membrane (oval window) that leads to the inner ear. There is also a passage, the eustachian (auditory) tube, that leads from the middle ear to the throat.

The inner ear contains the cochlea, a fluid-filled structure shaped like a snail's

The three main parts of the ear are the outer, middle, and inner sections. Within this overall structure the ear is a complex collection of tubes, canals, containers, fluids, membranes, bones, cartilage, and nerves.

shell. Stretched inside the cochlea is the basilar membrane, along which are the sound-receptive hair cells that make up the organ of Corti.

How the ear works

Sound waves, which are disturbances of molecules of the air, are funneled by the pinna in the outer ear through the auditory canal, causing the eardrum in the middle ear to vibrate. Although the vibrations are very slight, they set up corresponding vibrations in the three little bones of the middle ear, which are then transmitted to the inner ear via the oval window (see diagram above). Movement of the oval window causes movement in the fluids of the inner ear, setting up wavelike motions of the basilar membrane. They cause the hair cells of the organ of Corti to move. As those cells bend and twist, they activate nerve cells at their base. Impulses in those nerve cells are then transmitted to both hemispheres of the brain via the auditory nerve.

Locating sounds

Many sound waves reach our two ears at slightly different times. If the sound comes directly from one side, it will reach the farther ear about 0.8 milliseconds later than it reaches the nearer ear. In addition, the nearer ear receives the vibrations directly; the vibrations are less intense when they reach the farther ear because they have been diverted around the head. If the sound comes directly from above, in front, or behind, it reaches both ears at about the same time and with the same intensity. But the shape of the pinna changes the waves in different ways depending on the direction from which they come. We use those three cues—time difference, intensity difference, and distortions resulting from the angle at which the vibrations strike the ear—to judge the direction of a sound.

Perceiving pitch

In daily life we want to know far more about a sound than just where it came from. We want to know whose voice it is, what song, what bird, or what animal. We need to be able to detect, learn, and recognize sounds. For that we need to be able to perceive pitch (as experienced in the high and low tones of a musical scale). One theory, the frequency theory, suggests that sound waves give rise to brain activity that corresponds directly to the frequency of the wave.

In other words, a wave at 500 cycles per second (500 Hz) would give rise to 500 nerve impulses per second. There is evidence that this does happen, but only for the lower frequencies, because a nerve cannot ordinarily fire more than about 1,000 times per second. A second explanation, called place theory, suggests how we perceive higher pitches. It seems that high and low frequencies affect different parts of the cochlea. If the base of the cochlea is most active, we hear higher frequencies; if the upper end is most active, we perceive lower frequencies.

Hearing and language

Spoken language is hearing's most important contribution to our lives. Language helps us create cultures. It works close up or at great distances, in daylight or in darkness. Its evolutionary

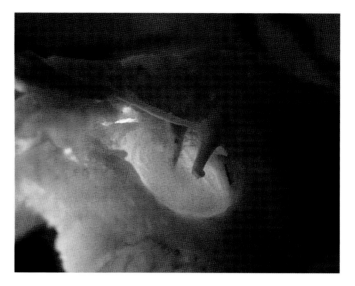

significance can hardly be overstated; neither can its contribution to our thinking and to our ability to solve problems and to adapt. In oral (spoken) language we use sounds for which we have widespread agreement concerning their referents (meanings). Language can also consist of visual rather than auditory symbols—now, for example, you are reading the words written on the page. In some cases, such as American Sign Language, it can consist mainly of gestures. Spoken language depends on our hearing, which, like our other perceptions, depends on the activity of our brains. Information from each ear is transmitted via the auditory nerve to either side of the brain. Our brains hear and process sounds. Processing a sound might consist of nothing more than recognizing that a sound has occurred, or it might mean recognizing the meaning of a sound. How the brain associates sounds with meanings is still largely a matter of speculation, but scientists do know where in the brain that activity takes place.

Research on brain activity

In 1861 surgeon Paul Broca (1824–1880) met a patient with a severe speech disorder—he could only produce one word. When that patient later died, Broca

The tympanic membrane, more commonly known as the eardrum, is the part of the ear that vibrates when sound waves enter. The tiny bone in the image is the hammer of the middle ear. It transmits sounds from the eardrum to the inner ear via the anvil and stirrup.

performed an autopsy and found damage to a small area on the left side of the frontal lobe of his brain. Broca correctly concluded that the injury explained the man's inability to produce the ordinary sounds of language. That area of the brain has since come to be known as Broca's area (*see* Vol. 1, pp. 90–95).

A short time later the neurologist Carl Wernicke (1848–1905) identified another area of the brain that is more closely related to the production of speech than the comprehension of it. That part of the brain, now known as Wernicke's area (*see* Vol. 1, pp. 118–125), is also on the left-hand side of the brain (the left hemisphere). Very close to Wernicke's area is a third structure, the angular gyrus, which is also involved in language. Researchers generally agree that in most people the left hemisphere is more dedicated to language than the right one.

> *"Any sufficiently advanced technology is indistinguishable from magic."*
> — *Arthur C. Clarke, 1972*

Event-related potentials

Electroencephalograms (EEGs), positron emission tomography (PET scans), and functional magnetic resonance imaging (fMRI) give information about brain activity either in the entire brain or in regions of the brain (*see* Vol. 1, pp. 96–103). Recent studies typically make use of sophisticated methods for detecting brain activity. For example, EEGs give general recordings of brain activity; PET scans show the level of activity in different regions of the brain; and fMRI provides a picture of nerve activity in various structures of the brain.

When EEG recordings are taken while a person is exposed to a special stimulus, it is possible to detect electrical activity that relates directly to that stimulus. That activity is called an event-related potential (ERP). ERPs are now among the most often studied variables (that is, something whose value is subject to change) in brain research. Much of the research with ERPs uses auditory stimulation. Some studies show that responses to spoken words as well as responses associated with producing words are stronger in the left hemisphere than in the right. Nevertheless, ERPs in response to stimulation of hearing tend to occur in both hemispheres. And when signals are fed into only one ear, the ERP is usually stronger in the opposite hemisphere. Those findings support both the conclusion that the left hemisphere is very involved in language and the general principle of contralaterality.

Contralaterality means that each brain hemisphere tends to control functioning in the opposite side of the body, as shown in our knowledge of how visual fields correlate to the brain (*see* diagram p. 70). Although we know that Broca's area is involved in producing speech and Wernicke's area in understanding speech, ERP research shows that many other areas of the brain participate in those processes. The nerve architecture that underlies language is complex and not yet very clear. For example, ERPs produced by auditory signals occur earliest in the brain stem and then in several other brain structures before they occur in the auditory cortex. In addition, ERPs arise not only in response to external stimuli; they also happen in response to thoughts and emotions that are independent of external stimulation. For example, ERPs often occur when a person is expecting a signal. ERP research is still in its infancy, but it may eventually tell us much more than we now know about the specific areas of the brain involved in different perceptual, mental, and physical processes.

TOUCH, TASTE, AND SMELL

Our world does not simply have sound, color, and movement; it also has odor, taste, and texture. It can be hot or cold. Sometimes it can be painful. And it can be upright, sideways, or upside down—or

THREE IS SOFT AND YELLOW: SYNESTHESIA

Normally our senses, our perceptual antennas, are tuned to different features of our world. They give us separate but related images of the same scene. For example, imagine a woman teaching a class. We hear the sounds of her voice, we see the numbers she writes, and we smell the perfume she is wearing. But there are some rare individuals who might see colors—the number three as yellow, for example—when the teacher speaks, who might feel the smell of her perfume, or who might hear the melodies that belong to each of the numbers she writes. Those people have a rare condition termed synesthesia in which stimulation of one perceptual system leads to their experiencing imagery in another.

The most common forms of synesthesia involve visual images. The images are usually highly consistent and predictable. For example, Mike Dixon and his associates at the University of Waterloo, Ontario, Canada, studied a synesthetic person who consistently saw colors while looking at black digits or even when simply asked to imagine a digit. Others see colors or other visual images when they feel certain moods or when they are in pain. Still others feel tactile (touch) sensations when they hear music. We have no widely accepted explanation for synesthesia in spite of a spurt of recent research. It is possible that some artists experience especially rich mental imagery because they have the condition.

There is some evidence that mental images relating to one perceptual system can help improve performance associated with a different system. For example, many athletes, whose performance depends very much on their body senses, such as balance, try to improve their performance by using visual images—that is, by imagining and mentally rehearsing their actions. They are using their visual systems to enhance the performance of their body senses. Note also that our everyday speech often makes use of synesthetic language—we speak of sounds that are dull or bright, of colors that are warm or cold, and of drinks that are either heavy or light.

---

sometimes we can be in a sideways or upside-down position. Fortunately, we have other perceptual systems, other dedicated senses, that allow our brains to know those things about our worlds.

The body senses

We know much more about seeing and hearing than we do about our other senses. A lot of research has focused on vision in particular. That is partly due to the apparently greater evolutionary importance of vision and hearing— especially for communication and locomotion—and partly because of the greater difficulty of studying the other perceptual systems. Yet those other senses are very important to our functioning. Take, for example, the body senses, sometimes known as the somesthetic senses. Among other things, they are essential for moving around, for staying upright or knowing about body position (*see* box p. 81), and for avoiding things that are painful and that might damage or kill us.

Touch: the haptic system

The word haptic comes from the Greek meaning "to be able to lay hold of"— hence its use for the sense of touch. The haptic perceptual system is also called the skin senses. They consist of various receptors that give us information about bodily contact. Some receptors are sensitive to pressure; others react to warmth and cold; still others provide sensations of pain. The senses rely on more than one million nerve cells that have endings in or near the epidermis (the outer layer of skin). More receptors lie in the skin of our faces and hands than anywhere else because they are the most sensitive areas. It is possible that sensitivity in these areas evolved to ensure the survival of the species.

Pressure

Pressure receptors are unevenly distributed throughout the body. You can easily demonstrate that by using the "two-point threshold" procedure. Ask someone to touch different parts of your body lightly with the two points of a compass, systematically varying the distance between the two points. The higher the concentrations of pressure receptors, the better you can sense that there are two points close together and not just one. In less sensitive areas the points have to be further apart for you to feel them individually. For most people the two-point threshold for the fingertips is about 0.08 of an inch (0.2mm). It is about five times farther apart on the forearm and even farther apart on the back. Those measures of sensitivity to touch are very approximate. Nor do they necessarily reflect a person's normal sensitivity to

A patient receiving acupuncture treatment. According to the gate-control theory, the insertion and manipulation of needles into the body stimulate the neurons in the midbrain and stop them from transmitting pain.

FOCUS ON

PHANTOM LIMB PAIN

Psychologist Guy R. Lefrançois once worked in an army kitchen with Nicolao Kovach, who had lost his left forearm in the Hungarian Revolution (1956). That missing arm hurt him a lot, he said. At first Lefrançois imagined it would be the stump, the scar of the amputation, that still hurt. No, said Nicolao, it's my darned hand! It's my fingers! But of course, Nicolao had no hand, no fingers. What he had was a phantom limb. Psychologist Krista Wilkins and her associates studied 60 children and adolescents who lacked a limb. Nearly half of them had been born with a missing limb; the others had undergone surgical amputation. Only a small fraction of those born with a missing limb experienced phantom sensations. But even after their surgery had healed, almost 70 percent of the amputees had phantom pain. Some of them had stump pain, where the site of the surgery itself hurt. But many also had phantom limb pain in which the pain seemed to be located in the absent limb. For more than a third of those amputees phantom limb pain mirrored the pain they had felt in the limb before surgery. Phantom limb pain is real pain. Patterns of brain activity are much the same in people experiencing pain in a missing limb as they are in people experiencing pain in a real limb. That seems to be evidence that phantom limb sensations are produced in the brain by the same processes that underlie other sensations of pain, but without the external stimuli.

The Melzack-Wall gate theory provides another explanation for phantom limb pain. The theory suggests that because there is no stimulation from the limb after removal, A-fibers remain inactive, and the "gates" remain open (see p. 82).

unexpected stimulation. That is because we are significantly more sensitive when we are expecting a touch or a vibration. Our responses to unexpected stimulation are less certain and slower.

Temperature

Two different kinds of receptors allow us to sense changes in temperature. One kind is sensitive to heat and the other to cold. There are about five times more cold receptors than heat receptors. Like our sensitivity to pressure, our sensitivity to temperature diminishes with age. The face is the part of the body most sensitive to temperature; the extremities are considerably less sensitive. Cold receptors increase their rate of firing when the temperature is dropping; heat receptors increase theirs when temperature climbs. Information from cold and heat receptors is essential to our brains if they are to maintain our body temperatures within a normal range. The brain readjusts our temperature by sending out signals that lead to blood-vessel dilation and increased perspiration when we're too warm or blood-vessel constriction when we're too cold. If those measures are not sufficient, and our temperature receptors continue to signal that we're too hot or too cold, our brains might suggest that we make a fire or jump in a lake full of cold water.

THE BASIC ORIENTING SYSTEM

There is a complex structure in our inner ears that has nothing to do with hearing. It lies in the part of the ear named the labyrinth because of the complexity of the tunnels it contains. The labyrinth includes not only the snail-shell-shaped cochlea but also three other tubes called semicircular canals (see diagram p. 76). The tubes are set at right angles to each other and are filled with fluid. They are the main sense organs of our basic orienting system that detects bodily movement and position.

If you take a sealed glass partly filled with water and swirl it around, tilt it, or turn it upside down, the movements of the water are predictable. That is how our inner-ear receptors (our vestibular senses) work. When we move, lie down, spin, or stand on our heads, the fluid in our semicircular canals moves in expected ways. Hair cells inside the canals translate the effects of those movements into nerve impulses that our brains interpret to determine that we are doing those things—moving, lying down, spinning, or standing on our heads. Our basic orienting system relies not only on our inner-ear receptors, but also on sensations we get from receptors in our muscles, tendons, and joints (our kinesthetic senses). The kinesthetic senses allow our brains to know that our arms and legs are bent this way or that, or that we are moving forward or backward. In addition, our other perceptual systems are brought into play. For example, we know when we are moving because sensors in our muscles and joints or movements of the fluid in our semicircular canals tell us so. We know we are moving not only because sensors in our muscles and joints or movements of the fluid in our semi-circular canals tell us so. Our visual system also tells us that we are moving. Some aspects of movement are coded by specific cells in the visual cortex, and these cells respond to particular aspects such as speed or direction.

Pain

Pressure receptors habituate (adapt) to stimulation very rapidly. You might feel the gentle pressure of your sweater when you first pull it over your head, but within moments you no longer sense it. In contrast, pain receptors do not habituate nearly as rapidly. That is usually useful

> *"One of the greatest pains to human nature is the pain of a new idea."*
> — *Walter Bagehot, 1869*

because pain is a signal that something is wrong. One of the functions of pain is to keep us from doing things that are harmful—like walking on broken glass or leaning on a hot stove. Pain results from the stimulation of nerve endings by pressure, heat, or sometimes chemicals. Certain areas of the body, such as behind the knee, the buttocks, and the neck, have more pain receptors than areas such as the tip of the nose, the bottom of the thumb, or the soles of the feet. In addition, there are pain receptors in the internal organs. When they are stimulated, we feel visceral pain, that is, pain in the internal organs. Visceral pain is often felt in parts of the body that are far removed from the true source of the pain. For example, people suffering from heart pain may have the sensation of pain in their arm, their neck, or perhaps even in their hand.

Two distinct types of nerve pathways transmit pain sensations to the brain. One is rapid, and the other is slow. Each results in a different kind of pain sensation. The first, transmitted by the rapid nerve pathways, is the instant, sharp pain you feel when you first burn your hand or step on a thorn. The pain message reaches your brain very rapidly and is sharp and insistent because its function is to make you pull away from the cause of it in time to prevent serious damage. The response is swift and automatic. The second type of pain sensation, which is transmitted by the slower pathways, is the dull ache that continues after you have pulled away.

One explanation of how the body processes pain is the gate-control theory proposed by the scientists Ronald Melzack and P. D. Wall. According to them, we feel pain when the nerve cells that connect pain receptors to the brain are active. Those nerve cells, called C-fibers, have to pass through a series of "gates" to reach the brain. However, those gates are not always fully open and are sometimes completely shut. That is because there is a second kind of nerve cell, called an A-fiber, that can close some of the gates, preventing the passage of pain signals. C-fibers, which carry pain signals, transmit at a faster rate than A-fibers, which hinder pain sensations. That explains why we quickly sense sharp pain when we hurt ourselves. The "neural gate" involves a region of the midbrain, and the neurons in this area inhibit the cells that would normally communicate pain from the pain receptions. When the neurons are active, the neural gate is closed; and when the neurons are not active, the neural gate is open. Gate-control theory may also explain why acupuncture relieves pain. The reasoning is that if acupuncture is effective, it is because the insertion and manipulation of the needle stimulate the A-fiber nerve cells that hamper the transmission of pain signals, thus closing the "gates." The theory is also sometimes used to explain phantom limb pain (*see* box p. 80) when a person has lost a limb but continues to feel pain in that area.

THE CHEMICAL SENSES

Taste (gustation) and smell (olfaction) are especially important biologically. One of their functions is to prevent us poisoning ourselves; another is to entice us to eat. Both are essential for survival. The organ that makes it possible for us to smell is the olfactory epithelium, which is located toward the top of our nasal (nose) passages. It is a small membrane covered by a mat of tiny hairlike structures called cilia. The hairs respond to molecules dissolved in the mucus (thick, slimy fluid) lining the nasal passages, transmitting impulses directly to the olfactory bulb, a small protrusion at the front underside of the brain above the olfactory epithelium.

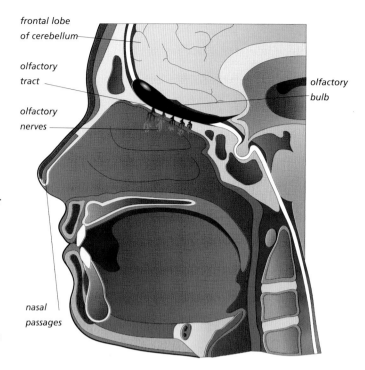

A side view of the nose showing the olfactory epithelium and the olfactory bulb. The ability to detect odors depends on cilia, hairlike extensions of the cells that make up the olfactory epithelium. The olfactory bulb, the brain organ involved in olfaction, is immediately above the olfactory epithelium.

In many animals, including people, the nostrils that lead to the olfactory epithelium are slanted upward. That gives two distinct advantages. One is that odors rise from warm objects and are therefore more likely to be trapped by a nose that opens downward. The second is that a nose that points downward is less likely to become blocked by rain or any object falling from above.

Our vocabulary for smells is vague. We cannot easily describe what something smells like other than by comparing it to other objects with strong and familiar odors. Although there have been many attempts to classify smells, none has been widely accepted. Yet research indicates that we often have powerful recollections of odors and strong associations with them. And it seems that in spite of our poor vocabulary for odors, we can distinguish more than 10,000 different smells. The sense of smell is far less developed in people than it is in many other animals. The part of our brain devoted to smell is very small in comparison with the total size of our brain; in contrast, about one-third of a dog's cortex is involved in smell. Some scientists estimate that the dog's sense of smell is as much as one million times more powerful than that of a person (*see* box on p. 85).

GUSTATION

We have seen that smell depends on an airborne molecule being dissolved in mucus and brought into physical contact with receptor cells. In the same way taste depends on chemicals being dissolved in fluids that surround taste-sensitive cells. Those cells are found on the tongue in clusters of about 40 or 50, in little protrusions known as taste buds. The taste buds are dotted with tiny openings through which dissolved chemicals reach the taste cells. Taste cells have a life cycle of only about 4 to 10 days, after which they die and are regenerated. But regeneration becomes slower as we age and sometimes stops completely. People sometimes add more salt and spices to their food as they get older to compensate for their decreasing number of taste cells.

Our language for taste is no more exact than that for smell. When asked what something tastes like, we are most likely to compare it to some other, familiar food. Or we might simply say that it is sweet, sour, salty, bitter, or some combination of those terms. Psychologists generally agree that those four tastes are universal. Furthermore, it seems that different parts of the tongue are most sensitive to each of those tastes (see diagram p. 84). That does not mean we have taste receptors for sweet tastes and different receptors for salt, sour, and bitter. Receptors seem to respond to combinations of tastes, although it is not clear which combinations give rise to which impressions of taste.

What we think of as taste is only partly based on what our tongues tell us. People

who are anosmatic (unable to detect odors) do not taste food in the same way as the majority of people. In fact, smell is sometimes more important than the reaction of our taste buds in the tasting of food. If you were to pinch your nose tightly

> *"Smell is a potent wizard that transports us across thousands of miles and all the years we have lived."*
> — *Helen Keller, 1902*

while taking alternate bites of an apple and an onion, you would be unlikely to detect any difference in taste between the two. Temperature and texture also influence taste. Cold mashed potatoes do not taste anything like hot mashed potatoes. Certain fish such as squid can be unappealing because of their slimy texture for example. What tastes good or bad also depends on learning and experience. In certain cultures

A perfumer testing fragrances. People can identify more than 10,000 different smells, but do not have a comprehensive or precise vocabulary to describe them.

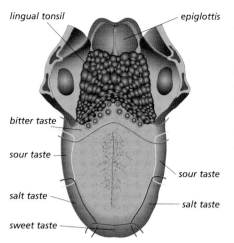

lingual tonsil

epiglottis

bitter taste

sour taste

sour taste

salt taste

salt taste

sweet taste

A surface view of the tongue showing areas of sensitivity. Different areas of the tongue are most sensitive to one of four basic tastes: sweet, salt, sour, and bitter. These areas overlap considerably.

grubs, beetles, intestines, fish eyes, caribou stomachs, and animal brains are considered to be great delicacies. The junk foods such as burgers and chips that some of us love might taste very bad to people who like orange beetles. Taste preferences also change with age.

Future research

Scientists now have sophisticated instruments that can detect and map brain activity in people. These advances in technology have enabled psychologists to use brain-imaging techniques to study the relationship between what people

Is Beauty in the Mind?

According to neuroscientist and psychologist Vilayanur Ramachandran, if a rat is given a reward for responding to a rectangle and not to a square, it will outdo itself later in responding to a more exaggerated rectangle than the original—say, a rectangle that is much longer and narrower. We may be a little like the rat, says Ramachandran, in that we too might respond to things that are overstated and embellished. An awareness of that might guide artists in the use of certain principles that seem to underlie our notions of beauty in art.

The principle illustrated by the rat that responds to the exaggerated rectangle is this: If something is good, more of it is even better. In art, if form is beautiful, more or clearer form might be even more beautiful; if a color is especially appealing, more of it might be even more appealing. Artists might consciously or unconsciously intensify particular features in their work, as Pablo Picasso (1881–1973) did during his blue period, when blue tones dominated his paintings. Artists might group elements in a painting to highlight distinct features, such as the figure rather than the background. They might draw attention to contrast or use different techniques to emphasize a single element, such as line or form or color. Ramachandran's studies of brain activity in people while they are looking at paintings provide evidence that each of those techniques can lead to nerve-cell activity associated with our perception of attractiveness or beauty. Those studies also show that visual areas of the brain are most stimulated when looking at more appealing visual art. At least to some extent beauty itself may be a pattern of nerve-cell activity in the brain.

Pablo Picasso in front of one of his paintings. If we perceive a particular feature in an artist's work to be beautiful, then is a work of art containing more of that feature especially attractive?

PHEROMONES

A male moth flitting around on a dark night might suddenly become aware of a female moth several miles away—and will then go and find her! A dog does not have quite so far to go when a neighbor's bitch becomes receptive. His nose tells him the exact location of the dog in heat. Among nonhuman animals almost all receptive females give off airborne molecules called pheromones. Pheromones are very potent and highly attractive to the male of the species. A handful of pheromone molecules smacking into a male moth's antennas is all it takes to arouse his sexual interest. Then, in the same way as we use our two ears to locate the direction of a sound, the male moth computes differences in reception time between his two antennas to locate the female moth. And then he will fly through adverse conditions such as storms to find her.

Scientists have tried hard to find human sexual pheromones; cosmetics companies are very interested. We know there are human secretions, especially certain steroids, that are pheromonelike. Many occur on male armpit hair (one example is androstadienone); others occur in urine. Some studies have shown that females are more sensitive to those substances than are males, especially when they are releasing eggs (ovulating). Some research also indicates that exposure to pheromones may positively affect women's moods. But no clear link has yet been found between human pheromonelike substances and sexual behavior. Besides, not all pheromones send out sexual messages. Many insects produce pheromones designed to keep other insects away. The well-known unpleasant odor of the skunk is also a pheromone with the same warning message—keep away!

perceive—how they see, hear, and feel the world around them—and the nerve activity happening in the brain. More research has been conducted into how we see than any of the other senses, and scientists know more about vision and hearing than any other senses. Knowledge about how the senses work is incomplete, and research into the complex processes involved in perception is ongoing.

Summary

Perception involves sensation and the brain's interpretation of it. The brain plays an important role in perception as it interprets information from complex neural connections (*see* Vol. 2, pp. 20-39). Particular areas of the brain control each of the senses. The brain receives and interprets information and also filters out unwanted or unnecessary information so that we are not overwhelmed with different perceptions. Research suggests that there are critical stages for the development of the brain and, as with other abilities (*see* Vol. 4, pp. 58–77), deprivation at an early age results in impaired perception. Gestalt principles (that people perceive the whole rather than elements of it) explain some elements of perception (*see* Vol. 1, pp. 46–51). Less is known about touch, taste, and smell (the last two senses are sometimes labeled the chemical senses) than about hearing and vision. The eyes are the most complex sensory connection from the outside world to the brain. Technological advances such as the development of brain-imaging techniques will enable psychologists to study these senses in the future. Future research will also focus on analyzing the relationship between what we perceive and the nerve activity happening in the brain. This is a complex area, and we do not always have a vocabulary to describe our perceptions or even a conscious awareness of what we are perceiving.

CONNECTIONS

• The Biology of the Brain: pp. 20–39
• Artificial Minds: pp. 140–163
• Gestalt Psychology: Volume 1, pp. 46–51
• Neuropsychology: Volume 1, pp. 90–95
• Brain-imaging Techniques: Volume 1, pp. 96–103
• Psycholinguistics: Volume 1, pp. 118–125
• Perceptual Development: Volume 4, pp. 40–57

Emotion and Motivation

"Humankind has always been in awe of the power of emotions."

Susan Greenfield

Emotions play a vital role in everyday life and in mental health. Understanding emotions helps us understand human behavior. Since ancient times people have attempted to explain what emotions are, how they are caused, and which parts of the brain coordinate them. Although many advances have been made in our understanding of emotions, we are still just beginning to unravel the complex relationship between emotions and the body.

The philosophers of ancient Greece (*see* Vol. 1, pp. 10–15) explored the nature of emotions, as did later scientists. However, current views about emotions are based on the discoveries made by the naturalist Charles Darwin (1809–1882) and the psychologists William James (1842–1910) and Wilhelm Wundt (1832–1920). Research into emotions became increasingly popular in the 1950s and is now a major aspect of psychology and the related sciences.

THE NATURE OF EMOTION

Imagine you are walking alone through the woods. Suddenly you come face to face with a large black bear. What would happen next? Although we could not predict the outcome of this encounter, we can be sure that many things would affect your body, mind, and behavior—and that you would experience emotion. Your emotional reactions would probably begin with a startle response, then your heart would start to pound, and you would direct your whole attention toward the bear in front of you. You would immediately stop and freeze, while feeling a strong need to run away. If someone were to ask later you how you felt, you would probably say you were afraid.

Clearly, your emotions when facing the bear would be complex, and your response would include physiological, behavioral, and subjective elements. As in this case, we can say that any emotion has three components:

• Physiological changes, such as acceleration of heart rate and activation of specific regions in the brain.
• Behavioral responses, such as a tendency to escape from or prolong contact with whatever is causing the emotion.
• A subjective experience, such as feeling angry, happy, or sad about the person or thing causing the emotion.

Meeting this large black bear would probably elicit the startle response followed by a complex mixture of physiological, behavioral, and subjective reactions.

- Behavior is given both energy and goals by emotional reactions. In this sense emotions tell us what to do.
- Charles Darwin viewed emotions as a means of communicating information quickly. Emotions have enormous importance in the survival of individuals and species. He compared emotions in people and animals.
- Some emotions, such as fear and disgust, originate in primitive parts of the brain and are shared by all animals, while others, such as humor, guilt, and envy, involve the cortex and are thought to be known only by humans.
- The autonomous nervous system uses neurotransmitters and neuromodulators to translate emotional responses into finely tuned physical responses.
- Joseph LeDoux believed the emotional brain has two pathways: a short route for instant, life-preserving responses, and a slower, more considered, route.
- Antonio Damasio proposes that memories of emotional experience cause bodily changes to occur in emotional situations. He believes these changes, which he calls somatic markers, help us make quick decisions by following what folk wisdom calls gut feeling.
- Jaak Panksepp argues that different emotions each have nerve circuits in the brain dedicated to them, some of which interact to produce complex emotions.
- There are some differences in the way the two hemispheres of the brain process emotional responses. However, no one side of the brain exclusively processes emotions in the way that the left brain exclusively processes some intellectual functions.
- The brain is where emotions are processed and experienced, but they can also be provoked or influenced by feedback from the body. Therefore some researchers believe that machines could not have emotions in exactly the same way that people do.

Emotions are therefore a specific and automatic set of consciously experienced responses in reaction to a real or imagined stimulus. People experience emotions when they are afraid, angry, or proud of something specific. An emotion is not the same as a mood, which is a temporary disposition to react in a specific emotional way. If you feel content, tired, irritated, tense, or depressed, you are experiencing moods rather than emotions. Temper is a more permanent disposition than mood to react in specific emotional ways. "Affect" is the term used by some psychologists for the current emotional state of a person.

The functions of emotions

In 1872 Charles Darwin's highly influential book *The Expression of the Emotions in Man and Animals* was published. In this book Darwin argued that emotions are a beneficial product of evolution and thus shared by different species. He also believed that species retain their emotional capabilities during evolution because they play an important role in communication, which improves the species' chances of survival.

According to Darwin, each emotion that was important for survival developed a very specific type of expression. In humans two aspects of expression are most important: facial expressions, such as smiling or frowning, and behavior (also called posture), the tendency to come toward or avoid something. Returning to our earlier example of an encounter with a bear, imagine that a woman saw you in this situation. She would realize that you were facing something scary merely by looking at the expression on your face and

> "We have seen that the senses and intuitions, the various emotions and faculties . . . of which man boasts may be found . . . in the lower animals."
> —Charles Darwin, 1872

posture even if she could not see the bear. This information would probably prompt her to leave before the bear saw her. The communicative function of your expression of fear could thus save her life, and maybe yours as well if she did not just leave you there but brought help.

The expression of emotions helps in our social life by allowing us to communicate quickly. Experimental studies have shown that people can accurately recognize the emotional states of other people merely by glancing at their faces. However, failures to recognize emotions accurately can have severe consequences. For example, a warm smile universally expresses pleasure, and an unsteady one conveys unease; anyone who is unable to tell these different smiles apart is at a great social disadvantage. This can even apply to whole cultures, since some expressions—such as maintaining a fixed smile for strangers as a gesture of submission—occur in some cultures but not others.

While Darwin emphasized the importance of emotions in the survival and evolution of species, philosophers

> "Darwin's (1872) pioneering studies began a century-long debate about whether observers can accurately judge the emotion shown in a facial expression."
> —Paul Ekman et al., 1992

before his time had adopted the view that emotions are disturbing states of mind inherited from our early ancestors that battle with our powers of reason. As a consequence, they believed that emotions are a major cause of mental disease and behavioral problems. In the 1940s Darwin's view of emotions as advantages bestowed by evolution became more influential, and today psychologists assume that emotions have an important adaptive function in enabling people to adjust to new circumstances.

One of the ways this comes about is through providing motivational impetus—in other words, an emotion "moves" an individual toward a response. Emotions—such as the fear you feel when meeting a bear in the woods—allow individuals of any species to make an instant, possibly life-saving, response to events. It is the feeling of fear that motivates you to avoid close contact with

BASIC EMOTIONS

CASE STUDY

In 1971 psychologists Paul Ekman and Wallace Friesen tested whether facial expressions of emotion are shared universally among all humans. They showed photographs of Americans portraying different emotions to people from a variety of cultures, including New Guinea tribes, and asked them to identify the emotion. The results suggested that expressions of six "basic" emotions—happiness, fear, anger, sadness, disgust, and surprise—are indeed shared irrespective of culture.

the bear. Emotions, therefore, are powerful guides to behavior, since they provide clear goals to pursue, such as escaping a wild bear or staying close to someone who attracts you. In addition to telling you what to do to survive in a dangerous situation, emotions also mobilize the energy you need to carry out these behaviors. The experience of emotion includes changes in the activity of the autonomic (involuntary) nervous system, which is the communication network by which the brain controls all parts of the body except for contraction of skeletal muscles (*see* pp. 20–39). In the sudden encounter with the bear the feeling of fear causes the autonomic system to increase the heart rate and blood pressure. That supplies the muscles of the voluntary system with the oxygen and glucose they need to move you speedily away from danger.

In addition to their communicative and motivational functions, emotions also provide information. Emotions guide your attention toward important stimuli and provide a stream of information about whether or not you have attained your action goals, such as escape. Likewise, you will stop eating ice cream when it finally disgusts you, or you will stop talking to a person whose statements are making you angry. Seen from this functional perspective, emotions are very important guides for behavior: They provide fast, clear communication about current stimuli and goals and energy for behavior, as well as telling the person what to do. Emotions therefore have a role in evolution, since they help ensure survival.

Are basic emotions innate?

The functional view of emotions has dominated the research of scientists who share Darwin's evolutionary view. In this view there is a set of basic emotions shared by all humans (*see* box opposite) that are important for the survival of the species. Strong evidence that basic emotions are innate (inborn), rather than learned, stems from the work of psychologist Carroll Izard. He and his colleagues have demonstrated that people who are born blind and have never seen faces still display the typical facial expressions of the basic emotions—such as smiling when happy or wrinkling the nose when disgusted.

But are such basic emotions linked to more than facial expressions? Of course, certain basic emotions trigger specific types of behavior, such as escape, aggression, or care. This suggests that different basic emotions might prompt specific patterns of response in the autonomic nervous system (changes in heart rate, breathing, digestion, and other systems) to enable the body to carry out the appropriate behavior.

In 1983 Paul Ekman, Robert Levenson, and Wallace Friesen found that different basic emotions were linked to specific changes in the autonomic nervous system. They asked people to adjust their face muscles to show a particular basic emotion. At the same time, they assessed several physiological factors relating to the activation of the nervous system.

A happy, smiling baby. Happiness is one of six basic emotions that have the same facial expressions in every country in the world.

Ekman and his colleagues found clear evidence that the expression of different emotions is accompanied by different adjustments of the nervous system. This finding suggested that there is a link between the facial expression of a basic emotion and how the body prepares itself for action, adding support to the notion of basic emotions.

However, few studies of the autonomic nervous system have confirmed such active links between facial expression and autonomic responses. The most consistent finding is that the expression and experience of anger are associated with increases in blood pressure. There is also consistent evidence that emotions do influence the activities of the autonomic nervous system and thus have the power to mobilize the body's energy. Today there is no convincing evidence for a fixed set of basic human emotions linked to specific physiological and behavioral responses.

In 1980 the psychologist Robert Plutchik proposed a different view of emotions. Plutchik's model (*see* diagram p. 90) included eight primary, or basic, innate emotions—joy, acceptance, fear, surprise, sadness, disgust, anger, and anticipation. According to Plutchik, all these primary emotions have an important role in survival because they are linked to distinct behavioral programs, such as "destruction" in the case of anger or "approach" in the case of joy. An important aspect of Plutchik's model is that it also considers more complex emotions, such as guilt and love. Plutchik suggested that such complex emotions are derived from combinations of the primary

Plutchik's 1980 model of basic and derived emotions (left). The more complex emotions are derived by combining these eight basic emotions. For example, surprise combined with fear produces alarm, while joy mixed with fear produces guilt.

example, should both express joy and sadness in the same way. Yet many Westerners have observed that the Japanese are considerably less expressive than Americans. Researchers Ekman and Friesen attempted to address this apparent discrepancy by introducing the concept of display rules. In this theory cultural rules determine the appropriate way for

> "What constitutes a human is
> not simply naturally given. It
> is also created by us."
> —Kennan Malik, 2002

emotions. For example, anticipation and fear combine to produce anxiety.

One criticism of the idea of basic emotion has come from the observation that, despite the findings of Ekman and others, people from different cultures do not in fact always express the same basic emotions in quite the same way. If the basic emotions are innate and a shared evolutionary inheritance of all humans, people from America and Japan, for

individuals to display emotions in social settings. Culture, therefore, can regulate the actual expression of emotions, but the fundamental human way of the emotions does not differ between the cultures. That is because display rules do not operate all the time. When people are alone in private (and thus the influence of culture is minimal), they should show the true, innate expression of an emotion rather than a public display (see box opposite). However, other evidence has led to further criticism of the idea that humans share a

Anger may lead to fighting – but, as with the display of other basic emotions, the way in which anger is expressed can vary depending on culture and situation. Here, these two young men perform a ritualized form of fighting developed as a culturally acceptable expression of real or simulated anger.

PRIVATE AND PUBLIC BEHAVIOR

To demonstrate that people react differently in public and private settings and so provide support for their theory of display rules, Ekman and Friesen conducted a clever experiment. They showed different stressful film clips to Americans and Japanese, and recorded their facial expressions. The participants watched the film clips either alone or in the presence of an experimenter of the same ethnic group. When they were alone, the participants showed similar expressions; but when the experimenter later interviewed them while they were watching a replay of the film clips, the Japanese participants tended to mask their responses more than the Americans, providing evidence of cultural differences in display rules.

fixed set of basic emotions. In 1995 the psychologist James Russell reported studies in which he and his colleagues presented pictures of mimed facial expressions to participants in the study. He found that people did not describe the facial expressions in terms of the standard six or so basic emotions. Instead, the terms they used seemed to form just two basic dimensions: pleasure–displeasure and calmness–arousal. As a result, Russell argued that previous evidence for the accurate recognition of expressions of basic emotions was merely the result of flaws in the methods used in the studies. However, although Russell dismissed the lists of basic emotions suggested by other psychologists as largely the product of cultural assumptions, he did concur with the idea that there is much overlap in the way different cultures describe emotions.

The emotional circumplex

Russell's two-dimensional theory was not new, however. More than 100 years ago the philosopher and psychologist Wilhelm Wundt (see Vol. 1, pp. 30–39) suggested that all emotional experiences can be classified using the dimensions of pleasure and arousal. This model, called the emotional circumplex, has become the main alternative to explaining emotion in terms of a set of basic emotions.

In 1988 psychophysiologist Peter Lang and his colleagues published a large set of emotion-provoking pictures called the International Affective Picture System. The pictures are rated on the dimensions of pleasure (they may be pleasant or unpleasant) and arousal (they may be calming or arouse emotion in the viewer). Pictures of flowers, for example, are pleasant but not arousing; pictures of erotica are pleasant and arouse sexual emotion; and pictures of a mutilated body are unpleasant and arouse disagreeable emotions.

Lang used the pictures in a study in which two separate aspects of participants' emotional response were noted: the viewers' subjective ratings of arousal and pleasantness, and objective measurements of their autonomic nervous system activity. The level of arousal can be assessed by measuring changes in skin conductance and activity in the cortex (measured by functional magnetic resonance imaging, or fMRI; see Vol. 1, pp. 96–103). Pleasantness and unpleasantness, which are related respectively to approach and avoidance systems in the brain, can be assessed by measuring the activity of two facial muscles, the zygomatic major and corrugator supercilii muscles. The more pleasant a picture, the more electrical activity of the zygomatic major muscle

Russell's circumplex model of emotions. According to Russell, emotions can be represented as a combination of degrees along two dimensions—arousal and unpleasantness— rather than by basic emotions. For example, a feeling of elation combines high degrees of arousal and pleasantness.

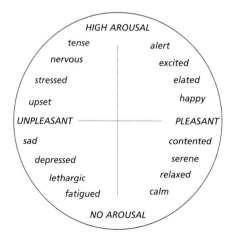

CHOOSING OUR EMOTIONS

In the early 1960s Stanley Schachter and Jerome Sugar conducted experiments to prove that bodily arousal (which causes increased heart and breathing rates and other effects) is only linked with emotions when people believe the arousal is caused by external situations. In one experiment he divided the participants into two groups, giving one group an injection of the drug epinephrine (which speeds up the heart and breathing) and the other group a placebo (an inactive substance). Only some of the epinephrine-injected individuals were informed of the effects of the drug. The participants were then exposed to a situation likely to elicit an emotional response: They were insulted or amused. From their reported responses and behavioral expressions it was clear that the epinephrine-injected individuals who were unaware of the effects of the drug they had been given had experienced more intense emotion and fear than either the placebo group or the informed epinephrine-injected group. They attributed their heightened state to the qualities of the stimuli to which they were exposed; they felt anger at the insults, for example, while the other groups felt only irritation. The group of epinephrine-injected individuals who understood the drug's effects attributed their jittery feelings to the drug, and their responses to the stimuli were similar to those of the placebo group. Schachter's experiment suggests that we experience arousal, we interpret it, and then the emotion occurs, in that order.

can be detected. This muscle is activated by the brain to draw back or tighten the cheek for a smile. The more unpleasant a picture, the more electrical activity of the corrugator supercilii muscle can be measured. This muscle plays a part in lowering and contracting the brows to form a frown. When Lang compared the participants' own ratings of their emotional reactions to the physiological measurements, he found a high rate of agreement between them. This matching supports the idea that pleasure and arousal are key aspects of how emotions differ from one another—but sheds little light on the question of whether humans share a set of basic emotions.

Causes of emotions

What causes the emotional experiences we are all familiar with? Let us go back to the bear in the woods. In this situation you would probably believe that you are running away from the bear because you feel fear. According to common wisdom, all your responses—pounding heart, freezing—occur because you feel afraid of the bear. However, William James (*see* Vol. 1, pp. 30–39), who first used the bear-in-the-woods example to illustrate his theory, turned this idea on its head.

According to James' theory of emotions, you are afraid of the bear because you show fear behaviors—your conscious fear is the result of your physical reactions to the threat, not the other way around. Your heart pounds, you stop still, and you feel fear. In short, James put forward the idea that it is emotional behavior that causes emotions.

> *"How to gain, how to keep, and how to recover happiness is in fact for most men at all times the secret motive for all they do."*
> —*William James, 1902*

Although James' theory is now more than 100 years old, it still influences research today. James proposed that specific emotions follow specific patterns of visceral changes (the viscera are the organs within the chest and abdomen) and skeletomotoric adjustments (movements of the muscles attached to the skeleton), and that feeling an emotion only becomes possible through changes in the body. The "facial feedback hypothesis" has been formulated by researchers influenced by James' idea.

Psychologist Jim Laird has conducted several studies of this hypothesis. The studies show that if people adjust their facial muscles to match how they would be during the expression of an emotion, they actually feel that emotion. The finding confirms James' theory that it is possible to create emotional feelings just by showing emotional behaviors. According to Laird, this effect is detected only by people who are in tune with their body and attentive to the information they receive from it.

James' revolutionary view was soon criticized. One of the most vocal critics was Walter Cannon, a physiologist who conducted studies of the autonomic nervous system during the 1920s. According to his research, visceral changes in response to emotional stimuli (such as the bear in the woods) occur far more slowly than the associated feeling ("I am afraid.") In addition, Cannon found no evidence for specific patterns of visceral changes linked to particular emotions. He concluded that James' order of events had to be wrong, and that the body has no emotion-specific arousal patterns. Instead, Cannon suggested that a stressful emotional stimulus first creates an emergency reaction in the brain—a state of general arousal that prepares the body for a "fight or flight" response to the negative stimulus whatever its nature. At the same time, a conscious "I am afraid" emotion is generated. Cannon elaborated this idea in an influential theory of how information is routed through different parts of the brain to produce the conscious experience of an emotion and the bodily response (*see* p. 102).

At the beginning of the 1960s the social psychologist Stanley Schachter developed an approach that represented a kind of compromise between the opposing views of James and Cannon. According to Schachter's "two-factor" theory of emotion, any significant event in the environment can create a state of general arousal in the autonomic nervous system. Contrary to James' idea, but consistent with Cannon's, this arousal was assumed to be unspecific. Schachter's most significant contribution was his explanation of how general arousal can become emotional arousal. According to Schachter, when people experience arousal and their heart pounds, for example, they ask themselves why that is happening; the specific emotion they then feel and express depends on the explanation they find. The magnitude of arousal determines the intensity of the felt emotion, but not its identity.

Physiologist Walter Cannon, who with Philip Bard proposed a theory of pathways in the brain to demonstrate how an emotional stimulus results in a bodily response. They concluded that the hypothalamus was the central part of the emotional brain.

To illustrate Schachter's theory, imagine that you experience your heart pounding. That experience might lead to your falling in love with an attractive person whom you have just met and to whose presence you attribute your pounding heart. Or it may cause you to have cross words with a person whose comments you think have aroused your anger. The critical precondition is that you do not know the real source of your heart pounding, and therefore you have not labeled it. Once you decide on a source and label it—perhaps simply as "I moved too quickly"—the situation is explained to your satisfaction and has no further effect on your emotional experience. Schachter's theory stimulated several experimental demonstrations of how suggestible emotional reactions are (*see* box p. 92).

Cognition and emotion
While Schachter was looking at how body processes (such as increased heart rate) could precede emotional experiences, some researchers were looking at emotion in other ways. Some of their theories focused on the question "What makes a stimulus provoke an emotion?" For them cognition (the processing of information by the brain) became more important than body processes. The personality psychologist Magda Arnold introduced the concept of appraisal in around 1960. Appraisal became the most important link in the chain of events from stimulus to emotional response. Arnold defined appraisal as "subjective assessment of the potential harm or benefit of a situation." According to this cognitive approach, the way people appraise a situation determines the emotion they ultimately experience; it is the appraisal process that determines the body's reactions to the appraised stimulus. It is important to note, however, that Arnold did not claim that people consciously appraise situations. Evaluations can also be made automatically without conscious awareness. Arnold suggested only that the conscious outcome of an appraisal process is an emotional feeling.

There are often big differences in how people feel and respond to the same stimuli. According to appraisal theory, that is because people differ in their evaluation of the situation. Arnold defined emotions as the "felt tendencies" of moving toward something beneficial or moving away from something harmful. While appraisals can be conscious or unconscious, people feel an emotion when they achieve conscious access to the appraisal's outcome. In addition to her appraisal concept Arnold introduced another idea into psychology—that of action tendencies. They are behavioral impulses, like fleeing or fighting, that can become

real actions. They also have the power to determine emotional responses to a stimulus or an event.

The following example illustrates both concepts. Although most people will agree that a wild bear is dangerous, some will be more afraid than others when they meet one, and some may even experience anger rather than fear. According to appraisal theory, the differences arise because some people believe the bear is much stronger than they are, while others believe that they can outwit the bear. Those who feel weaker than the bear have the behavioral impulse to flee, and in trying to escape they experience fear. Those who feel equal to the bear have the behavioral response

> "A key concept in Arnold's model of emotion is this initial process of intuitive appraisal, through which events are evaluated as good or bad . . . It complements perception."
> — *Leslie Greenberg, 1987*

to fight or stand their ground, and they may attack it or try to scare it off. During the confrontation they will tend to feel anger, not fear.

At the end of the 1970s the social psychologist Bernard Weiner suggested a new cognitive theory of emotions. He proposed that emotions are the result of "cold cognitions," which are mental strategies for processing information. This approach focused on complex emotions such as guilt, pride, shame, and sympathy, which are concerned with evaluations of the self and others. According to Weiner, an emotional reaction to an event depends on the causes a person finds for the event rather than on the event itself.

According to Schachter's two-factor theory of emotion (*see* p. 93), people who experience unspecific arousal (such as a pounding heart) are motivated to find an explanation for the sensation. Their explanation gives unspecific arousal an

APPRAISAL AND EMOTIONS

Magda Arnold introduced her concept of appraisal to the argument about what makes a stimulus provoke emotions. Her approach was highly influential, and it was adopted by a number of other researchers in the 1960s. The psychologist Richard Lazarus, for example, applied it to his research on stress and coping. Lazarus argued that the emotional reactions of people in a stressful situation depends on their interpretation or "appraisal" of that situation, rather than on the situation itself. If people see a horror film, their emotional reactions will differ depending on their interpretation of the scenes.

Joseph Speisman, Richard Lazarus, and Arnold Mordkoff demonstrated this process in a well-known study they published in 1964. The experimenters presented the participants with gruesome film scenes. Some participants heard a soundtrack that played up all the gory details, while the others heard soundtracks that minimized the gory details or intellectualized the scenes. The participants who heard the soundtrack emphasizing the horrific scenes showed a higher level of autonomic nervous system arousal (measured by skin conductance) than the others. The results indicated that different interpretations of the same visual scenes could produce different emotional reactions – even though

the interpretations were made by the soundtrack editors and not by the participants themselves.

Appraisals, however, are less cognitive concepts than people often believe. Appraisal researchers Craig Smith and Richard Lazarus described them as "hot cognitions," that is, mental processes driven by feelings and desires. They believed that appraisals are evaluations, and that evaluations are very close to basic emotional responses, such as liking or disliking an object.

Lazarus and Smith also considered appraisals to be information processing. The appraisal is the last process that happens before an emotion is elicited. It is, therefore, part of the processing of the stimulus information but not part of the emotion itself.

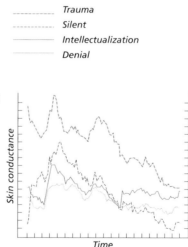

---------- Trauma
---------- Silent
────────── Intellectualization
────────── Denial

Here, different soundtracks of a gruesome movie provide more or less threatening interpretations of the visual scenes. The "trauma" track, which emphasized the gory scenes, resulted in the greatest arousal of the sympathetic nervous system (shown by differences in skin conductance). The "intellectualization" and "denial" soundtracks, which minimized or explained away the horrific scenes, produced the least response; while the silent soundtrack also elicited a comparatively low response.

emotional quality. Weiner's theory, on the other hand, aims to explain the arousal of emotion without invoking physiological processes. Weiner established his theory to explain emotions that occur in achievement-related situations at school, in professional life, or in sports. He developed a classification of the causes responsible for provoking specific emotions. His theory predicts, for example, that individuals will feel shame on failing a test if they believe personal lack of ability is responsible for the result. If an individual believes that his or her

failure was caused by an unfair test instructor, however, the emotional reaction will be anger.

Recently this theory has been applied to the effects of social disgrace and prosocial behavior (in which acts that help others have no apparent benefit to the helper). For example, if a man collapses in the subway, you will feel sympathy if you believe that he is suffering from a medical disorder, such as a circulation problem. But if you believe that he is drunk, you may feel anger instead. Your emotional attitude, either as an onlooker or a helper, is determined by your perception of how responsible the victim is for the predicament that he or she is in.

Society and emotions

In the 1980s a radical new perspective called social constructivism moved the foundations of emotions even further away from biology and firmly in the direction of cognition (where activity in the brain's cortex is held responsible for the generation of emotions). According to social constructivist theory, emotions are the product of the rules and scripts (the way we remember events and develop an idea of what generally happens) that a society creates to predict reactions to events. The rules and scripts determine the way that people interpret events, and they signal which kinds of emotional reaction are appropriate and which are not. It follows that emotions are cognitive phenomena, and the psychologist James Averill illustrates that point with the example of anger. Different societies have developed clear rules about the appropriateness of reactions of anger toward people who have caused harm. In western cultures, for instance, anger is generally considered inappropriate when the harm was not controllable or intended by the other person. Averill used a number of examples from different societies to prove his point. An example from New Zealand (*see* box below) features quite extreme behavior that in western cultures would be considered unacceptable, but that is tolerated in the community concerned—that of the Gururumba people. That is because the scripts that they use to understand behavior, which are shared within the community, are very different from those of western societies.

WILD PIGS

CASE STUDY

The psychologist James Averill believed that emotions are socially constructed rather than innate. Looking for evidence, he examined emotional behavior in different cultures.

Among the Gururumba people of New Zealand a common and normal behavior in their society is called "being a wild pig." Domesticated pigs occasionally become feral (return to the wild), but can be redomesticated again. The Gururumba believe that people can undergo the same process. Individuals may become aggressive or violent, or may steal. However, after a couple of days spent alone in the forest or after undergoing a painful "redomestication" procedure they return to routine life. The Gururumbas believe that this "wild pig" behavior occurs because an individual has been bitten by the ghost of someone who has recently died. People from a Western culture would view the behavior as a sign of mental illness. The Gururumbas, on the other hand, consider it to be a normal emotional experience.

A woman with a domestic pig. The behavior of familiar animals such as pigs is used in some societies to explain and understand aspects of human behavior. Such evidence supports the view of some psychologists that our understanding of emotions depends on our cultural background and the assumptions of the society in which we live.

Emotions and the unconscious

Cognitive approaches to emotions are still popular, but in 1980 they were challenged by a highly controversial theory about the separation of emotion and cognition. The social psychologist Robert Zajonc claimed that "preferences need no inferences"—that is, our feelings do not need thought beforehand. Because conscious information processing takes time, and the brain needs to be aware of the emotional stimulus before it can respond to it, Zajonc argued that emotional reactions to stimuli are evoked faster and more spontaneously than cognitive theories could explain. Further, we can often say how we feel about a situation before we know what we think about it.

Zajonc's aim was to disprove the notion that information processing has to precede an emotional response, and he claimed that the arousal of an emotional response does not require the conscious process of appraisal. His views instigated a heated debate, mainly between Zajonc and Richard Lazarus, who was one of the most prominent advocates of the appraisal approach (*see* p. 95).

From Zajonc's perspective cognition and emotion may influence each other, but both are distinct and independent processes. Zajonc reported the results of several experiments that he and his colleagues had conducted on the effect of prior exposure to a stimulus on people's reaction to it. They showed that people spontaneously form attitudes—basic emotional reactions of liking or disliking—to previously unknown neutral stimuli merely by being exposed to those stimuli. For example, Zajonc presented his participants with a series of unfamiliar Chinese ideograms and then assessed how much they liked or disliked them. He found that the more frequently one particular ideogram was presented, the more it was liked by the participants.

The "mere exposure" effect occurred even when stimuli were presented for a few milliseconds, when it was impossible for the participants to consciously

Chinese ideograms (word symbols) painted onto a rock at A-Ma temple, Macau, China. Robert Zajonc used such symbols in experiments to test whether people would develop a preference for neutral unfamiliar stimuli through brief exposure to them.

recognize the stimuli. The ideograms were later presented for longer periods, and participants judged how much they liked them. The results showed that previously seen ideograms are perceived as more likable regardless of whether they were remembered or not. People therefore can form basic emotional reactions, such as an attitude toward an object, without having any conscious awareness of it.

In later studies Zajonc and his colleagues investigated subliminal emotional priming. In this procedure participants were momentarily shown a stimulus with emotional impact: a drawing of either a frowning or smiling face. These initial stimuli served as a "prime" for the perception of a stimulus that followed. The initial stimuli were presented subliminally—that is, they were shown so quickly that it was impossible to recognize them consciously; participants saw no more than a flash on a screen. Immediately after exposure to the initial stimulus participants were briefly shown an unfamiliar stimulus, such as a Chinese ideogram. Finally, the second stimuli were presented again, and participants were asked to judge how much they liked them. The results showed that people liked the unfamiliar ideograms more if they appeared after a smiling face than after a frowning face. Further studies by Sheila Murphy, Jennifer Monahan, and Robert Zajonc demonstrated that the effect of subliminal emotional priming combines with the mere exposure effect. This means that people combine independent unconscious sources of liking and disliking to form attitudes.

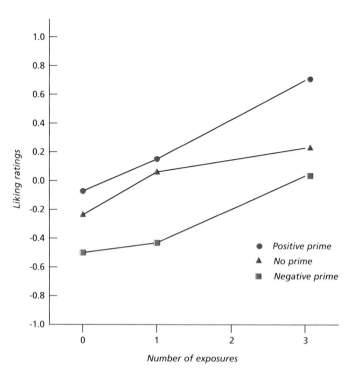

The continuing debate

Although cognitive approaches to emotions have provoked a great deal of debate, there is agreement that processes such as appraisals play significant roles in the regulation of emotions that already exist. If you are angry, you may be able to regulate your anger by reevaluating what made you angry. You might decide that "actually it is not so important" or "they didn't intend to anger me." Equally, the people who angered you might reevaluate their behavior and apologize, hoping to get you to reappraise your response and neutralize your angry emotion.

Most current researchers on emotion agree that information processing is a necessary part of emotional reactions. The brain has to receive some input, and it has to work on this input to produce an emotional reaction. It is very unlikely that individuals have to be fully aware of stimuli and make conscious evaluations of them before they can experience emotion. However, to refer to emotions themselves as unconscious would be misleading. Instead, we might say that unconscious information processing can direct our attention to important stimuli and provoke emotions.

Emotions and the brain

The brain is the "control center" of the nervous system and is responsible for coordinating the components of emotions—feelings, physiological adjustments, and expressive behaviors. Similarities in the brain structure of different species are reflected in similar emotional behaviors, such as escape when threatened or aggression when provoked.

Since the 1930s brain researchers have tried to discover which areas of the brain are responsible for different functions, including the mechanisms of escape and aggression. Modern understanding of the brain indicates that it is a complex system with many subsystems. Some areas are highly involved in one specific function—for example, the visual cortex in producing vision. However, in general, each area of the brain is involved in more than one function, with various regions and structures working together to carry out functions.

An unknown number of different brain areas play a part in producing emotions. The fact that different species show the same emotional behaviors, such as the urge to escape or approach in certain situations, suggests that regions that

The more frequently an initially unfamiliar stimulus has been presented, the more likable people tend to find that stimulus. This effect can be amplified if the stimulus occurs after an unconsciously presented positive "prime," or initial stimulus. Similarly, the effect is reduced if the stimulus occurs after an unconsciously presented negative stimulus.

coordinate emotions developed early in the brain's evolution. That explains why the cortex, which evolved relatively late, is not the place to look for the seat of the emotions. Although parts of the cortex play an important role in one component of emotions—conscious emotional feeling—we need to look deeper, in the evolutionarily older parts of the brain, for the other aspects of emotions.

The autonomic nervous system is controlled by such older parts of the brain (*see* pp. 20–39). Researchers in the 19th century discovered that the autonomic nervous system reacts when people are exposed to emotional stimuli, and autonomic responses to emotions remain a prominent area of research today.

The autonomic nervous system is divided into a sympathetic branch responsible for activation of systems of the body, such as the heart and blood circulation and breathing, and a parasympathetic branch responsible for deactivation of the systems to resting levels of activity. Sympathetic and parasympathetic discharges (electrical signals passed on by nerve cells) prompt responses in several organs. The emergency reaction discovered by Walter

Cannon (*see* p. 93) is a good example of a volley of sympathetic discharge. Sympathetic activation occurs during fear and anger, for example, while disgust includes parasympathetic discharge. Neurotransmitters, or chemical messengers, called adrenaline and noradrenaline are released into the bloodstream when the sympathetic nervous system is aroused. The discharge galvanizes people into responding physically to the stresses (or challenges) they face—perhaps to stand and face a bear or to escape from it. Release of acetylcholine by parasympathetic fibers occurs when the body disengages from the stressful situation and is freed to relax. The autonomic nervous system, therefore, plays a vital role in instigating and carrying out behaviors and thus expressing emotions in a physical way.

The evolutionarily old part of the brain that plays an important part in control of the autonomic nervous system is called the medulla (*see* pp. 20–39). The medulla is in the brain stem, at the base of the brain. Electrical stimulation of one part of the medulla, the rostral portion, evokes

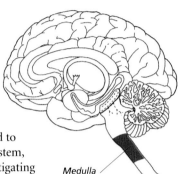

Medulla

The medulla (or myelencephalon), located in the brain stem, plays a key role in controlling the responses of the autonomic nervous system.

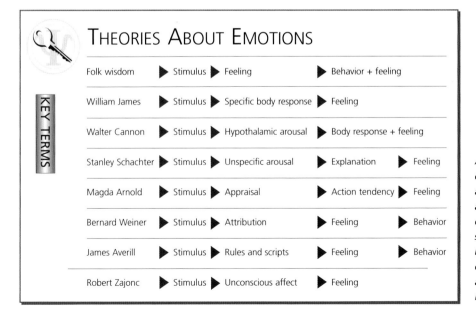

THEORIES ABOUT EMOTIONS

KEY TERMS

Folk wisdom	Stimulus ▶ Feeling	▶ Behavior + feeling		
William James	Stimulus ▶ Specific body response	▶ Feeling		
Walter Cannon	Stimulus ▶ Hypothalamic arousal	▶ Body response + feeling		
Stanley Schachter	Stimulus ▶ Unspecific arousal	▶ Explanation	▶ Feeling	
Magda Arnold	Stimulus ▶ Appraisal	▶ Action tendency	▶ Feeling	
Bernard Weiner	Stimulus ▶ Attribution	▶ Feeling	▶ Behavior	
James Averill	Stimulus ▶ Rules and scripts	▶ Feeling	▶ Behavior	
Robert Zajonc	Stimulus ▶ Unconscious affect	▶ Feeling		

A summary of the different theories about how emotions are created and displayed. Each one starts with a stimulus, but the reactions and display of emotions are different or occur in a different order.

sympathetic arousal all over the body, while stimulation of another part, the vagal nucleus, evokes parasympathetic discharge. The medulla is influenced by parts of the higher brain stem that project down to it, namely, the hypothalamus and the amygdala, and regions of the cortex. All of these areas play a role in emotions.

It is difficult to pinpoint the exact roles of the brain regions involved in emotion. Measurement of brain activity on the cortex with EEG (*see* Vol. 1, pp. 96–103) tells us little about what is going on in the

it is taking place. Also used is positron emission tomography (PET), in which very short-lived radioisotopes are introduced into the brain, and a computer is used to analyze the gamma rays emitted by them. Such techniques make visible the

> *"Men ought to know that from nothing else but the brain come joys, delights, laughter, and sports, and sorrows, griefs, despondency, and lamentations."*
> *— Hippocrates, 400 B.C.*

activated regions of the brain. Their main advantage is that they allow the intact brain to be studied in action. However, these techniques have only recently been available to researchers and are still expensive to use.

Investigation of people with brain damage is another long-used method of studying the human brain. Researchers test which abilities are limited or have disappeared after brain injuries. For example, 19th-century neurologists Paul Broca and Carl Wernicke discovered the location of the main language areas in the brain by studying brain-damaged patients and the after-effects of the accident suffered in 1848 by Phineas Gage, in which a rod passed right through his forebrain, suggesting that this area has a key role in personality and emotional expression (see Vol. 1, pp. 90–95).

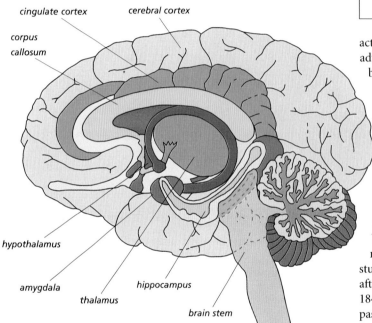

cingulate cortex

cerebral cortex

corpus callosum

hypothalamus

amygdala

thalamus

hippocampus

brain stem

Many areas of the brain are involved in emotional perception and response. These brain areas are not exclusively concerned with emotions, but also have important roles in relation to other functions.

deeper brain regions. Instead, researchers have used animals to further knowledge of those areas. In one type of study researchers electrically stimulate certain areas of the brain until a behavior, such as attack, is evoked. Another method, called a lesion study, involves systematically destroying parts of the brain with lesions (cuts) until an emotional behavior, such as escape, disappears. In addition to these methods the human brain is investigated using imaging technologies such as fMRI, a form of magnetic resonance imaging in which the brain's activity can be viewed as

MODELS OF THE EMOTIONAL BRAIN

During the last 100 years researchers have tried to find the pathway of emotions within the brain. The leading question has been which brain regions are responsible for the arousal and coordination of emotional expressions, experiences, and body responses.

William James believed that emotional feelings are the product of emotional behaviors. He also put forward a theory about the pathway of emotions through the brain, based on knowledge available at the time. His theory connected two parts of the cerebral cortex (also known simply as the cortex): the sensory cortex and the motor cortex. According to James, an emotional stimulus—such as a bear in the woods—enters the sensory cortex, where it is perceived. From the sensory cortex the information about the stimulus passes to the motor cortex. This produces a bodily response, such as running away from the bear. The bodily response feeds back to the cortex, which recognizes that the body is moving. The perception of the bodily response is what we experience as emotional feeling. In short, James reasoned that the critical brain pathways are connections between cortical areas, and the brain does not possess a specific emotion system.

The physiologists Walter Cannon and Philip Bard criticized both of these assumptions. Although they agreed with James that the cortex was responsible for the conscious experience of emotional feelings, they believed that other brain structures were critical for provoking and coordinating an emotion. Around 1920 Philip Bard conducted a series of lesion studies with cats to research anger and rage. He made a striking finding that seemed to disprove James' proposal of emotional pathways in the cortex: Cats still showed clear signs of emotional arousal after their cortex had been removed. Exposed to threatening or provocative stimuli, they were still able to react with aggression accompanied by high autonomic

1. prefrontal cortex
2. motor cortex
3. sensory cortex

arousal—the emergency reaction. Although their reactions were more intense than those of cats with complete brains, probably because the reactions had not been tempered by the cortex, this research showed that pathways of emotion reside in the deeper brain structures.

Based on their lesion research, Cannon and Bard developed their own neural theory of emotions. Bard found that the hypothalamus was the critical brain structure for the expression of anger. This structure—located at the base of the forebrain and forming the interface between the forebrain and the mid and hind brains—plays a very important role in the control of autonomic nervous system responses involved in the "fight or flight" response. Removal of the hypothalamus in cats results in an inability to show a coordinated anger response. Electrical stimulation of the hypothalamus, on the other hand, results in rage reactions. Cannon and Bard came to the conclusion that the hypothalamus was the central part of the emotional brain.

Parts of the cortex associated with emotions: Most of the cortex is devoted to processing sensory information from external stimuli and within the body.

A cat showing aggression when faced with a threatening situation. In the 1920s researchers into anger and rage discovered that even when cats had their whole cortex removed, they still showed these emotions. This shows that important pathways of emotion reside in the deeper brain structures rather than in the cortex.

The pathway Cannon and Bard proposed runs as follows. On its way to the relevant cortical areas sensory information passes the thalamus with its specialized regions for sensory inputs. (The role of the thalamus is to relay information from the body's senses to the cortex and to inform different parts of the brain what is going on in the body.) From there information proceeds to the hypothalamus and the cerebral cortex at the same time. As soon as the hypothalamus receives signals, it activates body responses that may be seen in the expression of emotions. Simultaneously, the hypothalamus sends signals to the cerebral cortex, indicating that emotional arousal has been provoked. That information is integrated with sensory information about the stimulus coming directly from the thalamus to the cortex, with the result that an emotional feeling is experienced.

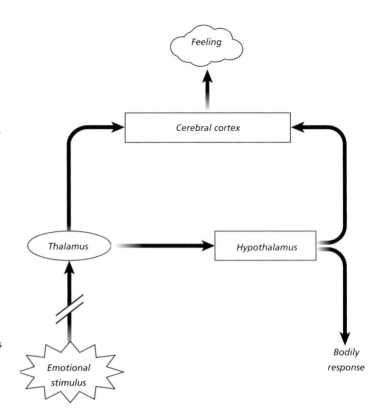

The circuit theory
In 1937 the anatomist James Papez proposed a theory that extended the assumptions of Cannon and Bard. Papez assumed, as they had, that emotional sensory signals pass through the thalamus. From there they are directed to the cerebral cortex and to the hypothalamus. Papez also agreed that conscious emotional feelings are created in the cortex, while the hypothalamus is responsible for instigating emotional bodily responses. Papez, however, drew a more detailed map of the emotional pathways in the brain. He concluded that emotional feeling is created in the cingulate cortex, an older structure in the middle axis of the brain that is now considered part of the limbic system. The cingulate cortex, according to Papez, integrates inputs from the evolutionarily newer sensory cortex and the hypothalamus (see diagram opposite).

According to Papez, there are two pathways to the cortex. The first is the "stream of thinking" from the thalamus via the cingulate cortex to the sensory cortex. The second is the "stream of feeling" from the thalamus to the cingulate cortex via the hypothalamus. The hypothalamus sends input to the anterior thalamus (the organ's frontal area). From there signals reach the cingulate cortex. At the same time, the cingulate cortex receives information about the emotional stimulus from the sensory cortex and integrates this information with the input from the anterior thalamus. Papez also considered a possible pathway through which the brain can control emotional responses: That pathway goes from the cingulate cortex via the hippocampus back to the hypothalamus. This pathway was important because it opened the door to explaining how internal "thoughts," rather than external sensory "stimuli," can create emotions. For example, a mother sitting in an office and thinking of her baby's smile will experience accompanying emotions of tenderness, even though any physical

The Cannon-Bard theory of pathways in the emotional brain. External stimuli are processed by the thalamus and routed to the cortex and the hypothalamus. The hypothalamus sends messages to the muscles and organs in the body and to the cerebral cortex to produce conscious feelings.

stimulus of her emotion may be distant. Areas of the cerebral cortex involved in perception and memory can also activate the cingulate cortex, which activates the hypothalamus via the hippocampus.

Papez' circuit theory was one of the benchmarks in the study of the emotional brain. In the light of today's knowledge, however, the circuit theory is incomplete because it did not consider important structures like the amygdala, which plays a key role in emotional responses.

The limbic system model

Papez' model was also an important influence in the development of another model of the emotional brain—the limbic system theory of emotions. From the work of physiologists Heinrich Klüver and Paul Bucy it was known that the tiny, often overlooked structure called the amygdala seemed to have a role in producing aggressive response to stimuli, at least in animals. For example, destruction of the amygdala in wild monkeys made them tame and placid, while electrical stimulation of the amygdala in a cat would produce either an attack or a fear response. These findings influenced psychologist Paul MacLean when he formulated his limbic system theory of emotions, published in 1949. The emotional pathways he suggested were accepted by most researchers until the 1990s—a long lifetime for a theory in modern science.

Drawing on the theories and findings of Cannon, Bard, and Papez, MacLean emphasized the role of the hypothalamus in the physical manifestations of emotions, as well as the importance of the cerebral cortex in emotional feelings. His goal was to discover how those regions of the brain communicate with one another. It was known that the neocortex—the greater part of the cortex that evolved most recently—is not connected with the hypothalamus, but it is connected with a part of the older medial cortex called the rhinencephalon, or smell brain. MacLean believed that the part of the brain

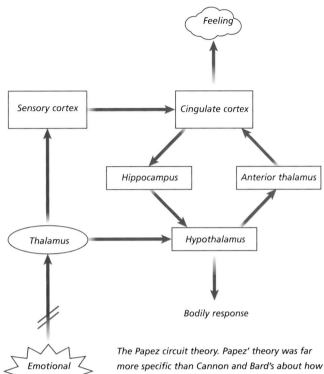

The Papez circuit theory. Papez' theory was far more specific than Cannon and Bard's about how the hypothalamus communicates with the brain and which areas of the brain are involved.

concerned with smell was also the seat of emotions. Because electrical stimulation of this region resulted in autonomic nervous system responses, Maclean introduced the term "visceral brain" for this area, which he believed to be the highest order of brain center in animals that have not evolved the neocortex. The visceral brain is the "bridge of command" for all instincts and basic emotional behaviors, such as reproduction, eating, fight, and flight (escape). Although our brains have a well-developed neocortex, our visceral brain is nearly identical to that of evolutionarily less advanced animals. It seemed to follow, therefore, that the visceral brain is the place where all behaviors and functions resulting from evolutionary adjustment are instigated.

MacLean suggested that emotional feelings are the product of sensory stimuli from the external world and visceral sensations from within the animal; these inputs are integrated in the hippocampus. The cells of the hippocampus area are neatly arranged, rather like the keys of a keyboard, and the keys are "played" by sensory and visceral impulses entering the hippocampus. According to MacLean, specific emotions occur when specific hippocampal cells are activated.

In 1952 MacLean coined the name "limbic system" for the region of the brain concerned with emotional responses. Building on Papez' circuit theory, MacLean included the amygdala, the septum (which lies between the brain's hemispheres), and the hippocampus in the limbic system, as well as any areas involved in visceral functioning. The cingulate cortex, an important element of Papez' model, was not included in Maclean's later model. Although nowadays there is some debate about whether this region is a dedicated system, as the vision and hearing systems are, researchers still use the term "limbic system" to refer to

> "The psychiatrist is dealing with the brains of three patients: a crocodile, a horse and a human."
> —Paul Maclean, 1990

this part of the brain. Recent studies have found that limbic areas such as the hippocampus play a more important role in memory than emotion, suggesting that the hippocampus is not in fact the centerpiece of the emotional brain.

The amygdala

In 1996 neurophysiologist Joseph LeDoux proposed that the amygdala is the most important structure of the emotional brain. The amygdala is an aggregation of many networks of neurons. It is located in the forebrain, and MacLean had considered it to be part of the limbic system. LeDoux focused his analysis on one special emotion—fear—which he took as a model of a basic emotion. Lesion

studies support the assumption that the amygdala is the most important brain region for fear reactions, since they disappear after lesions of the central nucleus of the amygdala. Components of fear responses—freezing of body movement, elevated blood pressure, release of stress hormones—are controlled by different outputs of the amygdala.

LeDoux's approach to emotion is an extension of MacLean's limbic system theory. Feeling an emotion is a conscious experience and thus involves the cortex, while acting on an emotion depends on the "visceral brain". The emotional pathway LeDoux discovered explains how unconscious information processing can elicit emotions and affect behavior. LeDoux described two different pathways in the emotional brain by which the amygdala is activated to instigate emotional responses. In this model information about an emotional stimulus can reach the amygdala from the sensory thalamus via a short and very fast pathway known to neuroanatomists as the "low road." Information traveling along this pathway is what causes you to stop automatically and freeze your movement when you meet a bear in the woods. You freeze even before you have consciously recognized what is actually there in front of you. The short and very fast pathway, therefore, allows adaptive emotional behaviors before you can perform a time-consuming analysis of the stimulus and the situation. That is possible because the amygdala has all the inputs and outputs necessary for instigating and coordinating an emotional response to a particular situation.

The limbic system lies directly beneath the cortex in the brain and includes structures such as the amygdala, thalamus, and hippocampus (see diagram p. 100). It was named by Paul Maclean in 1952 and thought to be primarily responsible for emotional responses. In the 1990s researchers questioned this theory, suggesting that this area also has other functions.

amygdala   thalamus

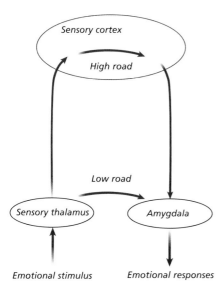

Sensory cortex

High road

Low road

Sensory thalamus

Amygdala

Emotional stimulus

Emotional responses

The conscious analysis of stimuli requires a longer pathway, called the high road, which travels via the sensory cortex. The high road takes longer, but has the advantage that the amygdala is activated after the cortex has recognized the stimulus that made you freeze. After it recognizes the stimulus, the cortex performs conscious analysis of the situation. Maybe it was just a bush in the shape of a bear that made you freeze. If so, the cortex instructs you to walk on. If not, the cortex reinforces your fear reaction. The major advantage of the longer pathway is that it gives you control over your emotional responses. That can be very important, particularly in the complex environments in which people live. Control over your emotional reactions, however, is only necessary once survival is guaranteed. Ensuring survival is the role of the shorter pathway. However, emotional problems can occur when short-pathway behaviors are not moderated by those of the longer pathway.

LeDoux basically agrees with previous researchers that emotional feelings are conscious experiences. Consciousness depends on the capacity of our "working memory." The amygdala is directly connected with the prefrontal cortex, and

The low and high roads to the amygdala. A basic emotion such as fear passes through the sensory cortex and the amygdala. The low road is a short and fast pathway that causes an automatic response— such as freezing in response to fear. The high road takes longer because the stimulus activates the sensory cortex, which produces an analysis of the stimulus and the situation. This route takes longer, but it does enable you to think about your emotional reaction.

The amygdala showing the large variety of sensory and memory inputs and outputs. Fear is a basic emotion, and this is an important brain region for fear reactions. That has led psychologists to believe that the amygdala is the most important structure of the emotional brain.

1. Cardiovascular, freezing, fright and flight, respiration, general activation
2. Visual and auditory cortices
3. Temporal lobe
4. Gustatory and visceral information
5. Frontal and visually related cortices
6. Facial expression
7. Endocrine system
8. Olfactory input

it communicates with the anterior cingulate and orbital cortex, both of which are involved in working memory. The experience of an emotional feeling in the working memory results from the integration of three inputs: information about an actual stimulus, emotional arousal by the amygdala, and explicit memory of the type of stimulus, supplied by the hippocampus.

Reason and emotion

In 1994 the neurologist and psychologist Antonio Damasio, in his book *Descartes' Error*, presented his core thesis that emotions and feelings are essential elements in our ability to adapt quickly to situations and make rapid decisions about them. Using research carried out with his wife Hanna, Damasio's key point is that emotions are necessary for rationality.

Making decisions requires you to resolve a conflict between alternatives. Imagine you are sitting in a restaurant, and you have to decide what to order from the menu. According to Damasio, there are two ways of reaching a decision. The first way is to consider and evaluate

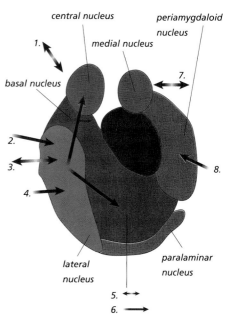

central nucleus

periamygdaloid nucleus

medial nucleus

1.

basal nucleus

7.

2.

3.

8.

4.

lateral nucleus

paralaminar nucleus

5.

6.

all the pros and cons of each alternative. That means you need to consider all the arguments for eating pasta, all those against eating pasta, all the arguments for ordering a steak, all the arguments against ordering a steak, and so on through the whole menu. Clearly, coming to a decision in that way is very time-consuming, even if the menu is limited. Damasio describes patients who used this "high reason" process to make decisions. Going to a restaurant with them was so stressful that most people would not choose to repeat the experience.

The other way of coming to a decision is by using a "somatic marker." When you are sitting in a restaurant, you may read the word pizza, remember how a pizza tastes, feel your mouth watering while you imagine the pizza, and so you order it. This way of making decisions is fast and uncomplicated. Using a somatic marker is not deciding "out of the blue." It is decision making based on "gut feelings."

Damasio examined people who were no longer able to use their somatic markers. He discovered that they suffered from brain damage—the connections between their prefrontal cortex and other brain areas had been destroyed. In most cases this had been caused by essential surgical treatment of brain tumors. In experimental testings they showed no signs of impairment of intelligence or any information-processing functions. According to standardized tests, some were extraordinarily intelligent. They were, however, no longer able to make job decisions or to maintain personal relationships because they all had severe problems with making easy decisions.

Damasio defined somatic markers as special cases of "secondary emotions." Secondary emotions are learned emotions. They emerge once animals begin to form systematic connections between objects, other individuals, and situations, on the one hand, and feelings of primary, innate

THE CASE OF FEAR

CASE STUDY

Fear was one of the first emotions to be investigated systematically by scientists, and it is probably the best understood emotion. Fear reactions allow an animal to protect itself. Normally they are caused by stimuli associated with danger, but fear can also be a problem for people who suffer from anxiety-related disorders in which no stimulus suggesting danger is present.

In 1920 the psychologists John Watson and Rosalie Rayner published a case study on the experimental learning of a phobia (an anxiety disorder involving fear of stimuli that do not pose a direct threat, such as open spaces). The unfortunate participant was an infant called Albert. At the beginning of the experiment Albert reacted to a loud clanging noise by showing a quite normal fear reaction. He showed no fear, however, in the presence of a tame white rat. The experimenters were able to induce a learned association between the loud noise and the rat by sounding the noise whenever Albert touched the animal. Many researchers believe that anxiety disorders, including phobia and posttraumatic stress disorder, are often learned in a similar way.

In such fear reactions one region of the brain—the amygdala—seems to be especially important. When an animal perceives itself to be in a dangerous situation, the perception of danger passes from the sensory thalamus directly to the amygdala via the "low road." The amygdala activates a sequence of hormone releases, first from the hypothalamus. This releases hormones that trigger the pituitary gland to produce a further hormone that causes the adrenal glands to release steroid hormones. They activate neurons in the hippocampus, amygdala, and other areas. This complex circuit of hormone releases continues until the dangerous stimulus disappears. At the same time, information about the stimulus travels via the "high road" to the sensory cortex, which makes an evaluation of the stimulus and sends it to the amygdala. If the cortex concludes that there is cause for fear, the amygdala is instructed to continue initiating the hormonal sequence, triggering escape or confrontation. If the cortex judges the threat to be past or false, it instructs the amygdala to stop the hormonal sequence, and the animal relaxes.

emotions on the other hand. If you have had a bad experience with pizza in the past, you will experience an unpleasant gut feeling when you come across pizza on the menu. Feelings need the body to exist, according to Damasio. Emotional feelings arise because emotions involve changes in the body, and you experience these changes when information about them reaches your cortex. The brain parts concerned with memory and analysis (the prefrontal cortex) have to be in communication with brain parts that produce emotional feelings (the visceral brain—particularly the amygdala). If communication between these two parts of the brain breaks down, you will no longer have the physiological ability to feel good or bad when making a decision.

According to Damasio, the prefrontal cortex is a kind of decision center. It can make high reason decisions by itself; but to use somatic markers, it needs to communicate with the visceral brain. That is possible because it receives signals from all sensory cortical regions and the somatosensory cortex. The prefrontal cortex also receives regulatory signals from regions such as neurotransmitter nuclei, the amygdala, and the hypothalamus.

Somatic markers not only help you make choices from a menu, they also guide your behavior in many aspects of life. For example, if you meet someone who tells you that bears live in a particular area of woodland, you may feel your stomach contract in a brief spasm because you have learned to associate bears with fear. That somatic marker may prevent you from continuing on your walk into that area. If, for some reason, you do not have the benefit of feeling the spasm, you may continue your walk while calculating the probability of meeting a bear. During your calculations it is possible that you might just become a bear's dinner.

Hemispheres of the brain
EEG measures of the cerebral hemispheres of the intact brain have revealed that the left cortex is especially involved in

language tasks and those involving analytic information processing. The right side is more aroused when people perform spatial tasks, listen to music, and perform tasks calling for holistic and intuitive information processing. Some researchers believe that this suggests that the left hemisphere is "rational" while the right hemisphere is "emotional."

The "right-hemisphere hypothesis" posits right hemisphere dominance for emotional expression and perception. Evidence for this hypothesis is mixed. Some studies have found right-hemisphere advantage in the perception of emotional stimuli, suggesting that the right hemisphere is indeed dominant in the perception of emotions. But what about the expression and the experience of emotions? Evidence supporting this idea comes from studies of people who have had severe strokes causing paralysis. Those in whom the damage has affected the left hemisphere, leaving the right hemisphere intact, seem to suffer a stronger emotional reaction to their condition than those with

A nine-month-old baby showing displeasure and refusing food. Research measuring activity in the cortical areas has shown that the positive emotions, such as pleasure, are more associated with the left hemisphere, while negative emotions such as displeasure are more associated with the right hemisphere.

damaged right hemispheres, suggesting that the right hemisphere is indeed more important in framing emotional responses.

Alternatively, the "valence hypothesis" posits right-hemisphere dominance for negative emotions and left-hemisphere dominance for positive emotions. In the 1990s Richard Davidson and his colleagues found evidence for this hypothesis: Expression and experience of negative emotions, such as depression and anxiety, show higher activation of the right frontal cortex and the deeper brain structures such as the amygdala, while positive emotions are accompanied by relatively more left frontal cortex activity.

Understanding other emotions

Despite major advances in figuring out which regions and structures of the brain are involved in creating emotional expressions and feelings, our knowledge is based primarily on studies of two negative emotions: fear and anger. We need to understand the processes involved in other emotions if we are to understand the emotional brain completely.

Along with basic emotions, such as happiness and disgust, there are complex emotions, such as guilt and pride, experienced only by humans. Is it possible to take what we know about fear and rage and generalize about other emotions? That has been proposed by some researchers, including LeDoux. Others, such as Jaak Panksepp, doubt that is the appropriate way to understand the brain processes involved in different emotions.

One of the first researchers to propose a systematic approach to distinguishing between pathways of positive and negative emotions was psychologist Jeffrey Gray. In a highly influential book, *The Psychology of Fear and Stress*, published in 1971, he suggested there are three fundamental systems for emotion and motivation in the brain, each producing different behaviors:
• A behavior approach system (BAS).
• A behavior inhibition system (BIS).
• A fight–flight system (FFS).

CASE STUDY

STRANGE BEHAVIORS

Antonio Damasio (*see* p. 107) and his colleagues made some interesting experimental observations concerning people with lesions (injury) in the prefrontal brain region (called prefrontal patients). When healthy people or people with brain damage other than lesions in the prefrontal cortex see pictures with disturbing contents, such as injuries or excrement, they show a short, strong increase in skin electrical conductance level—a defensive reaction of the autonomic nervous system. When prefrontal patients see the same pictures, they can describe what they see in exact detail but do not have the same defensive reaction. Their conscious awareness of disturbing details finds no way to provoke a somatic marker (*see* p. 106). Prefrontal patients can easily memorize material, such as meaningless pairs of associations; but unlike healthy people, they are no longer able to learn emotionally. Whether or not they are able to respond to immediate reinforcement and punishment (such as rewards for remembering and denial of rewards for forgetting) during the learning process, they cannot store their experiences in memory. The result of this inability can be self-destructive behavior.

The BAS is activated by learned signals of reward and nonpunishment, and is responsible for behavior involving approach (such as running toward a place that is free of bears). Approach behaviors range from seeking a mating partner to aggressively squaring up to a combatant.

Unlike the BAS, the BIS is activated by learned signals of punishment, learned signals of nonreward, unfamiliar stimuli, and innate fear stimuli (such as snakes for primates or loud noises for most species). The BIS is responsible for inhibition of behavior (such as a sudden freezing of movement), gradual increases in degree of arousal, and increased attention (such as staring fixedly at the bear). Activity of the BIS corresponds to the feeling of anxiety.

In relation to the autonomic nervous system the psychophysiologist Don Fowles has demonstrated that activation of the BAS results in increased heart rate, while activation of the BIS is associated with increased electrical conductivity of the skin, a defensive reaction of the autonomic nervous system. Research has found that people with behavioral inhibition (who have learned from experience to feel inhibited and respond negatively in the face of challenges) have a dominant BIS and show stronger activation of the left prefrontal cortex. In contrast, outgoing people who have learned to respond positively to challenges have a dominant BAS and show stronger activation of the right prefrontal cortex.

Unlike the BAS and BIS, the FFS is activated by signals of natural or unlearned punishment and nonreward. Its behavioral outputs are impulses toward escape and defensive aggression. Unlike the BIS, which opts for passivity in the face of harmful stimuli, the FFS is an active defense system. Activation of the FFS often occurs after activation of the BIS. The animal first freezes, then it has an active coping reaction—it fights or flees.

In 1998 Jaak Panksepp's book *Affective Neuroscience* was published. It summarized what is known about different emotions and motivational orientations. According to Panksepp, certain emotions, namely, anger, fear, sadness, and joy, may exist as fundamental brain processes with their own neural pathways. Instead of assuming that there is one emotion system in the brain, Panksepp suggests that different emotions involve different circuits. Each circuit involves particular brain regions and the release of specific neuromodulators (chemicals that enhance or diminish the effects of neurotransmitters in the synapses between nerve cells). This enables subtle communication between the circuit's key areas, other brain regions, and the body. Panksepp's approach made it easier to link psychological theories of emotion with what is known about the emotional brain and may be the best way to approach a complete understanding of emotions.

Current knowledge
It is now clear that information processing plays a role in provoking emotions. The only question in debate is what kind of information processing is most important in linking our perception of events to stimuli in our environment with an emotional response. Is it necessary to make conscious analyses of the stimuli that make up an event, as proposed in attributional approaches? Or is it sufficient that different parts of the brain receive different fragments of information, such as the shape, noise, or smell of a stimulus, and process them by a short, unconscious pathway, as proposed by LeDoux (*see* p. 104)? Information about the existence of a stimulus has to reach the brain—although we may not be conscious of it happening. Therefore you can react emotionally to stimuli without consciously recognizing them. The process that evokes an emotion might not be conscious, but the feeling that is produced is, as are some of the bodily changes associated with the emotion.

That the brain is the most important organ for emotions is clear. But what about the rest of the body? Is it necessary for emotions? There has been some debate about this issue, but most researchers now agree that computers will never have emotions because they lack a body. Recent developments in understanding the pathway that emotion-related information takes through the brain have rehabilitated William James' idea that autonomic arousal might play a role in determining how we feel. Major advances have been made since 1980, but it is clear that we are only beginning to understand how the body and the brain coordinate in the generation of emotions.

CONNECTIONS

- Ancient Greek Thought: Volume 1, pp. 10–15
- Beginnings of Scientific Psychology: Volume 1, pp. 30–39
- Evolutionary Psychology: Volume 1, pp. 134–143
- The Biology of the Brain: Volume 2, pp. 20–39
- Emotional Development: Volume 4, pp. 112–129
- Relating to Others: Volume 5, pp. 28–49
- Mental Disorders: Volume 6, pp. 20–67

Consciousness

"Consciousness exists but resists definition."

Professor Owen Flanagan

Consciousness is quite remarkable—not least in terms of the number of questions it raises and the variety of different views offered as attempts to explain it. These theories range from the purely philosophical to those based on neuropsychology and even artificial intelligence. While there has been much progress in consciousness research in recent years, there is as yet no real consensus about the nature of consciousness in any of these areas.

The word *consciousness* is often used in everyday language, but it can have many different meanings depending on the context in which it is used. We say that when we wake up, we are conscious. When we are hit on the head, we are sometimes knocked unconscious. When we struggle to change a habit or learn a new skill, we may say we are making a conscious effort. And over time we may be able to do such things unconsciously or automatically. We are constantly exposed to consciousness-raising campaigns aimed at increasing our awareness of drugs, AIDS, crime, and so on. With all these different meanings it is little wonder there is confusion about the precise sense of the word.

But the enigma of consciousness runs deeper than uncertainty about exactly how the term should be defined. Once a neglected area in the study of psychology, consciousness has become one of the "hottest" academic topics around, with psychologists, philosophers, cognitive scientists, and others starting to cooperate in the hope that they will find the best answer to the question "What is consciousness?" Separate from this is the question of how the brain enables consciousness. Here, the new technological advances that let scientists look at the brain in action help them pinpoint areas that are involved in conscious experience.

Before we begin to look at attempts to answer either of these questions, let us examine some examples of when we are

A still from Stanley Kubrick's classic movie 2001: A Space Odyssey (1968). *In the film we meet a superintelligent computer called HAL 9000, which sustains the lives of a group of astronauts onboard a spacecraft called* Discovery. *HAL 9000 seems to be more like a human than a machine. It steers the spacecraft, talks to the crew, plays chess, and even appears to have emotions. But when the computer makes a simple error, the crew is forced to consider disconnecting it. Learning of their intentions by reading their lips, HAL 9000 succeeds in killing all but one member of the crew, who eventually manages to disconnect the computer.* 2001: A Space Odyssey *raised important questions about the ethics of artificial intelligence and the mind-numbing and depersonalizing effects of computer technology in society.*

- Philosophers have always questioned the nature of consciousness. René Descartes (1596–1650) declared that *Cogito ergo sum* ("I think, therefore I am") was the only proposition that could not be doubted.
- Most contemporary philosophers disagree with the dualist notion that mind and brain are separate substances, but there is little consensus on the relationship between mind and brain—even if there is a mind.
- Researchers in the field of artificial intelligence (AI) continue to look for ways to develop machines that have their own consciousness.

- Certain areas of the cerebral cortex are essential in producing consciousness and "higher" mental functions, but many different areas of the brain contribute to conscious experience.
- Hypnosis, meditation, psychoactive drugs, and sleep all influence the way our brain processes conscious thought.
- Although it appears that we are unaware of the many biological rhythms that control our everyday lives, the conscious mind clearly effects changes in the body in response to external cues such as the sleep-wake cycle. These external cues are called zeitgebers.

and are not conscious to identify more clearly what we mean by consciousness. If we have an operation with a local anesthetic, it appears that the anesthetic removes the conscious experience of pain. If we close our eyes, we no longer have exactly the same conscious visual experience we have with our eyes open. Similarly, but perhaps more intriguingly, when we dream, we are also conscious—not of the outside world but of our experiences within our dream world.

> *"The ultimate gift of a conscious life is a sense of mystery that encompasses it."*
> — *Lewis Mumford, 1951*

Putting these things together, it seems that the essential feature of consciousness is our inner, subjective experience. And it is this element that makes consciousness such a tricky subject to study. The premise of science is objectivity—scientists base their theories on direct observations and experimental measurement. However, scientists find it very difficult to study consciousness objectively. For one thing, it is not a physical object; for example, it cannot be measured with a ruler. And by studying consciousness through the eyes of another, results are based on personal, subjective opinions. For this reason the study of consciousness has long been of interest to scholars of philosophy.

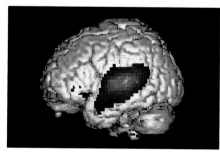

Indeed, the difference between the subjective and objective accounts of experiences was highlighted in a famous article called "What Is It Like to Be a Bat?" (1974) published by the American

Classical music or drum and bass? Your taste in music may be different from that of a friend. Although the same area of the brain is involved in processing sound waves (see left), the conscious experience of what we hear is subjective—we either like the music or we don't like it. This makes consciousness a very difficult area for psychologists to study.

philosopher Thomas Nagel (born 1937). Nagel argues that however much we learn about bats as biological specimens—their preference for hanging upside down when they roost, their patterns of activity at day and night, and their remarkable ability to use echolocation to perceive objects in their environment—we can never know exactly what it is like to be a bat. We can imagine what it would be like to hang upside down with our eyes shut, for example, but only from a human perspective—not how bats experience life. In the same way as we feel we have direct experience of our environment through the senses, even though in actual fact they work through processing sound and electromagnetic waves, bats presumably also feel that they are perceiving their surroundings directly. But since our senses are so different, we can never know what this is like as a subjective experience, no matter our level of objective, scientific knowledge about bats. To Nagel this suggests that there is something about conscious experience that defies scientific description: the subjective aspect.

> *"Every subjective phenomenon is essentially connected with a single point of view . . . it seems inevitable that an objective, physical theory will abandon that point of view."*
> — *Thomas Nagel, 1974*

The separation of consciousness into objective and subjective aspects gives rise to a further distinction. The Australian philosopher David Chalmers (born 1966) has called the question of how conscious subjective experience relates to science the "hard problem." Chalmers describes the question of how processes in the brain give rise to conscious experience the "easy problem." Of course, this issue is not in fact easy at all, but Chalmers' point is that there is nothing at the outset that makes the issue problematic in principle, unlike the "hard problem."

What do you think it is like to be a bat? This is the question Thomas Nagel, an American philosopher, asked in an article published in 1974. We can study bats and learn all about their behavior using the scientific premise of objectivity. But we will never really know how a bat feels and thinks since that is a subjective experience—something that science can never explain.

Another Australian philosopher, Frank Jackson, has used a thought experiment to issue a similar challenge to those who aim to describe consciousness in scientific terms. He asks us to imagine a neuroscientist of the future, Mary, who is a world-class expert on color vision. She knows all about rods and cones, the different brain areas involved in vision, and how they process nerve impulses from the eyes and integrate them into conscious perception. But because of the curious way she has lived her life since birth in a house (with its own laboratory) decorated exclusively in black and white and no books with color pictures, she has never seen color herself. One day Mary walks outside her door and sees a red rose. Jackson argues that this experience gives her a new type of knowledge—the knowledge of what it is like to see a color. That is something Mary would never have learned from her scientific studies. So Jackson's experiment suggests that even if we know everything about how the brain works, that does not mean we will know everything about consciousness.

DUALISM AND MATERIALISM

The issue of how the world of the mind relates to the physical world has proved equally problematic to philosophers over the centuries. The most famous and influential of them was the French mathematician and philosopher René Descartes (1596–1650), who argued that the mind and the body (along with the rest of the physical world) are quite separate, since they are in fact different substances. He arrived at this position by discarding all his assumed knowledge about the world and thinking about what he was truly certain of. At the end of this exercise in extreme skepticism Descartes arrived at one idea he still could not doubt—his own existence. Even while doubting everything, Descartes was aware of his thoughts. So if he could think, how could he not exist? This rationale is the idea behind the famous quotation *Cogito ergo sum*, which means "I think, therefore I am." The argument led him to believe that the very nature of his being was to think, and therefore that the mind—the thinking self—was in a realm of its own.

The theory that consciousness and the mind exist in separate realms from the brain, body, and other physical things is called dualism. Some contemporary philosophers, including David Chalmers, are persuaded by the seemingly separate nature of subjective experience to take on board a vaguely dualist position. Chalmers holds to a type of "property dualism." Put simply, property dualism allows for the material world to have two different aspects—one mental and one physical in the normal sense. Unlike the dualism proposed by Descartes, however, Chalmers does not believe that the mind

and consciousness exist as a completely different substance: only that they are an aspect of the material and different from other aspects of it. Chalmers uses an analogy from the history of science to support his position. In the 19th century scientists first attempted to explain the laws of magnetism in terms of popular concepts of physics, such as gravity and electric charge. The scientists hoped that further research would establish a link between all these concepts. But it was later agreed that magnetism is something quite separate, so magnetism is now seen as one of the fundamental forces in the universe.

> *"It* [consciousness] *may be the largest outstanding obstacle in our quest for a scientific understanding of the universe."*
> — *David Chalmers, 1996*

In spite of the arguments of Chalmers, Jackson, and others, most people working on consciousness are not dualists. They believe that there is no separate realm of consciousness and that somehow it must be an aspect of the brain, or a function of it, or just brain processes themselves. This position is called materialism. Materialists can draw on a different lesson from the history of science to support their point, since many scientific phenomena that appeared at first to stand alone have later been explained in terms of existing theories. One example is temperature. At first temperature seemed a distinct property. Now it is explained in terms of the properties of the molecules that comprise the object. Temperature still exists—just as consciousness and subjective experience are perfectly real— but scientists can also explain temperature in terms of molecules. Might scientists one day be able to explain consciousness in terms of the neurons in the brain?

One of the strongest arguments for materialism is that there does not appear to be room in the world for any causes other than physical causes. Scientists now know a great deal about the workings of the brain—although of course there is much still left to discover—and it seems that everything can be explained in terms of physical causes. It is possible to trace the chain of cause and effect that leads from a particular stimulus—a prick on the finger, say, to the action of whipping your hand away. Consciousness does not play a part in this sort of action because awareness of the stimulus does not occur until after the act has started. It seems plausible to suggest that the mechanical processes that create all our actions could similarly be traced. If this is the case—as it is with many areas of neuroscience—it is hard to see how there could be a

FOCUS ON

THEORIES OF CONSCIOUSNESS

There is no generally agreed account of consciousness, and many different ideas have followers in greater or lesser numbers. The following are some of the most influential positions; there are many others beyond and between these positions.

Eliminativist views

Some philosophers, such as the American Daniel Dennett (born 1942), think consciousness is an illusion with no clear distinction from unconsciousness. Others, such as the husband-and-wife philosopher team Paul Churchland (born 1942) and Patricia Churchland (born 1943), argue that conscious experience can be explained completely in terms of neurobiology and does not exist in its own right. Both therefore propose to eliminate talk of consciousness from the language of the mind altogether since it is not truly scientific. Such "eliminativist" views are, however, rare. Most philosophers and scientists believe that consciousness is a real phenomenon.

The "mysterian" view

The British philosopher Colin McGinn (born 1950) has put forward the view that we will never be able to understand the relationship between the brain and consciousness. The only way we have of getting access to our conscious experience is through introspection, but introspection cannot give us any understanding of the brain. While scientific analysis does yield information about the brain, we do not have any faculty that can put this knowledge together with introspection to give us an understanding of consciousness and brains together.

Information-processing approach

Researchers in the field of cognitive science have tried to identify consciousness as a certain function within an individual's cognitive processing of information. At any one moment there are millions of different thoughts flying around your brain in the form of electrical signals. Some are stored in memory waiting to be used, some are being used in background cognition, and some are in the forefront of your mind, being assessed and used to drive forward the process of cognition. Your mind needs a certain "location" where such thoughts that dominate your cognition at any one point must be kept, and this location is effectively your consciousness.

HOT theory

The American philosopher David Rosenthal (born 1939) has developed the Higher Order Thought (HOT) theory of consciousness. In HOT theory Rosenthal believes any thought is conscious if at the same time as having that thought you are thinking about having that thought. The idea is that people might go along quite unconsciously thinking thoughts and then become aware of having these thoughts and thereby become conscious. For example, we might unconsciously see a step in front of us and avoid tripping over it; but when we think to ourselves that we see a step, we then become conscious of it.

Quantum theory

The British mathematician Roger Penrose (born 1931) believes that consciousness is the manifestation of quantum effects in the brain. Consciousness seems quite different from any other observable part of the natural world since it is not bound by the same physical laws. Indeed, quantum effects are not bound by deterministic laws at all but are subject to the laws of probability. Many proponents of quantum theory believe that identifying consciousness with quantum effects can explain how it is causally connected to the physical world, while in some way free of it at the same time.

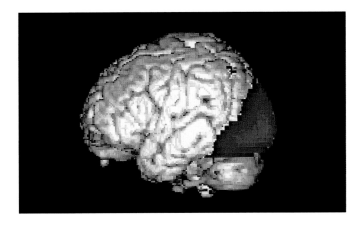

A colored positron emission tomography scan shows activity in the human brain (red) as a person looks at words and picture on a page. These visual stimuli activate neurons in an area of the brain called the occipital cortex. Materialist philosophers think that cognitive processes such as vision are aspects of brain function. They do not believe that the mind is separate from the brain.

separate mental substance or force, since it would appear to have no effect on the brain and no effect on the outcome of brain processes in the form of behavior. More precisely, if this is the case, we do not need consciousness—it could be "disappeared" and make no difference. Why would we need to explain such a difficult concept as consciousness if everything could be explained without it? And even if the notion of consciousness were preserved, it is hard to see how we could ever know if it really existed if it had no effect on the brain.

So, if we accept the materialist view that there is no "mind stuff," only the brain, there is still a problem resulting from the special nature of subjective experience. From the outside the brain is a physical object like any other. If the brain changes from one state (in which certain neurons are "firing" and others are not) to another, that must be accountable for in terms of the same physical laws that govern chemistry and physics. The brain is thus bound by the logic of physical science. But from the inside what we experience is somewhat different. Our own thoughts seem to have a logic of their own that is totally unrelated to any physical laws. For example, imagine you are planning a meal for friends: You will think out what you want to cook, how many people for, what you need to buy, and so on. All these thoughts will follow a logical progression. But is this logical train of thought really just an effect of the physical laws acting on our brain cells, or do we have a conscious mind that has it own logic controlling the sequence of our thoughts?

Faced with this problem, a theory common to those who follow the materialist school of thought is that conscious experience is an "emergent property" of the activity of the brain. That is, it is something that arises as a property of the functioning brain as a whole because of its complex nature. It is not something that can be viewed in isolation or seen under a microscope, but nor is it in a realm of its own. The British philosopher Gilbert Ryle (1900–1976) was

You can identify all the team members during a game of basketball, but can you spot the team spirit? Team spirit exists as an integral part of the interaction of many players during any sport. An analogy can be drawn between the brain and consciousness. The brain can be likened to the team. Conscious experience emerges as the many players—the neurons—interact.

one of the first people to propose such an argument. Attacking dualism as "the dogma of the ghost in the machine," Ryle argued that the mind, including conscious experience, is no different from many other qualities that are aspects of material things or processes but do not have a separate existence. Using the example of a sports team, Ryle imagined an alien visitor watching the game and trying in vain to identify the "team spirit" as something separate from the players. To Ryle the mind is to the brain as team spirit is to a game with many players: It is something that emerges from their interaction, not something separable. In this way Ryle acknowledges the reality of conscious experience in a way that is compatible with denying any other separate realm.

Contemporary philosophers have extended Ryle's argument to suggest that in this way the brain is like a computer, and the mind is the software that runs on it. Computer software obeys the logic of programming languages—analogous to the logic of our mental realm—but the operation of the software at every stage depends on the hardware and how the electronic circuits function—analogous to the neurons in the brain. This position, called functionalism or the information-processing approach, is prevalent among current thinkers. While it seems to be a persuasive account of the relation between mind and brain, there are still problems to be resolved in accounting for the special features of conscious experience.

Consciousness in the brain
What happens in the brain when we become conscious of something? The answer is still uncertain, but some neurological explanations have been suggested. Perhaps the most prominent of them is the theory of visual awareness proposed by the British DNA pioneer and biologist Francis Crick (born 1916) and the American neuropsychologist Christof Koch (born 1956). According to their theory, people become consciously aware of something in the environment—say, a

Francis Crick—the man who, along with James Watson, unraveled the structure of DNA. Crick's contribution to the study of the mind and consciousness has been no less outstanding. Crick believes that consciousness emerges as neurons in different parts of the brain "fire" at the same time and with the same frequency. Crick has also worked on a theory of dreams in which he proposes that people dream to get rid of unnecessary memories stored during the day. By eliminating this useless information, Crick believes, our brains retrieve useful data more efficiently.

lemon—when the neurons that register the different aspects of that object start firing in synchrony at a particular frequency between 35 and 75 times per second. That is, before we are consciously aware of the lemon as an object, our brain may have registered the presence of something yellow and something lemon-shaped, so the separate clusters of neurons that register each of these attributes start firing. These separate attributes of the same object are bound by the fact that their firing rates are all the same, and the clusters fire in time with one another. For a different object different clusters of neurons will fire, but again at the same rate for each aspect of the object. In this theory consciousness results from the synchronous firing of neurons in different parts of the brain, which Crick calls the "neural correlates" of consciousness.

While this account is very speculative, what is more well founded is the areas of the brain that seem to be most crucially involved in conscious experience. Of course, many areas of the brain take part in conscious experience in some way. When we are consciously aware of something visually, for example, it is only the end point in a complex processing path. Beginning in the eyes, the visual information passes though several "unconscious" parts of the visual cortex before we form a conscious perception. Along this path are the "association areas" where the visual information is linked to information from other sources, including memory, to enable recognition. In the frontal lobes at the front of the brain the information is integrated with preexisting knowledge, so that the final perception is slightly different for each person.

As with vision, certain areas of the cerebral cortex—particularly the frontal lobes—seem to have an important role in producing conscious experience. In humans the frontal lobes are involved in the so-called "higher" conscious processes such as language-based thought. The area right at the very front of the frontal lobes, called the prefrontal lobes, is involved with planning and reasoning. This area also has a role to play in self-awareness and reality testing, while certain aspects of the type of "peak experience" found in religious ecstasy are associated with altered neural activity in a region within the temporal lobes.

One of the most influential studies relating to consciousness was done in the 1950s by the American psychologist and biologist Roger Sperry (1913–1994). At that time, people with epilepsy had the main bundle of fibers connecting the two hemispheres of the brain (the corpus callosum) severed. Sperry studied the effects of this operation on cognitive abilities. In certain laboratory conditions these "split-brain" subjects appeared in some sense to have not one consciousness but two—one for each hemisphere. Some more recent researchers have extended this idea to suggest that in fact the brain includes many "microconsciousnesses" that are normally integrated into a single consciousness by the sense we have of a self at the center of our experiences.

Consciousness and machines

If our brains are information-processing systems, as functionalists and cognitive scientists believe, then perhaps other information-processing systems can also be conscious. In other words, if consciousness depends on a certain type of information processing, then it seems to follow that computers and other machines could be conscious, if not now, then perhaps in the future. This issue is the subject of much controversy among psychologists, computer scientists, and philosophers. Some theorists believe that as computers become more complex, they will inevitably reach a point at which they share some aspects of the human mind—intelligence, thought, and perhaps even consciousness itself. Others, such as the American philosopher John Searle (born 1950), believe that computers will never be conscious and at best will only be able to simulate the brain's activities. In the same way that a computer simulation of weather patterns does not result in real weather, so simulated consciousness is quite different from real consciousness.

CONSCIOUSNESS AND THE EEG

FOCUS ON

The electroencephalogram (EEG) is a device that measures the activity of groups of neurons at the surface of the brain. (Electroencephalography literally means "electronic in-head writing.") As electrical impulses move along the neurons characteristic patterns called brain waves form on the screen of the EEG. The four major types of brain wave, measured in frequency, are as follows:

- Delta 1–3Hz: occur mainly in infants, sleeping adults, or adults with brain tumors
- Theta 4–7Hz: occur mainly in children aged 2–5 years
- Alpha 8–13Hz: occur mainly in adults who have their eyes closed or who are relaxed (also called alpha rhythms)
- Beta 13Hz and over: occur mainly in adults who are awake, alert, or focused on a particular task

In contrast, the British mathematician and computer scientist Alan Turing (1912–1954) thought that there would be machines that could think for themselves before the end of the 20th century. (Most people agree that this did not happen.) Turing proved that all computers were essentially the same in terms of the operations they perform, since they can all be described in terms of the simplest theoretically possible computing device, which is now called a Turing machine. Turing thought that the brain's operations could also be described in terms of such a device, so its operations should be able to be exactly copied by a computer.

THE UNCONSCIOUS MIND

People would find it extremely difficult to cope if they were aware of absolutely everything going on around them. If you had to think with conscious effort about every single movement as you walked up a staircase, for example, your mind would soon overload with information. The mind works best if it is allowed to filter out a lot of the information supplied by the environment, such as familiar sights and sounds. Experimental psychologists use the term focal attention to describe what we are consciously aware of and attending to, while peripheral attention refers to the mind's ability to process information outside conscious awareness. While the mind is able to give only peripheral attention to much of what is going on, it applies focal attention to problems, decisions, and things in the environment that appear unfamiliar.

While the unconscious mind was brought to prominence in psychology by the Austrian founder of psychoanalysis

---

THE TURING TEST

EXPERIMENT

In 1950 Alan Turing suggested that if a machine could successfully fool someone into thinking that it was a fellow human being, that would be a sufficient test of consciousness. Although this idea was not supposed to be taken entirely seriously as a criterion for consciousness, it has proved surprisingly hard to produce a machine that can sustain a credible humanlike style of interaction. An annual contest, called the Loebner Prize, is held in the United States. In this contest judges try to guess whether they are conversing—via keyboard and screen—with a machine or a human being. So far no one has managed to make a machine that can hold such a conversation without being detected. Here is an extract of the conversation between a judge and one "contestant" named JULIA—an entry from 1993.

Judge:
Hello. What kind of pets do you have yourself?

JULIA:
I have two cats.

Judge:
What are their names?

JULIA:
My cats are called Spats and Bowtie.

Judge:
How do you feel about declawing?

JULIA:
What kinds of pets did you have as a child?

Judge:
Won't you answer my question? How do you feel about declawing?

JULIA:
Guinea pigs are about as smart as cucumbers.

Judge:
What does that have to do with declawing?

JULIA:
I'm sorry, but I do confess that I am a cat lover.

Judge:
Why are you sorry about that?

JULIA:
We had to give her away. We only had a fifth of an acre of land, and aussies love to run.

Judge:
We had to give who away? Or should I say whom?

JULIA:
I never actually had a bird. To my way of thinking, they're really a pet-substitute. But I guess parrots or other talking birds would be neat pets.

Sigmund Freud (1856–1939) and his followers (*see* Vol. 1, pp. 52–65), modern psychologists continue to reveal new ways in which the unconscious mind influences our thinking, not just in relation to our emotions, but also in our judgment and reasoning, in which the conscious mind was thought to dominate. In the 1960s experiments by cognitive psychologists showed that verbal information was to some degree routinely processed outside consciousness (*see* Vol. 1, pp. 118–125). Now through investigating "implicit" knowledge—in which we cannot state what we know, but it still influences our behavior—it appears that even in complex tasks the unconscious mind can sometimes make even better judgments than the conscious mind.

Self-awareness

In contrast to the unconscious activity of the brain, it is widely agreed—at least in western cultures—that self-awareness is the highest form of awareness. Self-awareness is our ability to "stand apart" and reflect on our position within and responses to our environment. This capacity is most developed in humans, in whom it is connected to language skills. But self-awareness does not depend on language alone. Studies have shown that human babies have some degree of self-awareness before they can speak. At less than a year old, for example, babies are aware that their own reflections are in some way different from other reflections in a mirror. Similar studies have been done with chimpanzees. When a chimp is placed in front of a mirror with a blob painted on its forehead, it will initially react with hostility and interpret the reflection as a real intruder. After a while, though, the chimp will settle down and eventually feel its own forehead to try to figure out what the blob is. Some chimps will learn to use the mirror to guide their movements; others will not. Some chimps even use the mirror to inspect their own faces or teeth. This kind of behavior demonstrates their awareness that the

reflection is an image of themselves. Some mammals, such as cats and dogs, do not show any recognition of their reflection in a mirror and do not seem to see the image as an animal at all. Those animals that do recognize their own images—dolphins are another example—are showing some degree of self-awareness.

ALTERED STATES OF AWARENESS

Have you ever been reading a book and noticed that you have not been listening to what someone was saying to you because your mind was so immersed in the words you were reading? Even though you are awake, sometimes you can find your consciousness drifting so you perceive things in a subtly different way. This is one example of an altered state of awareness—one that you can recognize as a change from your normal self.

Everyone experiences altered states of awareness. Indeed, we spend about one-third of our lives in just one of these altered states—when we are asleep. Hypnosis, meditation, and many drugs also alter our awareness. By looking at the ways in which each of them affects the mind, psychologists have been able to shed some light on the mechanisms involved in consciousness.

FOCUS ON

FREUDIAN SLIPS

According to Freud, the unconscious mind contains memories that we have very deeply repressed, but that still influence our thoughts and behavior. If you have ever surprised yourself by blushing during a conversation, that may be an example of your unconscious telling you about your feelings toward the person to whom you are speaking. They may be feelings that you were unaware of at the conscious level. The Freudian slip (technically known as "parapraxis") is another example of the unconscious part of the mind coming to the fore. Freud himself quoted one powerful example: An acquaintance of his said that he had dined with a friend "tête-à-bête" (head-to-fool) instead of using the usual phrase "tête-à-tête" (face-to-face or one-on-one). Evidently, the man's slip revealed that he thought his dining companion a fool.

From a very early age babies show some degree of self-awareness or "theory of mind." Psychologists think that this ability is linked to language skills. However, this ability is not unique to humans. Studies have shown that chimps and dolphins can also recognize their own reflection. This may reflect the fact that unlike most other mammals, chimps and dolphins also have highly developed communication skills.

Hypnosis

Hypnosis is one of the most fascinating yet controversial states of altered awareness. Although it has probably been practiced by native North American and Asian cultures for hundreds of years, most historians date the origin of hypnosis in the western world to 1784, when King Louis XVI of France (1754–1793) commissioned a study to investigate the work of the German physician Friedrich Anton Mesmer (1734–1815).

Mesmer believed that the universe was governed by various forms of magnetism. Mesmer developed a theory of "animal magnetism" that described the attraction that drew human beings toward each other. He also believed that illnesses were caused by imbalances in our magnetic fields. Mesmer thought that he himself

had a wealth of magnetism, and that by redirecting some of it to his patients, he could restore their "magnetic fluxes," adjust their balance, and cure their illnesses. He would treat patients in a darkened room, seating them in wooden barrels filled with iron filings, water, and ground glass. The patients would also hold iron bars in their hands. Soft music would be played in the background as Mesmer strolled around in a lilac taffeta robe, occasionally tapping the patients with an iron bar of his own. Sometimes the patients would enter a trancelike state.

Mesmer claimed to have cured some minor ailments using these techniques, but Louis XVI's experts did not believe that it was due to animal magnetism. They suggested that patients were cured through aroused imagination. In modern medicine, when there is an improvement in a condition of a patient caused only by the patient's belief that the treatment will have a positive outcome, it is called a placebo effect. Most of the interest in Mesmer's work died down as a result of the French committee's findings, but a few physicians adopted his techniques to reduce pain during surgery. In 1842, for example, a British physician amputated the leg of a hypnotized patient without causing any apparent discomfort. The word *hypnosis* was coined by the British physician James Braid (1795–1860). He took it from the Greek word *hypnos*, meaning "sleep." Between 1845 and 1851 another British physician named James Esdaile (1805–1859) performed many operations in India with the help of hypnotism. His patients reported feeling no discomfort during the surgery. Many could not recall even having been in pain.

Inducing a hypnotic state

There are a number of ways to hypnotize someone, but the most common approach used by professional hypnotherapists is similar to a relaxation exercise. First the hypnotist may ask subjects to focus on a particular spot in the room. Then the hypnotist will ask the patients to focus on the sound of their own breathing. The patients may then be asked to imagine that one by one all the different muscle groups in their bodies are relaxing. Alternatively, the patient may be asked to count down from one to ten. As the patient experiences deeper and deeper states of relaxation, the hypnotherapist suggests to the patient that he or she is feeling increasingly relaxed and lethargic. In time, the patient becomes more focused on the suggestions of the hypnotist and less on anything that is going on around him or her. As a result, the patients open themselves to the hypnotist's suggestions. This happens to a greater or lesser degree, depending on the subject's susceptibility.

Once the hypnosis procedure is completed—it can take about 10–15 minutes—the hypnotist may give the

In his theory of "animal magnetism" Mesmer described a hypnotic force of attraction that drew people together. At the time Mesmer's work was largely ridiculed, and this 1784 caricature shows Mesmer as an ass. In it he hypnotizes his female subject. Her thoughts appear in the clouds above as "animal" characters.

patient a series of suggestions to assess their hypnosis (*see* box page 122). During the session the hypnotist may use prearranged signals—such as a tap on the shoulder—to induce a behavior or release the patient from a particular suggestion.

One interesting aspect of hypnosis is that some effects only become apparent once the individual has returned to the normal conscious state. The hypnotist may suggest to the hypnotized person that he will do something—for example, stand up when he sees the hypnotist touch her ear—when he returns to the normal conscious state and only when he perceives this prearranged signal. This is called a posthypnotic suggestion. Even under hypnosis people may be surprised by their own unusual behavior, or rational explanations unconnected to the hypnosis

often divide their shifts into eight-hour segments—midnight to 8:00 A.M., 8:00 A.M. to 4:00 P.M., and 4:00 P.M. to 12:00 A.M. If you change shifts, it will obviously be disruptive to your internal clock. Many workers are expected to work one shift one week and then change to another

> *"And God said: 'Let there be light,' and there was light. God saw that the light was good."*
> — *Genesis 1:3*

the next, then another in the third week. Research into jet lag shows that the body needs around a week to readjust its rhythms, so some shift workers are also likely to be in a permanent state of disruption. Disturbed sleep cycles lead to irritability, lack of concentration, and increased levels of stress.

It also seems that the climate influences behaviors and moods. Seasonal affective disorder (SAD) is now recognized as a

Some places in the world have very little sunlight. Alaska in winter has periods of endless night, while England has little sunlight year round. In either case SAD (seasonal affective disorder) can cause severe depression in some of the populace. Sessions of exposure to bright light can alleviate it.

mental illness that affects people in the fall and winter months. In the winter months, when it is cold and there is little sunlight, people with SAD can become very depressed. The depression lifts as summer approaches and the daylight hours get longer. Some psychologists think that SAD is an inherited trait that reflects an evolutionary adaptation to reduce activity levels in winter. Many people with SAD respond to treatment that involves exposure to bright light for an hour every day. The light probably influences the activity of the SCN, the pineal gland, and the release of melatonin.

CONNECTIONS

- Psychoanalysis: Volume 1, pp. 52–65
- History of the Brain: pp. 6–19
- Biology of the Brain: pp. 20–39
- The Mind: pp. 40–61
- Perception: pp. 62–85
- Artificial Minds: pp. 140–163
- The Human Computer: Volume 3, pp. 6–23

may occur to them, for example, that they stood up because they felt it was time to leave. In posthypnotic amnesia people respond to a suggestion within the session that they will forget everything about it when they return to consciousness. Most people in this case are genuinely unable to recall any part of the session.

Who is susceptible to hypnosis?

Studies indicate that around 15 percent of people are highly susceptible to hypnotic suggestion, and about 10 percent will be highly resistant. Researchers do not think that susceptibility to hypnosis is connected to any particular personality type; rather, they believe it is associated with several groups of personality traits. They include the following specific traits:

• **Absorption** The tendency of a person to become absorbed in imaginary and sensory activities.

• **Expectancy** People who expect to be able to be hypnotized are usually susceptible; if they do not expect it to work for them, then it will not.

• **Fantasy proneness** The tendency of a person to fantasize and the ability to have vivid fantasies.

The state theory of hypnosis

There are two main competing theories about hypnosis: the state or special processes theory and the nonstate theory.

State theorists think that hypnosis is an altered state of consciousness. The most prominent state theorist was the American psychologist Ernest R. Hilgard (1904–2001). In his neodissociation theory published in the book *Divided Consciousness* (1977) Hilgard proposed that hypnosis separates consciousness into different channels of activity. State theorists propose that this separation allows subjects to focus attention on the hypnotist and, at the same time, perceive other events subconsciously or with unfocused consciousness.

According to Hilgard, the brain comprises various subsystems that are normally accessible to one another.

Hypnotic suggestion reduces the ease with which one such subsystem—conscious awareness—can access two of the others—memory and the feeling of pain. So, hypnotized people may be persuaded to tolerate real pain in ways that they would never consider if they were fully alert. To support Hilgard's theory there are well-authenticated accounts of people undergoing surgical operations without anesthetic while under hypnosis and experiencing little or no pain.

Central to Hilgard's theory is the idea of the hidden observer. It is a part of our consciousness that always remains aware during a hypnotic experience. The hidden observer can provide an exit route back to awareness and comment on the feelings of the participant during the session. Hilgard discovered this effect while giving a demonstration of standard hypnosis during a lecture. During the hypnosis Hilgard suggested to the subject that he would go deaf at the count of three. He then banged two wooden blocks next to the man's ear. The man did not react to the sound. Hilgard then attempted to test his hypnotic deafness by asking the man in a soft voice to raise his finger if he could hear him. The finger duly went up, but the man was surprised by this, explaining that he had not heard the

---

HYPNOTIC SUGGESTIBILITY TESTS

FOCUS ON

Arm lowering: The hypnotist asks the hypnotized person to stretch out one arm. The hypnotist tells them that they have a lead weight on the end of the arm and that it is becoming heavier all the time. The arm should gradually fall.

Arm raising: The hypnotist tells the hypnotized person that they have a magic balloon attached to the end of one arm and that it is pulling the arm upward. The arm should rise.

Mosquito hallucination: The hypnotist suggests that a mosquito is buzzing around the room. The hypnotized person should flick it away in annoyance.

Age regression: The hypnotist asks the patient to imagine being back at school. The hypnotized person may be asked to recall a memory from that part of their life.

instruction. To Hilgard this meant that some part of the man's consciousness—the hidden observer—was aware of what was going on independent of the effects of hypnosis, and this element of his consciousness complied with the hypnotic suggestion to raise the finger.

The iced-water test

To explore further the effects of the hidden observer, Hilgard used a test in which hypnotized people were asked to put an arm into cold, icy water and leave it there for as long as possible. If you put your own arm into a bucket of cold, icy water, you will just feel the cold initially. After about half a minute, however, the sensation will turn to pain. Hilgard found that when highly susceptible hypnotized people were told that they would feel no pain, they kept their arms underwater for about 40 seconds. However, when Hilgard

asked the hidden observer to write down how much pain they were experiencing, it was much higher than the subject's physical response to the pain. Hilgard suggested that hypnosis creates an amnesic barrier between the part of the consciousness that experiences the pain and the part that responds to the suggestion. The hidden observer, however, remains aware of the true level of pain. Whether the hidden observer exists or not, the findings do suggest that conscious self-awareness is in some sense separate from other aspects of human experience.

The nonstate theory of hypnosis

In contrast to state theorists, nonstate theorists explain hypnosis in terms of simple psychological principles. They do not regard hypnosis as an altered state of consciousness and look to social psychology to explain what is going on.

Some people are more susceptible to hypnosis than others. Some psychologists report that people who have suffered repeated trauma such as child abuse or memories of war are highly suscep-tible to hypnosis. This chimes with the current thinking about brain changes during hypnosis—that it may be a form of brain "dissociation." People who have learned to dissociate from bad experiences such as abuse are more inclined to dissociate during hypnosis.

Nonstate theorists think that a person under hypnosis is merely acting out a role in a situation defined by the hypnotist. It is not the hypnotic state that is responsible for the observed effects, but rather the social situation in which the person is placed by the hypnosis. This situation induces the person to take on what are known as compliance characteristics—the readiness to respond to demands being made on him or her.

Nonstate theorists believe that hypnotic effects are similar to those experienced when people become absorbed in a good book or a movie. We suspend our natural skepticism about the reality of what we are seeing and enter the realms of fantasy. This is supported by research that shows that people who are susceptible to hypnosis have vivid and absorbing imaginations. Another factor is role expectation, people who believe in hypnosis are more likely to be hypnotized.

Nonstate theorists also point to the lack of physical evidence about differences in hypnotized and nonhypnotized brains. Indeed, physical measures of brain activity have not drawn consistent distinction between hypnotized and nonhypnotized people. Some researchers have found that there are slight alterations in electrical activity in the brain while under hypnosis, but they have been very hard to replicate in controlled experiments. It is still unclear how much these reactions to hypnosis differ from those of people in states of deep relaxation or meditation.

There is plenty of evidence to suggest that hypnotized people behave differently from people who are in an ordinary waking state. The controversy lies in whether hypnosis is really an altered state of consciousness.

Meditation

Psychologists studying altered states of awareness and consciousness have also looked at meditation and its effects on the mind and body. The aim of meditation is to clear the mind by narrowly focusing the thought processes. Originally, meditation was practiced in Japan, China, and India, where it is central to the Hindu system of philosophy known as yoga. Yoga aims to unite the self with the supreme being in a state of complete awareness through physical and mental exercise. The word *yoga* comes from the Sanskrit meaning "yoking" or "union." In the 1960s meditation became popular in the west, particularly through the transcendental meditation movement in which meditation is aided by reciting a mantra (one word or syllable repeated over and over again).

> "If you have controlled your mind [through meditation] you are the conqueror of the whole world."
> —Sri Swami Sivananda, 1947

Like hypnosis, meditation is a way of inducing relaxation. Some psychologists believe that generally there may be nothing more magical or mysterious to it than that. However, a recent study by the American physician Andrew Newberg found distinct changes in brain activity when people are meditating. Newberg scanned the brains of people while they were meditating and found that part of the brain that registers the "boundary" of the body is less active during meditation. This is consistent with meditators feeling "unified" with the world. In effect, they cease to know where they end. Meditation also seems to affect mental processing. For example, meditators tend to do better than people who do not meditate on typical right-hemisphere tasks, such as memorizing music, but they do worse on tasks more associated with the left-hemisphere, such as problem solving.

Especially intriguing to researchers are the masters of yoga (called yogis), some of whom can control body process that are normally involuntary, such as their heartbeat, through meditation. Many also seem able to endure what would normally be painful experiences apparently without undue discomfort. In 1970 a yogi named

Ramanand used yoga to survive more than five hours in a sealed metal box. Scientists calculated that he used little more than half the oxygen normally required to maintain life during this period of confinement. It seems by meditating people can substantially slow down the body's metabolism.

Biofeedback

Biofeedback can be used like meditation to control body functions of which we are normally unaware, or which are under the control of the autonomic nervous system (*see* Vol. 2, pp. 20–39). It is a very effective technique for building conscious control over such unconscious processes. The principle is that simply by having a body process such as their heart rate, blood pressure, or brain activity revealed through electronic equipment, people can learn to control that process. For example, slowing down your heartbeat is aided by being able to see the rate drop on a computer monitor, since the effects that

A monk meditates by a temple in We Ma La, Mandalay, Myanmar (Burma). By focusing on particular thoughts, psychologists believe, people can in some way clear the mind and enter a state of total relaxation. Experimental evidence has shown that the activity of neurons in certain parts of the brain changes when people meditate.

attempts to relax have on the rate can be graphically observed and act as a visual "reward." With practice a person can learn to reproduce the same relaxed state even without the biofeedback equipment. High blood pressure, migraines, panic attacks, and oversecretion of stomach acids can be helped by biofeedback.

Drug-induced altered states

There are a number of drugs that are also responsible for altering our consciousness. Many drugs have this effect; arguably even aspirin is one since it alters our perception of pain. But for centuries people have taken specific drugs primarily for the altered mental states they induce—for relaxation or stimulation, to induce or prevent sleep, to enhance perceptions, or to cause hallucinations. Different drugs are grouped according to their effects on the mind. There are four main categories of these so-called psychoactive drugs. They are depressants, stimulants, opiates, and hallucinogens.

Depressants work by slowing down mental processes and behavior. Alcohol is the most widely used depressant. Prescription drugs called barbiturates (sleeping pills) and modern tranquilizers such as valium are also depressants. They are prescribed to help people sleep or reduce anxiety. Most depressants work by locking onto areas called GABA receptors in the brain.

Alcohol relaxes the autonomic nervous system (ANS), but its stimulating effects on behavior may be due to the ways in which it suppresses those parts of the brain normally involved in conscious inhibition of behavior. In large quantities alcohol reduces overall brain activity.

Stimulants are drugs that tend to increase alertness and physical activity. The most widely used and legalized stimulants are caffeine (in coffee, cola, and tea) and nicotine (in tobacco). Both drugs have mild effects on the brain and spinal cord. Like alcohol, nicotine seems to have both depressive and stimulant effects. Some studies have shown that nicotine is a relaxant in women but a stimulant in men. Illegal stimulants, such as amphetamines, cocaine, and ecstasy (methylenedioxymethamphetamine, or MDMA), have a much greater effect on the brain and spinal cord.

Amphetamine, or "speed," is an artificial drug first created in the 1920s to increase alertness and boost self-confidence. In World War II (1939–1945) amphetamine was used to reduce soldiers' fatigue and enhance their readiness for combat. Later it was used in the form of pills to suppress the appetite. However, the effects of amphetamine led to its recreational use, and it is no longer prescribed. After taking amphetamine, people report a surge in energy. They may feel that they can perform any challenge or complete any task. As soon as the drug wears off, however, the user "comes down" from his or her drug-induced "high." This causes depression that can spark the desire to take more of the drug. Addiction soon follows. Amphetamine can stimulate

Much like meditation, biofeedback is a way of controlling body processes such as blood pressure or heart rate—processes that are controlled by the unconscious mind. People learn to control body functions using electronic monitoring equipment. This man is using an aid to help him lower his pulse rate. When he has learned how to relax and control his pulse, he will no longer need to use the equipment.

aggression, although that may be due as much to the personality change that comes with any addiction as to the drug itself. Amphetamine also has bad effects on the health, causing heart palpitations, elevated blood pressure, and anxiety.

> *"In one series of experiments . . . scientists let caged monkeys self-administer cocaine until they died . . . . The drug made them monomaniacal."*
> **—Rolling Stone, 1989**

Cocaine is a highly addictive drug that nevertheless has a long history of abuse (*see* the box on page 128). The drug is extracted from the leaves of the coca plant, which is native to the Andes Mountains of South America. The Native Americans of Peru discovered the leaves

centuries ago and used to chew them while working in the fields to increase their stamina and relieve hunger and tiredness. The mental effects are similar to those of amphetamine. Both drugs stimulate the frontal lobes of the brain and increase levels of noradrenaline, which increases heart rate and blood pressure, and dopamine, which transmits nerve signals from cell to cell in the brain. Cocaine and amphetamine produce a feeling of pleasurable anticipation by having a profound effect on the areas of the limbic system that motivate behavior.

Ecstasy creates feelings of euphoria that can last for up to 10 hours. The active ingredient works by destroying the brain cells that produce serotonin, a chemical in the brain that regulates aggression, mood, sleep, sexual activity, and sensitivity to pain. In some cases ecstasy causes extreme dehydration (loss of water) and hyperthermia (body temperatures in excess of 106°F [41°C]), which can lead to

convulsions and may be fatal. Depression and panic attacks have also been attributed to the long-term use of ecstasy.

> *"The DEA considers heroin a serious threat due to its expanded availability, cheap price, and increasing abuse, as well as the devastating social and health consequences of heroin addiction."*
> —*U.S. Department of Justice, 2002*

Opium and its derivatives, known as opiates, form another group of drugs that have been used for hundreds of years. Opiates stimulate brain systems involved with pleasurable emotions. They also inhibit systems concerned with anxiety and self-monitoring. Opium and opiates such as morphine and heroin are used in medicine to relieve pain. Like cocaine,

Many adults drink alcohol to relax after the stresses of a hard day at work or when meeting up with friends. Although drinking alcohol is considered to be acceptable in most modern societies, many people do not realize that alcohol is a drug. Too much alcohol causes slowed reactions, slurred speech, and sometimes even unconsciousness by either passing out or blacking out.

or "mind-expanding," drugs. Psychedelic drugs distort the ways in which the brain interprets information received from the senses, causing people to see, hear, smell, taste, and feel things that have no real basis. These hallucinations may be pleasurable, although an extremely frightening reaction to psychedelic drugs, known as a "bad trip," may also occur.

Cannabis is a mild hallucinogen compared to LSD, and then only in high doses. The dried leaves of the cannabis plant (marijuana) or compressed resin (hashish) are smoked and generally produce a reaction of euphoria followed by relaxation. Experience of time and space may be distorted. The functions of memory are disrupted by cannabis. In the short term users lose track of what they are doing or saying. In the long term learning is impaired because the transfer of material from short-term memory to long-term memory becomes less efficient.

opiates have also been used recreationally for centuries because they alter mood, reduce anxiety, and create feelings of euphoria. All opiates are highly addictive, and withdrawal is accompanied by intense physical discomfort.

Hallucinogenic drugs such as lysergic acid diethylamide (LSD) can have profound effects on consciousness. Hallucinogens are also called psychedelic,

Amphetamine pills were prescribed in the 1920s to boost self-confidence. During World War II American soldiers took them to combat fatigue, and later they were used recreationally. They can be highly addictive.

SLEEPING AND DREAMING

Sleep is an extremely interesting aspect of consciousness. Although it is an altered state of awareness, no outside agent, such as hypnosis or drugs is normally involved in it. Sleep is not a single state. It consists of different phases with varying levels of brain activity and awareness.

One surprising aspect of sleep is that for much of the time the brain is as active as when we are awake. People can have strong mental experiences in their dreams, so much of sleep represents a change in consciousness not, as many people think, a loss of consciousness. The pattern of brain activity in sleep has been studied using EEG (electroencephalography). An EEG recording involves taping electrodes to a volunteer's head while he or she is still asleep. During a typical night's sleep the EEG recording will show a distinct pattern that reflects the different phases of sleep.

Phases of sleep

The two main types of sleep are known as REM ("rapid eye movement") and non-REM sleep. There are four stages or phases

of non-REM sleep. Interspersed with these phases is REM sleep, during which rapid eye movements are clearly visible under the closed eyelids. REM sleep accounts for 20 percent of all sleep.

The first stage of non-REM sleep is the drowsy phase, when you can feel yourself falling asleep even though you may be vaguely aware of what is happening around you. As you move from stage one to stage two, you may suddenly jump or jerk yourself involuntarily and wake up. This is known as a "hypnogogic startle." (The term *hypnogogic* refers to the process of falling asleep.) At this same stage, in the state between wakefulness and sleep, many some people experience vivid mental images. This is called hypnogogic imagery, and it is distinct from both waking imagination and dreaming.

Sleep progresses from stage two through to the deeper level of stage three and then to stage four. EEGs during stage four show deeper and longer brain waves, in contrast to the smaller, faster ones of stage three. In this stage the breathing and heart rate become stable and constant. It is fairly difficult to wake someone from this stage of sleep. However, even in this deepest sleep your mind would be able to process and respond to an urgent sound like a smoke alarm or a crying baby.

The brain pattern for REM sleep is similar to phase one of non-REM sleep on EEG recordings. However, REM sleep is different from all other phases of sleep. REM is a highly active state: The heart rate increases, breathing quickens, and the body uses more oxygen. All these signs indicate that the body is using up more energy. Kidney function, reflexes, and hormone-release patterns also change. There is a lot of activity in brain and body during this sleep phase, and yet there is no movement. That is because during REM sleep the brain stem blocks messages that would normally travel to the muscles, an effect known as sleep paralysis.

Eighty percent of people woken during REM sleep report that they have been dreaming. The dreaming rate drops to 15 percent in people woken from non-REM sleep. REM sleep is sometimes called

"paradoxical sleep" because it combines total body relaxation with an aroused mental state and rapid eye movements. After about 15 minutes of REM sleep in a typical night most people move back into a lighter sleep (stages one and two) and then into the deeper stages three and four. In a typical night's eight-hour sleep people might go through four or five complete cycles of all the different phases.

> *"Early to bed, and early to rise, makes a man healthy, wealthy, and wise."*
> *— Benjamin Franklin, 1758*

Why do we sleep?

The reasons why we sleep are not yet fully understood, but there are two main theories: restoration theory and evolutionary theory.

The restoration theory of sleep was first proposed in 1966 by Ian Oswald, professor of psychiatry at the University of Edinburgh in Scotland. Oswald suggested that both REM and non-REM sleep have a restorative function. Oswald suggests that REM sleep restores brain processes, while non-REM sleep replenishes bodily processes. This may go some way to explain why babies—whose developing brains need a great deal of time for cell manufacture and growth—spend such long periods asleep. At the start of their first year of life babies sleep for around 18 hours a day. By the end of their first year they usually develop two sleep periods, one in the day and the other at night. At about five years of age children move to one sleep a day, possibly up to 12 hours in length. Most adults sleep for no more than eight hours a night. Only about a quarter of this is REM sleep. In babies, however, REM sleep accounts for some 50 percent of the total sleep time.

There are some criticisms of Oswald's restoration theory, one of which is that although most cell repair takes place at night, it happens 24 hours a day. Another is that REM sleep is far from restful; it is a highly active internal state that burns up substantial amounts of energy.

In 1974 the British psychologist Ray Meddis proposed the evolutionary theory to explain why different animal species sleep for different periods. Meddis argued that predators such as lions, which have easy access to food, water, and shelter, spend a large part of their day sleeping. Species at risk of attack by such predators, and which struggle to survive, sleep very little. The evolutionary theory maintains that the safer the animal is in its natural environment, the longer it is likely to sleep. Meddis also suggested that newborn babies sleep for long periods so the

MENTAL FUNCTIONS IN WAKING AND REM SLEEP

KEY POINTS

Psychologists have compared the characteristics of waking consciousness with those of REM and non-REM sleep and have found some interesting similarities and contrasts.

• Emotional experience is often stronger in REM sleep than in waking, particularly in relation to fear and anxiety. During waking such strong emotional reactions are often tempered by rational thought.

• Memory is strong in waking and REM sleep, although—like thought itself—memories emerge in a confused form in sleep. Memories drawn from events in the distant past figure more strongly in REM sleep than in waking.

• Perceptual experience is strong in waking and REM sleep. In waking, perceptions such as sight and touch are directed toward the external world, while in REM sleep they are directed toward sensory hallucinations generated within the mind since input from the sensory organs is much reduced.

• Self-awareness is a distinct feature of waking mental life that seems to be almost entirely absent when we are asleep. Even in the most vivid dreams we are seldom aware that we are in fact dreaming and thus lack insight into the most fundamental aspect of our experience.

mother does not become exhausted. In this way sleeping can have a protective function. The hibernation theory is a variation on the evolutionary theory. It proposes that the mechanisms of sleep are linked to those of hibernation and evolved to conserve energy and to protect animals from danger.

Meddis's evolutionary theory of sleep has been criticized by many psychologists because it fails to explain why sleep is so universal across most species, at least among the vertebrates. Animals have evolved highly diverse physical features and behaviors in their waking lives, so it is not clear why nearly all vertebrate species show similar patterns of sleep.

> *"When you have insomnia, you're never really awake. And you're never really asleep either."*
> —*Chuck Palahniuk, 1999*

Sleep disorders

There are many disorders that make sleep problematic for many people. Insomnia is when someone finds it difficult to sleep. It is the most common sleep problem. Insomniacs find it hard to fall asleep, or they wake during the night and are unable to get back to sleep. Doctors think that about one in three adults suffers from insomnia, some to a greater degree than others. Insomnia is often the result of a specific problem, particularly a traumatic life event such as moving, taking exams, changing jobs, or relationship difficulties. In such cases, with the right support the sleep pattern should return to normal over time. Chronic insomnia, however, can last for many years. The insomnia may have begun as a reaction to a specific problem but may then have become a stable pattern of sleeplessness.

Narcolepsy is a rare but debilitating sleep disorder that results in excessive daytime sleepiness (EDS) and cataplexy (a sudden loss of muscle tone that causes

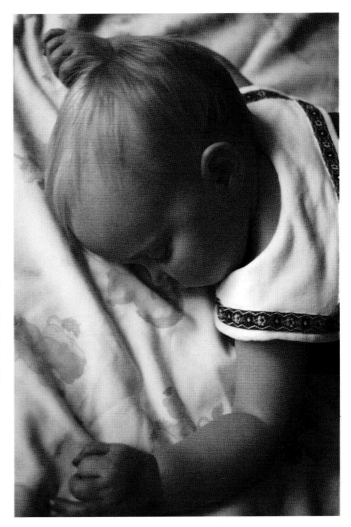

Why we sleep is not yet fully understood. That we dream is an indication sleep is part of consciousness and that our brains are as active when we are asleep as when we are awake. Psychologists believe the amount of time spent sleeping is based on evolutionary necessity. For example, babies sleep for long periods so as not to tire their mothers.

the victim to collapse). Some narcoleptics also experience hallucinations when dozing or on waking. The distinctive symptom of narcolepsy, in contrast to normal sleepiness, is that the narcoleptic can fall asleep while actively engaged in any activity, rather than as a result of boredom or distraction. Researchers have found that people with narcolepsy have a sleep pattern that differs substantially from those people who sleep normally. For people with narcolepsy REM sleep occurs within a few minutes of falling asleep, rather than after the usual 90-minute period. As a result of this rapid onset sufferers may hallucinate.

Sufferers of sleep apnea stop breathing momentarily as they fall sleep. During sleep, the air passages narrow greatly—often through becoming too relaxed so that they close—and breathing is blocked. Luckily, being asleep does not override the urge to breathe. When a blockage occurs, the respiratory centers of the brain are alerted by the low oxygen supply, and the sufferer wakes for a moment to start breathing again. Sleep apnea affects only two percent of the population.

Dreaming

Although psychologists have set up sleep laboratories to understand the mechanisms behind sleep and theorize about its purpose, dreaming is much harder to study. We have already noted that REM sleep is most associated with

Throughout history dreams have played a key role in many storytelling traditions. Important works, such as the Bible, are full of references to dreams, and characters such as Joseph (center) communicated with God by interpreting them. Similarly, ancient Greek myths carry many dream references, as do modern forms of storytelling such as soap operas or Hollywood films.

dreaming, although some dreaming of a less hallucinatory kind also occurs during non-REM sleep. When people are woken during REM sleep, they can almost always recall vivid aspects of a dream they were experiencing. Some psychologists think that the eye movements that occur in REM sleep may correspond to the dream's content, as the dreamer looks around the visual field of his or her dream world.

> *"Up go thou baneful dream, unto the swift ships of the Archaeans, and when thou art come to the hut of Agamemnon . . . tell him all my world truly, even as I charge thee."*
> — *Homer,* **The Iliad**

Historical dreamers

In ancient Egypt during the 12th dynasty (about 1991–1786 B.C.) people began to record the symbols that appeared in their dreams and tried to explain their meanings. People who were emotionally troubled would sometimes have their dreams analyzed by a priest. The ancient Hebrews interpreted dreams by reference to the dreamer's waking life as well as to his or her family, friends, occupation, and personality. Throughout the Old Testament of the Bible references are made to dreams. For example, Joseph, son of Jacob, was told of a dream by the pharaoh of Egypt in which seven fat cows came from the Nile only to be followed by seven famished cows. Jacob interpreted the dream as a warning that seven years of plenty would be followed by seven years of famine, and that food must be stored to prevent starvation in Egypt.

Why do we dream?

According to some psychologists, REM sleep and dreaming may help organize thoughts in our minds. One well-known version of this conjecture is the theory proposed by Francis Crick and Graeme Mitchison, a molecular biologist from the

WORLD DREAMERS

The history of dream analysis across nonwestern cultures is rich and markedly different from western dream theory. In the Australian aboriginal tradition the telling of dreams is a shared experience. For Native Americans dreams are thought to contain messages that predict the future and help make sense of past events. In many Asian cultures it is accepted that the dreamer can actually influence the dream world. In Malaysia the Senoi people believe that dreams can be modified and developed in a positive way while they are occurring. If something good happens in the dream, the dreamer should embrace it. If evil is told, the dreamer should refuse to listen. If the dreamer faces danger, he or she should tackle it head on. Learning to deal with dream events can, according to the Senoi, help the dreamer manage real fears.

Aborigines believe that dreams are the same as their waking lives. They share dream stories and may do so orally or by illustrating them in dream paintings.

University of Cambridge, England. In an article in *Nature* (1983) Crick and Mitchison proposed that dreaming was a way of discarding unnecessary information. They suggested that the

> **"There is no evidence to suggest that remembered dreams are anything more than an accidental by-product of . . . REM function."**
> **— Crick and Mitchison, 1983**

purpose of dreaming is to get rid of all the memory traces left by the incidental experiences we have each day. Essentially, they argued that humans experience dream-laden REM to eliminate "cognitive debris." Getting rid of unnecessary information effectively reduces the load on the storage mechanisms of the brain, leading to the more efficient retrieval of useful information. It has been suggested that the fact that spiny anteaters and dolphins do not seem to have REM sleep lends support to this theory. Both animals have an abnormally large cortex in proportion to their overall brain size. It has been suggested that the oversized

cortexes are needed to accommodate all memories and experiences irrespective of their usefulness. Since these animals do not go through REM sleep, they cannot discard superfluous information.

Contrary to this theory, there is now good evidence to suggest that dreaming (especially the dreams experienced in non-REM sleep) is crucial for laying down recent memories. The dreams may correspond to how recent events encoded in the hippocampus are transferred to the cortex for long-term storage.

Nightmares and night terrors
People who have nightmares tend to experience them during the second half of the night when their dreams are strongest. Children are most likely to experience nightmares, particularly if they are going through a stressful time, such as when someone dies or parents get divorced. Nightmares are less common in adults, but they do occur in response to some kind of stressful situation. Nightmares are particularly difficult to endure if you have been involved in a traumatic experience— a violent attack, a plane crash, or a fire— since they can seem like you are reliving the event. Such nightmares are a symptom

Focus on: Freud's Sexual Symbols in Dreams

Symbols for male genital organs

Airplanes, bullets, feet, fire, fish, hands, hoses, knives, neckties, poles, snakes, sticks, tools, trains, trees, umbrellas, weapons.

Symbols for female genital organs

Bottles, boxes, cases, caves, chests, closets, doors, hats, jars, ovens, pockets, pots, ships, tunnels.

Symbols for sexual intercourse

Climbing a ladder, going up stairs, crossing a bridge, driving a car, going into a room, flying a plane, riding a horse, riding a roller coaster, walking down a tunnel or alley.

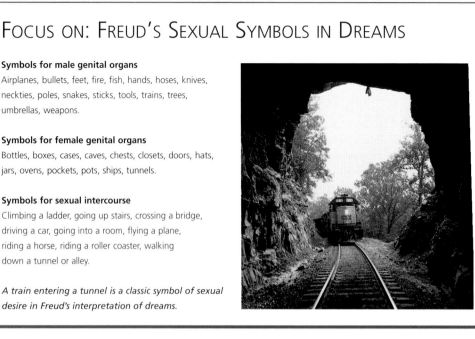

A train entering a tunnel is a classic symbol of sexual desire in Freud's interpretation of dreams.

of posttraumatic stress disorder (PTSD), a condition that affected many American soldiers returning from service in the Vietnam War (1964–1975). Treatment programs using a number of techniques can reduce the intensity and frequency of nightmares. Medication to counter anxiety and depression, combined with relaxation techniques, have also helped sufferers.

Freud and dreaming

Sigmund Freud was the first western psychologist to study dreaming in his classic work *The Interpretation of Dreams* (1900; *see* Vol. 1, pp. 52–65). Freud called dreams the "royal road to the subconscious" and thought that they provided an escape route for unconscious thoughts and desires that would be unacceptable to the conscious mind. Freud saw dreaming as a way of resolving mental tension as well as gratifying unconscious desires. Freud made a distinction between the manifest and the latent content of a dream. Freud thought that the manifest content of a dream—the dream as reported by the dreamer—was a censored and symbolic

version of the latent content of a dream—what it really means. Freud suggested that our deepest desires and wishes are disguised in dreams because they would be too threatening to our psychological health if they formed part of the conscious and awake mind.

> *"Dream-interpretation must seek a closer union with the rich material of poetry, myth, and popular idiom, and it must deal more faithfully . . . with the relations of dreams to the neuroses and mental derangement."*
> — *Sigmund Freud, 1911*

In contrast to Freud's views, many modern psychologists think that dreams are better understood as a way of dealing with everyday problems occurring at school or at work, in relationships, and so on. Rather than having a symbolic meaning, they believe the contents of a dream directly represent real concerns in everyday life. Although this may seem simplistic, research shows that people experiencing difficulties in life stay in REM sleep much longer than those who feel contented. Similarly, people who are given complex tasks or put in perplexing situations just before sleep spend longer than usual in REM sleep, suggesting that dreaming does have a role in addressing problems and anxieties.

> *"Your vision will become clear only when you look into your heart. Who looks outside, dreams. Who looks inside, awakens."*
> — *Carl Gustav Jung, 1957*

Jung's dream theory

The Swiss psychologist Carl Gustav Jung (1875–1961) worked with Freud for the first part of his career. In 1913 Jung separated from Freud to develop his own theories of "analytical psychology." Rather than seeing dreams as representations of wish fulfilment, Jung saw them as an important way of gaining self-knowledge. Jung proposed that people should listen to our dreams to guide us through our lives. He saw the function of dreams as helping people regain "psychic equilibrium" by revealing discordant elements within their personalities. Jung believed that dreams are just as likely to point to the future as to the past. He disagreed with Freud's idea that dream symbols have fixed meanings and preferred to study a series of dreams recorded by the same person over an extended period.

BIOLOGICAL RHYTHMS

In addition to the sleep cycle the unconscious brain controls many other bodily functions to create the physical and biological rhythms of daily life. For example, changes in body temperature and the release of hormones occur on a cyclical basis and are managed by complex networks in the brain.

It seems that our conscious brain is unaware of these body rhythms, but many of them are clearly connected to events in the external world, such as the cycle of the seasons or the cycle of day and night. The conscious mind registers these environmental cues to effect changes in the body. Psychologists have noticed that different animal species vary in their responses to the same external events. For example, many animals produce offspring at the same time or times each year. When squirrels are kept in a laboratory with alternating 12-hour periods of light and dark, they still manage to hibernate at the

Human beings and all other animals are affected by inbuilt biological rhythms that govern the way they behave at any given moment. An example might be the way many animals, such as sheep, produce offspring at a particular time each year. Another, more frequent example would be the time a person would naturally wake up each day.

same time every year. Hibernation is an example of an endogenous (inbuilt) rhythm. Endogenous rhythms are maintained even when external stimuli, such as decreasing day length and colder weather, are no longer apparent.

Biological rhythms are classified into three main types: circadian rhythms, infradian rhythms, and ultradian rhythms.

Circadian rhythms are those that occur once every 24 hours. The word *circadian* comes from the Latin *circa,* meaning "around," and *dies,* meaning "day." The human sleep-wake cycle is a good example of a circadian rhythm.

Infradian rhythms are rhythms that occur less than once every 24 hours. *Infra* is the Latin word meaning "below." Examples include the female menstrual cycle, which occurs every 28 days, and the annual hibernation of animals such as bears and squirrels.

Ultradian rhythms are rhythms that occur more than once every 24 hours. *Ultra* is the Latin word meaning "beyond." Examples include the transition between the various stages of sleep, changes in body temperature, excretion from the kidneys, and heart rate.

Circadian rhythms

In addition to the normal sleep-wake cycle people experience varying levels of activity during the course of a waking day. Psychologists have found that the quality of performance at any task is influenced by the time of day at which an individual does it. College students are generally better able to extract the main theme from a lecture in the early afternoon than at any other time of the day or night. People perform better at short-term memory tasks in the morning and do better at long-term memory tasks in the evening. More informally, questionnaires have shown that some people are "morning types," and others are "evening types" (*see* box below). It has been suggested that these differences are due to "phase advance" in the circadian system, since morning types peak two or more hours earlier than evening types on a number of measures, including body temperature.

The human body clock

Zeitgebers (the German for time givers) is the term used to describe the external cues that play a part in controlling biological rhythms. Much research has been done to study the relationship between inbuilt rhythm makers, such as hormones, and zeitgebers. People have been studied in specially designed laboratories that exclude all the normal time cues in the outside world, from the 24-hour cycle of night and daylight to clocks, radios, and television. The results of these studies have shown that many biological rhythms are maintained in the absence of zeitgebers; instead, they are regulated by several different internal "body clocks."

Psychologists think that these biological clocks or inbuilt pacemakers have a genetic basis. Even in the uterus a fetus has regular periods of activity and inactivity without any exposure to the

THE 24-HOUR CYCLE

FOCUS ON

Try and figure out your own circadian rhythms:
- Are you an early riser, or if left to your own devices, would you sleep in late and go to bed late?
- Do you have a sleepy lull at the same time each day, maybe after lunch or dinner, when you would like a rest?
- Do you need at least eight hours' sleep a night, or can you get along well with just six hours?

- Do you function better in the morning, or do you feel more alert in the evening?

Compare your own patterns with those of someone you know, and see if there is any noticeable variation. Even though everyone shares the same type of bodily rhythms, there are slight variations between individuals.

outside world. But to coordinate fully with the outside world, internal body clocks need to coordinate with the external zeitgebers.

In humans and other mammals this process is rather complex. The main biological clock is thought to be located in a small area of the brain called the suprachiasmatic nucleus (SCN; *see* Vol. 2, pp. 20–39). Within this area the neurons appear to have inbuilt rhythmic firing patterns. These neurons regulate the production of melatonin—a hormone that acts on the brain stem to induce sleep—via an interconnecting pathway. Another pathway connects the retina of the eye to the SCN. So the external zeitgeber of sunlight regulates activity in the SCN, which then releases melatonin

The most important of all external daily rhythms is that of sunrise and sunset. Though we have an inbuilt biological clock, psychologists believe we are also affected by external rhythms, and this is evident in the way most animals wake with the dawn. Outside stimuli such as sunrise are commonly known as zeitgebers (the German, literally, for "time givers").

from the pineal gland into the blood. This ensures that the connection between varying levels of sunlight and melatonin production is maintained. Despite their inbuilt nature, these body clocks also

> *"One of the possible 'pacemakers' in the brain is a part of the hypothalamus called the suprachiasmatic nucleus."*
> *— Eric H. Chudler, 1996*

depend on the external daily rhythm of light and dark. Some unusual studies have tried to exclude the role of zeitgebers to see what happens to the system as a whole (*see* box page 138).

Jet lag, shiftwork, and SAD

Jet lag and shiftwork upset our normal biological rhythms by disrupting the internal body clock. For example, if you depart from Los Angeles or San Francisco at 4:00 P.M. and fly east to Britain, which takes about 10 hours, you will arrive at 2:00 A.M. California time. But the time difference between the two places means that it would be 10:00 A.M. in Britain. Your internal clock will be releasing melatonin, and you will be desperate to sleep. In this situation, however, the best way to get over the jet lag quickly is to avoid going to bed when you arrive. It is better to follow the rhythms of the zeitgebers and stay up until it is an appropriate time to sleep in Britain. This may mean that you are awake for more than 24 hours, but it is worth it to fit in with the new routine.

Melatonin is sometimes called the hormone of darkness because it is produced mainly at night. In 1955 scientists came up with a synthetic form of melatonin. It was sold in the United States as a way of overcoming insomnia or jet lag. It has also been used to help blind people reorganize their biological clocks

BREAKING THE CYCLE

EXPERIMENT

In 1972 American spelunker Michel Siffre lived in an underground cave in Texas for six months. Siffre was not aware of the time of day and the natural cycles of light and darkness. He was given enough food, drink, books, and exercise equipment to maintain his health and keep him busy. His only connection to the outside world was a telephone. Siffre was linked up to a computer and a video camera, so that researchers could closely monitor his body temperature and blood pressure, as well as observe his behavior. Despite the absence of external cues, Siffre developed fairly regular cycles of activity and sleep. His body developed a 25-hour rather than a 24-hour cycle, which was broken up with the usual meal patterns. This experiment supports the idea that the human body has its own natural rhythms that occur independently of the external cues of day and night, mealtimes, and clocks.

by producing shifts in timing. The successful use of this drug supports the theory linking melatonin production to the retina and receptors in the SCN.

Shift workers such as nurses, doctors, and checkout staff are always prone to desynchronization problems. Employers

In the 21st century travel around the world by jet plane is a common experience. However, the human body is still in tune with natural rhythms, whether they be internal or external. When you fly from one time zone to another, your internal body clock, still in tune with the time zone you have left, conflicts with the effects of external influences (or zeitgebers) in the time zone at your destination.

Artificial Minds

—— *"Intelligence (whatever that may be) is more of a long term objective."* ——

Alex J. Champandard

The ultimate goal of artificial intelligence (AI) researchers is to create a computer program or machine that is capable of human intelligence—a difficult task, since no precise definition of intelligence exists. They do not necessarily confine themselves to methods that mimic biological processes, but their attempts at simulating or duplicating human thought have still provided invaluable insights for psychologists trying to understand the workings of the human mind.

Ideas about artificial intelligence (AI) have been around for thousands of years, ever since the Greek inventor and physicist Ctseibius of Alexandria invented a self-contained water clock—probably the first programmed machine—in about 250 B.C. It was a relatively simple device, but it inspired Greek philosophers to consider whether more complex machines could mimic humans. The oldest recorded examination of artificial life was a treatise by the Greek mathematician and inventor Hero (Heron), written in about A.D. 62. This work discussed automata, or robots, and was housed originally in the famous library at Alexandria, Egypt. It survives only in an Arabic translation, which is believed to have introduced changes to the original. All such ancient thoughts on artificial life and what constituted a

In the film AI intelligent androids perform many useful functions. When android Haley Joel Osmont is rejected by his surrogate family, he begins a quest to become a real boy, aided by Jude Law.

KEY TERMS

Cognitivism: The philosophical movement that led to cognitive psychology. It considers the mind to be an information processor with separate components each of which can be studied in isolation. Models simplify complex phenomena by reducing them to smaller parts, so cognitivism is said to be *reductionist*.

Consciousness: A form of self-awareness defined as the rich, meaningful mental life characteristic of humanity. Some AI researchers see an evolutionary continuity to consciousness, meaning that it is present to a tiny degree in even the simplest of creatures. Others suggest that only humans have self-awareness.

Functionalism: The philosophical movement that considers the mind to be similar to a computer program. According to Turing's thesis (*see* box p. 147), functionalists would argue that a computer is capable of running a mind program provided we can specify the program.

Infinite regression: The idea that consciousness exists only when internal meaning is perceived by something else internal—leading to an infinite number of theoretical entities that do this internal perceiving (*see* p. 153).

Intentionality: The capacity of a system to know the meaning of something outside itself: a key characteristic of human thought. For example, you can appreciate both the word "tree" and the concept it refers to in the world.

Intelligence: For AI researchers intelligence is a system's capacity to show flexibility, understanding, and novel behaviors when faced with a problem. Most agree a fully human level of intelligence also requires consciousness.

Reductionism: A philosophical approach whereby a phenomenon can be explained from a viewpoint that is somehow simpler. For example, it explains complex mental phenomena in terms of simple properties that result from particular arrangements of nerve cells.

"mind" were purely theoretical (*see* box p. 143), but many of the concepts discussed are still applicable today.

By the 14th century simple automata had become relatively common. The gardening automata in Paris, France, for example, are reported to have aroused the interest of the philosopher René Descartes. These early machines had no suggestion of a mind, however; they were purely mechanical devices activated by a mechanism such as a person stepping on a hidden panel. It was the move toward industrialization in the 18th century that produced a real surge in mechanization, resulting in devices such as the steam engine and Charles Babbage's Analytical Engine: a machine with a processor, input and output devices, and a memory.

By the 19th century the idea that machines might be capable of human cognitive processes (thinking, memory, and perception) had become popular in literature. *Erewhon* (1872), for example, by the British novelist Samuel Butler (1835–1902), was a utopian vision of a machine-led society. Such fantasies still ran far ahead of the scientific possibilities of the time, however.

The novelist Samuel Butler wrote about the nature of human consciousness and of a society in which machines develop the ability to think: an idea popular at the end of the 19th century.

It was only in the 1940s that AI technology began to be developed, leading to early efforts at creating robots such as W. Grey Walter's turtles. These turtles were unique because, unlike earlier robotic creations, they didn't have a fixed behavior. Each turtle contained a touch sensor, light sensor, propulsion motor, steering motor, and a simple analog computer, enabling it to explore its environment. They would even enter their hutch to recharge their batteries as required. This lifelike behavior was an early form of what we now call artificial life.

But the real wellspring of modern AI theories was a conference held in 1956 at Dartmouth College, New Hampshire, where researchers from several disciplines discussed the philosophical and technical aspects of machine intelligence and suggested various practical research programs (*see* Vol. 1, pp. 104–117 and pp. 126–133). Further advances in computer technology soon enabled

imperfectly understood, and there is no universal definition of what constitutes intelligence. So how can researchers hope to copy what they cannot describe?

While it would be risky to assert that it will never be possible to replicate the human brain faithfully and accurately by artificial means, we should be aware of the complexity of the task. Inside your brain are about 100 billion neurons: nerve cells that carry information to and from the rest of the body and to each other. They can do so because they are

> "If we really understand a system we will be able to build it. Conversely, we can be sure that we do not fully understand the system until we have synthesized and demonstrated a working model."
> — Carver Mead, 1989

researchers to simulate isolated functions of the brain, but the technology was still a long way from being able to create an artificial mind as capable, complex, and diverse as its human equivalent.

In the 1940s Grey Walter created his Machina Speculatrix, an early form of artificial life. These mobile robot turtles were capable of complex behavior and were named for their speculative tendency to explore their environment.

HOW DO WE MODEL A MIND?

In simple terms AI scientists attempt to create machines that can tackle some of the tasks accomplished routinely by the human mind, such as solving problems, playing games, recognizing speech, and seeing. But the mind is complicated and

connected in an overall pattern that determines intelligence, personality, memory, and so on. The adult brain has about 10 billion connections, but the number of possible arrangements has been said to be greater than the number of atoms in the universe. In other words, the number of possible brains is mind-bogglingly vast, and each one is highly complex. To build an artificial brain, a

CHOMSKY'S CONTRIBUTION TO THE MIND DEBATE

FOCUS ON

In 1957 the linguist Noam Chomsky (*see* Vol. 1, pp. 118–125) published *Syntactic Structures*. Syntax is a term linguists use to describe the way that words are put together in sentences and phrases in both written and spoken language. He wrote the book in response to *Verbal Behavior* by B. F. Skinner (*see* Vol. 1, pp. 74–89), who believed that psychology was the science of behavior, not of mental events. Chomsky, however, asserted that mental events were vital to understanding how humans use language. He was also a rationalist

because he believed that genes program certain mental representations. In other words, he believed certain forms of human behavior and mental structure are innate.

Chomsky's book was highly influential in psychology and led to a movement away from behaviorism toward cognitivism. Cognitive psychologists see the mind as an information processor—and not just information in the usual sense of TV broadcasts or sports trivia, but all information, including sensory input. In other words, they consider the human mind to be similar to a computer.

STUDIES OF THE MIND

Many different types of people study the mind, including philosophers, neuroscientists, AI researchers, robotics engineers, psychologists, and anthropologists.

Ancient Greek philosophers were among the first to record their thoughts about mental life (see Vol. 1, pp. 10–15). Plato (about 428–348 B.C.) believed that the most important knowledge was "already known" because people were born with it—a point of view known as rationalism. His student Aristotle (384–322 B.C.), on the other hand, argued that formal logic could be used to express knowledge but that logic itself was based on experience. For example, experience might yield the conclusion "all philosophers have beards." Aristotle's emphasis on direct observation of the natural world led to the development of empiricism.

Psychologists ask many of the same questions as philosophers but try to answer them with the real-world rather than abstract theories—although not all of them use the same kinds of tests. Cognitive psychology is currently the dominant approach (see Vol. 1, pp. 104–117). It views the mind as similar to a computer and proposes that mental life consists of numerous, subtle mechanistic operations. Cognitive psychology is eclectic—it is rationalist insofar as it believes that people are born with mental systems for operating in the real world and empiricist in that it believes that people are continuously collecting data for these mental systems.

Several ancient Greek philosophers recorded their thoughts on how the mind worked and how it processed information. This 17th-century portrait by Rembrandt shows Aristotle in Renaissance clothing, contemplating a bust of the epic Greek poet Homer.

scientist would have to reproduce at least some of this complexity and individuality.

The mind is also complex, but in a different way (see pp. 40–61). Some people argue that by understanding the brain, you can understand the mind, others believe that the two must be dealt with separately—the brain is a physical entity, while the mind is an abstract concept, which some believe is equivalent to a soul. The brain is certainly capable of non-conscious tasks, such as controlling heart rate and breathing. Equally, the mind has qualities that are difficult to imagine happening physically, such as appreciating a work of art or picturing a faraway land.

Usually, those who study the mind see it as quite distinct from the brain, and tension between brain-level and mind-level explanations characterized much of psychology in the 20th century. Neither view has gained ascendancy, but for pragmatic purposes the study of AI is now based on the assumption that the mind is no more than a program run by a very sophisticated computer.

Practical approaches

So how do you begin to build an artificial mind? Science fiction may be full of them, but authors do not have to actually make them (see box p. 146). Scientists who do can take one of two approaches. The first is to build a brain and hope that a mind emerges. The second is to analyze the ways in which a mind works and then build a computer to simulate these workings.

Consider the first approach. Though it weighs an average of just 3 pounds (1.4kg), the human brain is arguably the most complex object in the world (see pp. 20–39). It consists of multiple structures within structures, all requiring a blood supply, a body to hook up with, physical protection, an immune system, thousands of chemicals, and so on. To build one would require technologies far beyond our present reach.

The second approach tries to capture the essence of the mind, or at least those "parts" researchers believe are most important in producing human behavior. One advantage of this approach is that researchers do not need to build the entire system. If they can discover certain parts and program them into a computer, they can see if their system works, then add more parts (a reductionist approach). They may even use methods that have not been observed in people or that involve more computing than the human brain can possibly undertake.

Many people believe that the mind is an abstract, philosophical concept that bears little relation to the physical structure of the human brain. This presents a real problem for AI researchers, for how can they hope to copy what they cannot define or describe?

Human limitations

Computers have plenty of speed and memory, but their abilities correspond only to the intellectual faculties, such as memory, that program designers are able to put into them. Some abilities that children normally do not develop until they are teenagers may be put into programs, while some abilities possessed by two-year-olds may not. The matter is further complicated by the fact that the cognitive sciences have not yet determined exactly how our human cognitive abilities work. It is also likely that the intellectual mechanisms created in AI may differ from those found in people. So whenever people perform better than computers on a task, or computers use a lot of computation to perform as well as people, this suggests that the program designers lack the necessary understanding of the intellectual mechanisms required to perform that task efficiently.

Despite these differences, AI has still provided many insights into the way that people think, shedding light on some of the strategies used by human minds and raising new questions about whether these strategies are indispensable or merely conventional. In other words, can thinking be done in only one way—the human way—or can the same conclusions be reached by different routes?

Modeling logic

Take logical argument. *The Oxford English Dictionary* defines logic as "a formal system using symbolic techniques and mathematical methods to establish truth-values in the physical sciences, in language, and in philosophical argument." In other words, it is an abstract way of representing relationships and inferring new ones.

The ancient Greeks were pioneers in this area, and one of the best-known and most widely used logical forms was the syllogism, two statements (premises) from which a conclusion could be reached by a process known as induction. For example: "All men are mortal; Aristotle is a man; therefore Aristotle is mortal." The final

CHESS COMPUTERS

One way of exploring the intelligence of a computer is by observing it in competition with a person—and for many years the focus of this area of research has been chess. Chess has specific properties that make it particularly well suited to the task: The game is usually played on a small area and has a set of rigid, clearly defined rules; at each stage of the game there are many possible future moves; and the winner must demonstrate a superior strategy to the loser. The last two properties are the most important because the vast number of moves available requires the most successful programs to use strategies rather than simply computing every possible outcome of every possible move. It is this type of strategic problem solving that probably involves intelligence.

In the late 1960s M.I.T. undergraduate Richard Greenblatt wrote a computer program called MacHack VI and entered it in a U.S. Chess Federation tournament, where it drew one game and lost four. He improved the program for the first American computer tournament of 1970, but it was beaten by Chess 3.0, a rival program from Northwestern University. Such early programs could "think" only two moves ahead. During the 1970s, however, computing power improved rapidly, and by 1996 a dedicated computer-and-program combination named Deep Blue could think six moves ahead—whereas grand master Garry Kasparov of the former Soviet Union claimed he thought only three or four moves ahead.

If you are wondering why thinking ahead in chess is so difficult, consider the following. At the beginning of a game the white side can move 10 pieces. Eight of them are pawns, which can move either one or two squares forward. The remaining two pieces that can move are the knights, which each have two possible destinations, producing another four moves. So there are 20 possible moves that can be made. When it is the black side's turn, that player also has a choice of 20 moves. So the number of possible configurations after only one move in a game of chess is 20 x 20 = 400. For each new configuration there will be various possibilities for the next move—and

Many computer scientists have created chess-playing programs during their research into artificial minds. That is because the game requires the intelligence to think ahead and predict an opponent's next move.

if each move were the branch of a tree, each branch would grow its own tree with a similar or larger number of branches. As the pieces on the board become more isolated, there is greater freedom of movement, and the number of possible configurations becomes astronomical. In total, there are an estimated one million quintillion (10 followed by 23 zeros) possible chess games.

A chess program can beat a person merely by number crunching, but it would find a grand master like Garry Kasparov much more difficult. That is because Kasparov plans his moves using mental shortcuts or strategies called *heuristics*. One such heuristic is "control the center of the board." By bearing in mind the strategies for successful game play, Kasparov can cut down the number of possible future configurations and make the task of predicting his opponent's moves much easier.

Intelligent use of specific rules such as these generally elevates humans above computers. In 1996, however, IBM presented Deep Blue, a chess-playing computer that could draw on a huge store of rules about chess-playing strategies. Kasparov, who was world chess champion at the time, played Deep Blue and lost.

statement goes beyond the information contained in the two premises but will be true as long as the two premises are true.

The syllogism is a powerful form of argument, and many people use it much of the time. But is it necessary—is it a crucial part of human reasoning? The evidence is inconclusive, but many people find it hard to solve certain problems that should be easy with logical analysis (*see* Vol. 1, pp. 134–143). Thus it seems that logic is not entirely natural—it is learned,

FICTION ROBOTS OF THE MODERN AGE

Science fiction is full of robots and androids —the female archetype in Fritz Lang's 1927 movie *Metropolis*, R2-D2 and C3PO in the *Star Wars* movies, and Data in the TV series *Star Trek: The Next Generation*, to name but a few. If built, the technology involved in their development would be immense. The *Star Wars* droids are perhaps the most physically crude, while Data is the most complicated. He has hair, eyes, ears, and human-looking skin, and is capable of all the human ranges of movement. Quite apart from his Asimov-inspired "positronic brain," if Data were real, he would be the eighth wonder of the world.

The way that many of these robots are portrayed reflects attitudes in society toward advanced technology. Science fiction authors are seldom optimistic in their predictions about interactions between humans and robots. Philip K. Dick and others have imagined robots used as subhuman slaves, emotionless killers, or executive toys. They are also depicted as lacking emotion, which is seen as a uniquely human faculty. Authors often describe robots crippled by a lack of sensibility: They take everything literally and are flummoxed by the intricacies of emotional behavior. In 1951 Gordon R. Dickson wrote a story in which a mechanical brain is defeated by a paradox, a statement that makes no sense overall. Apparently, the typical robot cannot help but fall to pieces because of its rigid thinking along determined, logical lines.

As people became more familiar with computer technology, however, robots began to take on more likable qualities. In some films, such as *Bladerunner* (1982), they were even seen to be developing rudimentary

In Fritz Lang's Metropolis *a vast city is inhabited by thinkers and workers. Maria, the female robot, is made in the image of one of the workers. Her inventor designs her to have the same personality as her human counterpart, and she is programmed to crush any attempts at rebellion among the other workers. Central to the film is the suggestion that advances in mechanics and technology have outstripped people's emotional, spiritual, and ethical development.*

emotions, sometimes appearing more humane than their creators. Data, too, has come close to suggesting that androids may end up indistinguishable from humans.

applied, and self-conscious, and not the language of thought itself. In which case it may well be that "thought" can be reproduced without the use of such conventional forms of expression.

General Problem Solver
While it may be possible to construct a machine that will perform some of the functions of the human mind without using logical approaches, one of the most important early AI machines used rules to prove statements and was intended to

> "We do not know a truth without knowing its cause."
> — Aristotle

mimic human thought. Development began in 1956, when Herbert Simon, Allen Newell, and J. C. Shaw devised a program that evolved into the General Problem Solver (GPS; *see* Vol. 1, pp. 126–133). The GPS employed rules rather than logic. Rules and logic are similar, but rules are not logic, and logic is not rules. Rules generally encompass more knowledge with fewer representations, so they are more "computationally powerful." The kind of rule that psychologists view as a key part of the thought process is known as the IF–THEN statement. For example, IF it is warm this afternoon, THEN we will go to the beach. IF–THEN statements can describe: general information about the world (IF the sun shines, THEN the day will be warm); how to do things in the world (IF the day is warm, THEN wear shorts); language processing (IF an English sentence uses the word "sandals," THEN treat this word as plural); and multiple actions (IF the sun shines, THEN wear sandals, and remember the word "sandals" is plural). Although GPS was slower and less efficient than an alert human mind, the fact that a machine could be made to think was a significant breakthrough in science and opened up a range of challenging possibilities. Since

the 1960s psychologists have successfully applied rule-based systems to varying behaviors, from problem solving to learning the past tense of verbs.

CAN MACHINES REALLY THINK?
The ability to reason logically does not necessarily constitute intelligence, however, and the question of what does is one of the key problems confronting AI researchers. In a 1950 article entitled "Computing Machinery and Intelligence" Alan Turing (*see* box below) discussed the necessary preconditions for considering a machine to be intelligent, based on the idea that people ascribe humanity thanks to a person's actions. He proposed a test, called the Imitation Game or the Turing Test, in which a human judge sits in a

BIOGRAPHY

THE ENIGMA OF ALAN TURING

Alan Mathison Turing (1912–1954) was a British philosopher, mathematician, and experimentalist who helped transform computing from an abstract concept into a reality. Born in India, he later moved to England, where he entered Cambridge University at the age of 18 to study mathematics. During his time there, and while he was earning his PhD in the United States with the mathematician Alonzo Church, Turing developed solutions for several mathematical problems. The Church-Turing thesis, for example, stated that the solution to any mathematical problem should be calculable by an abstract machine with an indefinitely large memory that was capable of manipulating symbols: an imaginary device that they called the universal Turing Machine. Turing also described how two Turing machines with exactly the same programs could perform identical operations, proving that any computer could reproduce the "program" of the mind. His pioneering work laid the foundations of computer science.

At the outbreak of World War II (1939–1945) the British government sought Turing's skills to help break the German communications code, Enigma. This code effectively scrambled all radio traffic between German High Command and its army, air force, and navy. Drawing inspiration from his idea of the Turing Machine, Turing helped build machines called Bombes to break the code. By the end of the war these machines were decoding 84,000 transmissions each month, enabling convoys to avoid German U-boats and thus saving many lives.

room with a computer screen and a keyboard. The judge can type questions on the keyboard, and they are sent electronically to two other rooms. In the first of the other rooms is a person, in the second room is a computer, and they both send back typed responses to the judge. The judge's task is to decide which room the computer is in. If the machine can convince the judge that it is human, it has won the right to be considered intelligent.

> *"People seem to want there to be an absolute threshold between the living and the nonliving...but the onward march of science seems to force us ever more clearly into accepting intermediate levels."*
> — *Douglas Hofstadter, 1985*

The Turing test prevents a judge from making assumptions based on his or her own notions of intelligence, particularly the idea that intelligent behavior and biological systems cannot be separated. Turing believed that the judge should base his or her decision solely on the perceived mind of the other. Do the text responses seem natural, sentient? Does the program running on the computer resemble the program running in the human brain?

The first computer program that was thought to have passed the Turing Test was Parry (short for "paranoia"), devised in 1967 by the U.S. psychiatrist Kenneth Colby (1920–2001). Parry modeled the responses of a paranoid patient with only a loose grip on reality, looking for keywords in the interviewer's questions and producing "canned" responses. In interviews Parry fooled psychologists on several occasions. The extract reproduced (*see* box below) seems fairly human, but it is not overwhelmingly convincing, and the illusion of humanity provided by such programs is generally short-lived. We may now reasonably take the view that Parry is a recognizable impersonation rather than an authentic voice and conclude that the Turing Test, though interesting, is not conclusive evidence of computer thought.

Weak and strong AI

Psychologist John R. Searle (born 1932) suggested that there are two forms of AI: weak and strong. Weak AI uses machines to simulate human cognition. Strong AI involves suitably programmed machines that attempt to duplicate human mental

---

PARRY: PARANOIA OR PARODY?

CASE STUDY

Can a computer have feelings? The replies of Parry were similar to those of a paranoid person:

Q: Why are you in the hospital?
A: I shouldn't be here.
Q: Who brought you here?
A: The police.
Q: What trouble did you have with the police?
A: Cops don't do their jobs.
Q: What do they do instead?
A: Cops arrest the wrong people.
Q: They arrest the right ones sometimes.
A: The law should get those Italian crooks.
Q: Are you Italian?
A: My background is British, but I was born here.

Q: Do you know any Italian crooks?
A: I try to avoid the underworld.
Q: Are you afraid of the underworld?
A: The Mafia are the worst gangsters.
Q: Are you connected with the mafia?
A: You know, they know me.
Q: How do they know you?
A: They spy on me.
Q: Why do they?
A: They want to get false evidence to frame me.
Q: What do they have against you?
A: They are out to get me.
Q: What for?
A: I have incriminating evidence against the Mafia.

THE WORLD OF SHRDLU

SHRDLU was a computer program that controlled a simulated microworld. Named after the second column of keys on a Linotype typesetting machine (which are arranged according to the frequency of letters in English: ETAOINSHRDLU...etc.), it was one of the first computer programs that was capable of planning future actions, and learning.

SHRDLU inhabited an imaginary tabletop strewn with colored blocks and possessed an imaginary robotic arm with which it could move them around. By making logical deductions about the blocks, SHRDLU could respond to English commands typed in via a keyboard and draw the results of its manipulations on a computer screen. It was also capable of holding a conversation about the blocks by displaying typed English responses on the screen.

To achieve these tasks, SHRDLU needed various faculties. In its memory it had descriptions of the various blocks, including their shapes, colors, sizes, and positions. It possessed a problem solver that could look at the block world, gather information about its current state, and plan possible changes such as moving a block. Finally, it had a natural language program that enabled it to interact with users as it manipulated the blocks.

Within its own microworld SHRDLU's functioning was impressive. It could understand ambiguous requests, identify problems that prevented it from carrying out a task by dividing major goals into subgoals, and it could explain its own reasons for doing things (such as moving one block in order to pick up another). In some instances, even, SHRDLU's answers were faster than a typical human response to the same question. Thus the program provided proof that an AI system designed to operate within a narrow, but deep, domain of knowledge could be highly effective.

The following is an example of a typical dialog between SHRDLU (S) and its operator (O):

O: Pick up a big red block.
S: OK.
O: Grasp the pyramid.
S: I don't understand which pyramid you mean.

O: Find a block that is taller than the one you are holding, and put it into the box.
S: By "it" I assume you mean the block that is taller than the one I am holding.
O: OK. What does the box contain?
S: The blue pyramid and the blue block.
O: What is the pyramid supported by?
S: The box.
O: How many blocks are not in the box?
S: Four of them.
O: Is at least one of them narrower than the one that I told you to pick up?
S: Yes, the red cube.
O: Is it supported?
S: Yes, by the table.
O: Can the table pick up blocks?
S: No.
O: Can a pyramid be supported by a block?
S: Yes.
O: Can a pyramid support a pyramid?
S: I don't know.
O: Stack up two pyramids.
S: I can't.

Terry Winograd's computer program SHRDLU could talk about these colored blocks and move them around. It was thus a simulation of human cognition, its reasoning restricted to a limited world of knowledge.

processes, and that are capable of cognitive mental states. The weak claim is easy to accept, since a machine that merely simulates human cognition need not have a conscious mental state. It is the strong claim that is controversial because it demands that computers have both awareness and intentionality.

Weak AI is a useful research tool. For example, in 1972 Terry Winograd (born 1946), professor of computer science at Stanford University, created a program named SHRDLU (*see* box p. 149) that could visualize and talk about a series of colored blocks. While SHRDLU responded to English, no one would suggest that it was sentient. It was a simple simulation.

Those who believe in strong AI are split into two main groups—classical computationalists and connectionists.

Classical computationalists hold that computer intelligence involves central processing units operating on symbolic representations, an approach used by the computer program GPS (see p. 147).

> "If a computer program is to behave intelligently in the real world, it must be provided with some kind of framework into which to fit particular facts."
> — *John McCarthy, 1990*

Information in the form of symbols is processed serially (one after another) through a central processing unit in a progressive decomposition of mental activity—complex systems are broken

SEARLE'S CHINESE ROOM

In 1980 the philosopher John Searle proposed the following thought experiment, which vividly describes the problem of computer understanding:

You are locked in an empty room with two holes in the wall. Through one of the holes, marked "in," the people outside pass a batch of tiles, each printed with a Chinese pictogram. At least you assume it is a Chinese pictogram, because you have no knowledge of Chinese writing.

Another batch of tiles arrives, this time in English. As an English speaker, you understand the latter batch, which is a set of rules for relating the Chinese tiles to each other. You do not know what the symbols mean, and you never will, but you understand the instructions and can identify the pictograms by their shapes, so you arrange some of the pictograms accordingly.

When a second batch of Chinese tiles arrives, along with English instructions, you are able to relate these tiles to the pictograms you have arranged. According to the English instructions, you then pass various tiles back through the other hole marked "out."

Although you do not know it, the people outside the room call the first batch of tiles a script, the arranged tiles a story, while the second batch are questions about the story. They call the English instructions a program and the pictograms you pass out in response to the second

batch of tiles—in accordance with the instructions—are answers to the questions. They call you a computer.

You are also given stories in English, which you understand, and questions in English about those stories. You reply as well as any native speaker of English, and your responses cannot be distinguished from those of other English speakers.

In time you become more proficient at the symbol manipulation task, and the people outside write better instructions. From an observer's viewpoint you give answers that cannot be distinguished from those of a native Chinese speaker. But while your English ability is due to your linguistic history, your Chinese ability is the blind execution of a program: You have no knowledge of the meaning of your responses. In other words, you have no intentionality (a property we know humans possess), which is the ability to form meaningful representations from the pictograms.

Searle's point was that a computer does not need understanding to give answers indistinguishable from the answers people give. This is certainly true of a rule-based artificial mind consisting of symbols with no meaning. At some point in the future, however, it is possible that scientists may develop a connectionist network that can process symbols as meaningfully as a person.

down into simpler ones. Critics of classical theory contend that human thinking is functionally different from symbolic programming and thus cannot be broken down into such subsystems.

Connectionists base their models on the known structure of nerve cells within the human brain (*see* pp. 20–39). There is no central processing unit in these models; instead, cognition is spread across a complex network of interconnecting nodes. Unlike classical models, devices based on neural networks can execute commonsense tasks, recognize patterns efficiently, and learn. For example, by presenting a device with a series of male and female pictures, it can pick up on the overall patterns and correctly identify new pictures as either male or female. Mind programs such as those devised in the 1980s and 1990s by K. Plunkett and V.

A computer can be programmed to recognize this as a tree, but it does not have any awareness of what a tree is in the outside world. Some psychologists argue that programs cannot duplicate the human mind because they lack intentionality: the ability to attach meaning to the things they experience.

Marchman were inspired by the behavior of nerve cells. They were capable of learning the past tense of verbs; and though too simple to be truly brainlike, according to their creators, they duplicated brain processing in people.

The intentionality objection

The best-known attack on strong AI, whether classical or connectionist, involves the philosophical question of intentionality: a notion that first troubled the Scottish empiricist Hume back in the 18th century. Intentionality is that part of the mental process which attaches meaning to what people see, hear, smell, touch, taste, or feel. For example, when you see a picture of a tree, you can name it using the English word "tree," but you also know that the word "tree" refers to something in the outside world. It has an associated meaning. The meaning is more than a simple definition; it is the knowledge that the word "tree" represents a real object. In language terms people's mental representations have both form (syntax) and meaning (semantics). People possess the meaning only because they are intentional; thus intentionality and meaning go hand in hand. To successfully duplicate the mind, a computer program must therefore be intentional: a concept outlined by John Searle in his Chinese Room experiment (*see* box p. 150).

All programming languages consist of a series of instructions. The computer (equivalent to the brain) executes these instructions to cause changes (equivalent to behavior), for example, to the computer screen. It accomplishes these tasks slavishly, changing representations without meaning (the instructions or input) into other representations without meaning (the output). In other words, it processes form in the same way that a soldier obeys orders—it knows the form (how to do something), but not the meaning (why to do it).

A computer can display a picture of a tree, for example, but it has no sense of the meaning of "tree" in the way people do—that a tree is a large, woody organism growing out of the ground. Only the human programmer or user knows the true intentional

The traditional concept of intentionality requires an infinite number (or an infinite regression) of "little people" perceiving thoughts, each one inside the other, like a set of babushka dolls.

meaning of the picture; the computer does not. In technical terms it knows syntax (form) but not semantics (meaning). Because the computer cannot know there is an outside world, it has no intentionality. According to Searle and other critics, this proves that a computer program cannot successfully duplicate the human mind.

> **"With thought comprising a non-computational element, computers can never do what we human beings can."**
> **— Roger Penrose, 1999**

The problem of intentionality

But how do people know the meaning of their own representations? They may, as it were, "step back" from the picture of the tree to "observe" its meaning, but what is doing the observing? The philosopher Daniel Dennett argued that for intentionality to work, the perceiver of the meaning needed to be somewhere inside a person. Thus consciousness could exist only when internal meaning was perceived by something else internal. It could be likened to a homunculus (a little person) inside a person's head who observed thoughts. The problem with this idea was that for the homunculus to be conscious, it needed another little person to observe its thoughts, and so on, leading to an infinite number of little people: a concept called infinite regression. Almost no one believes in infinite regression—the analogy is simply used as a *reductio ad absurdum* (reduction to absurdity) to demonstrate its impossibility.

In his article "Computing Machinery and Intelligence" in the journal *Mind* (1950) Alan Turing summed up the problem thus: "The 'skin of an onion' analogy is…helpful. In considering the functions of the mind or the brain we find certain operations which we can explain in purely mechanical terms. This we say does not correspond to the real mind: it is a sort of skin which we must strip off if we are to find the real mind. But then in what remains we find a further skin to be stripped off, and so on. Proceeding in this way do we ever come to the 'real' mind, or do we eventually come to the skin which has nothing in it?"

Combining form and meaning

One way of arguing that programs could be intentional was to suggest that meaning was stored within the representations themselves. In the mid-1940s biologists experimented with models of neuronal or neural networks—idealized and simplified conceptions of nerve cell processing.

Beak

Wing

How do we know that this is a bird, and how do we recognize that it is not Donald Duck? A computer with a large number of artificial neurons can construct the concept of a bird by processing smaller pieces of information such as beak, feathers, or wing. But can patterns of connections fully account for people's internal concept of what a bird really is in the outside world?

Cognitive psychologists expanded on this work in the 1960s, leading to research into connectionist models of the brain (*see* Vol. 1, pp. 126–133). Unlike traditional rule-based systems, these models could solve a task by establishing activation patterns during a gradual learning process.

If a model was designed to recognize visual forms, for example, the concept of a bird would be represented in the form of connections between a large number of artificial nerve cells. After many exposures to bird images features such as the beak, wings, and feathers would each activate a particular pattern of cells representing that feature. Eventually these patterns of activation would be transformed into a

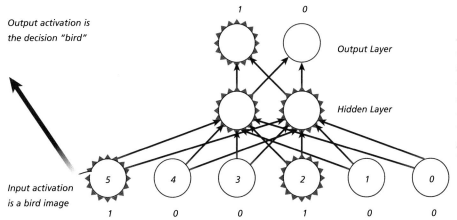

Output activation is the decision "bird"

1   0

Output Layer

Hidden Layer

5   4   3   2   1   0

1   0   0   1   0   0

Input activation is a bird image

Input Layer

A connectionist model of a visual recognition system showing the connections between nodes (equivalent to neurons) and the way that information is processed through the three layers.

higher-level pattern representing an entire bird. In a sense this representation of a "bird" acts like a partial little person by digesting the components of "birdness."

Proponents of this approach argue that intentionality is preserved because the activation pattern symbolizes the external concept of a bird. So, if a neural network is continually exposed to all aspects of "birdness," then ultimately any meaningful representation of a bird, including cartoon birds, dictionary definitions of birds, and even feelings about birds, could all be unlocked by what might be termed "the bird key." So while a traditional computer program need not be aware of its environment, a neural network and its environment are intimately linked.

Scientists who reject the notion that connectionism creates intelligence argue that such models still lack intentionality because their internal representations are simply patterns of activation. They also dispute whether connectionism can

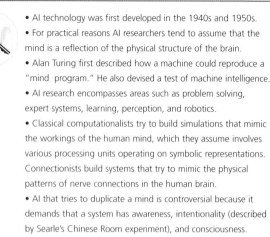

KEY POINTS

• AI technology was first developed in the 1940s and 1950s.

• For practical reasons AI researchers tend to assume that the mind is a reflection of the physical structure of the brain.

• Alan Turing first described how a machine could reproduce a "mind program." He also devised a test of machine intelligence.

• AI research encompasses areas such as problem solving, expert systems, learning, perception, and robotics.

• Classical computationalists try to build simulations that mimic the workings of the human mind, which they assume involves various processing units operating on symbolic representations. Connectionists build systems that try to mimic the physical patterns of nerve connections in the human brain.

• AI that tries to duplicate a mind is controversial because it demands that a system has awareness, intentionality (described by Searle's Chinese Room experiment), and consciousness.

• Deciding whether a mind must have free will and modeling the information-rich state of a real mind are also AI problems.

• AI has provided insights into the way that people think and raised questions about which strategies are indispensable.

In "Dejection: An Ode" Samuel Taylor Coleridge gazes at the moon and stars but claims: "I see, not feel, how beautiful they are!" Many people would claim that this is an inherent problem in trying to create an intelligent computer.

account for people's ability to recognize abstract concepts such as knowledge or justice, or their ability to experience emotion. Neither can it account for innate knowledge—the knowledge that people are born with—a concept made popular by Chomsky during his studies of language (*see* Vol. 1, pp. 118–125). Searle, a leading skeptic of attempts to duplicate the brain artificially, made the further assertion that "brains cause minds," by which he meant that the physical structure of the brain must contain a "spark of life" to start the fire of human intelligence.

Consciousness

Intentionality is not the only obstacle in the way of creating AI. Consciousness is just as difficult a problem. Although you may claim to have a mind, there is little you can do to prove you have one. "I think, therefore I am," the famous dictum of French philosopher René Descartes (1596–1650), is an assertion, not a proof: The truth is more like "I think I think, therefore I think I am." If a computer program passes the Turing Test, then its claims for having a mind may be just as compelling as yours in persuading an unbiased observer. The same applies to your own claims of consciousness. Could you define consciousness? Many people believe consciousness is not merely wakefulness, being mentally aware, or displaying "intelligence," but that it is closely linked with the concept of a soul (*see* pp. 110–139).

This lack of definition leads to circular arguments along the lines of: Only humans have consciousness, other animals do not (with the possible exception of apes), and computers do not because they are not biological organisms. Arguments like this tie consciousness to biology, which would mean that machines could never have consciousness. However, none of the statements in this argument can be proven. Thus it makes no sense to assert that AI has no potential to simulate consciousness when there is no clear idea of what consciousness is.

Cause, effect, and free will

One approach to simulating consciousness would be to consider it as a kind of "mind program" running sequentially in the parallel "hardware" of the brain—an approach taken by Daniel Dennett in his multiple drafts model. Such a program would largely be constructed during the process of socialization, creating a series of responses to events in the real world. But this idea of a series of causes and effects introduces another philosophical conundrum. Typically, people think of causes in terms of an original beginning causing an ultimate end, but things are not always that simple.

Imagine you are at a party talking to a friend when you feel a cold sensation down your back. The guy behind you has spilled his drink. He apologizes and says he tripped over a rug. It is annoying, but you cannot blame him because it was not his fault. So who should get the bill for cleaning your sweater? The cleaner moved the rug that morning, leaving it in the wrong place because he was in a hurry. His daughter is in the hospital, and the morning visiting hours are short. Do you

blame the daughter, who has a bad case of poison ivy because she ignored her father's warnings. If not, why not? If she had heeded his warning, your sweater might not be soaked.

When modeling the mind, researchers tend to assume a lawlike relationship between stimulus and response, just as a physicist sees the relationship between a

Will robots ever be able to respond to external events in the same way as people? Kismet (developed for the study of action recognition and learning) responds like a baby to visual stimuli by displaying appropriate facial expressions. When there are no stimuli, he displays a sad expression. During play he looks calm and happy. Too much stimulation causes him to become distressed.

ball and its bounce. More specifically, they assume that all behavior is determined (not random). But what determines behavior? We know that muscles connect to the central nervous system via nerve cells (neurons), which extend into and become parts of the brain (*see* pp. 20–39). Once in the brain, the signals generated interact in a complex—but determined— manner with other signals to and from other parts of the brain and body. The current state of your brain is determined by its state a split second ago, combined with any current incoming information from the changing environment (*see* pp. 62–85). The brain may therefore be described as a series of biochemical states in which there is no room for randomness; all reactions are the result of a stimulus.

A man who types words into a word-processor may think that the movements of his fingers are determined by the state of his brain, since his environment is quiet and unchanging. He thinks each sentence is the product of his free will. But what if his errors, omissions, and pauses are all the result of his previous brain state—where then is his free will? Cognitive scientists would say nowhere. If there is a lawlike relationship between stimulus and response, then the absence of free will is a logical conclusion, and modeling the mind becomes a real possibility.

The frame problem

Clearly, thinking is highly complex, and people are constantly updating their mental state by interacting with the world in many subtle ways. Thus at any given point the mind can be described as an information-rich single state. The many problems involved in representing even a single state bring us to the concept of frames. A frame is a way of representing knowledge about all the relevant objects and events common to a situation.

Roger C. Schank, director of the Institute for the Learning Sciences at Northwestern University, Evanston, Illinois, is a leading researcher in the field of AI. He gives this example of the frame problem: A man enters a restaurant and orders a burger. When the burger arrives, it is burned black, and he storms out without paying the bill. Did the man eat the burger? You and I know it is highly unlikely that he would have. But an artificially intelligent system might think he had because that would be normal restaurant behavior.

This undefined information about the state of the burger is just one piece of the fantastically large mass of information that people routinely receive or construct in such a situation. This is often called common sense. It was this lack of specific knowledge that impeded the development of programs such as GPS, which relied on broad problem-solving strategies but

IS THERE AN EXPERT IN THE HOUSE?

FOCUS ON

When people have a problem, one solution is to ask the advice of an expert. Unfortunately, human experts are often expensive, in short supply, and tend to grow old and retire. A computer model of a human expert, on the other hand, is usually cheaper, available 24 hours a day, and immortal. But are these systems better than their human counterparts?

MYCIN is an expert system that acts as a specialist in some medical emergencies in which immediate treatment is needed but it is not possible to consult a specialist in time. Its knowledge base derives from that of experts on bacterial infection. It can be run on any computer and is used by a medical doctor. The program starts by asking general questions about the patient, followed by more specific ones, as it attempts to formulate hypotheses and test them using a series of IF-THEN rules.

Most expert systems in current use are less complex than MYCIN. Philosophy professor Margaret Boden made the point that such systems are much less flexible than human experts. "In most cases," she says, "their explanations are merely summaries of previous IF-THEN rules." Humans cannot always explicitly state the rules that guide their performance; and even when they do, the system's performance is often inferior, indicating that there is insufficiency. Boden believes that expertise is really about high-level knowledge (intelligent overviews and syntheses) and analogy.

To get around this criticism, some expert systems adopt a more brainlike approach. CADUCEUS is based on the knowledge of one person, Dr. J. D. Myers, a specialist in internal medicine at the University of Pittsburgh. It tries to mimic the way Myers thinks, reasons, and arrives at decisions. The knowledge is not stored as IF-THEN rules but in a kind of spider's web called a semantic network. Whether CADUCEUS is more effective than MYCIN is unclear because the two systems solve different problems.

Expert systems raise ethical issues as well. If knowledge is power, do we want to give control to machines? And whom do we blame for any misdiagnosis—the expert the system is based on, the programmers, or the computer?

VISION AND INTELLIGENCE IN THE MILITARY

"We were looking out of our window...when a missile passed by on the line of the road on which the hotel stands . . . and it just went straight down the road."
John Simpson, BBC Foreign Affairs Editor, 1991

In the 1990s perceptions of AI improved thanks to memorable demonstrations of "smart missiles," which used machine vision technologies to intercept targets. One of the most startling was the Tomahawk Cruise missile, which appeared to sniff out targets like a bloodhound and politely swerve around civilians before burying itself at 700 mph. The technology behind such missiles has improved still further, and today they use contour maps of the target area obtained from satellite images. Missiles calculate their position on these maps using the Global Positioning System. By timing the return of signals sent to satellites in precisely known positions, they can pinpoint a target within centimeters of accuracy (although this is hardly a brainlike method).

Perhaps more interesting is the target acquisition system linked to the Heads-Up Display (HUD) and armament control in modern aircraft, which projects an image to provide the pilot with information. An important

An F-14 Tomcat launches an AIM-9 sidewinder, a heat-seeking missile.

component of this information is a "'crosshair" locked around a potential target, moving as shooters track a clay pigeon in their sights. To keep a target "locked" and known requires a program similar to a component of the human visual system. It detects objects by registering changes in light intensity—which tend to indicate object boundaries—and attempts to keep these objects in the middle of its camera. This "smart" system feeds location information to "dumb" missiles, such as those designed to seek out jet exhausts from enemy aircraft.

lacked world knowledge—a problem tackled by simulations such as SHRDLU. But could a computer ever handle the volume of data required to consider all different possibilities? The question is a technical one rather than a philosophical one, and there is no reason why a complex artificial neural network should not respond in the same way as a human brain given an equivalent computational power.

AI IN THE WORLD AT LARGE

All these inherent problems have not stopped researchers from trying to create artificially intelligent systems. After the Dartmouth conference in 1956 the pace quickened. During the 1960s research teams formed at M.I.T., at Carnegie Mellon and Stanford universities, and other institutions around the world, resulting in programs like the General Problem Solver, along with dedicated programming languages such as LISP, written by John McCarthy. The 1970s saw dissolution into specialized areas such as expert systems (*see* box p. 156) and connectionist networks, while corporate investment soared due to the potential of AI in business and the military. When results did not match expectations, much of the funding was withdrawn, but the public's perception of AI improved in the 1990s thanks to the demonstrations of "smart missiles" (*see* box above).

Expert systems

The problems involved in constructing a perceiving, intelligent learning machine led some researchers to scale down their efforts to concentrate on more specialized aspects of thinking, particularly in trying to model the intelligence of human experts (*see* box p. 156). Joshua Lederberg and Edward Feigenbaum made the first attempt to model an expert at Stanford University in 1965. Their system was called PROSPECTOR and helped analyze chemical compounds.

An expert system requires two major components: a knowledge base and an inference engine. The knowledge base is constructed from the data collected during a series of interviews with one or more human experts. A knowledge engineer then organizes this information into a searchable structure. Often this structure is of a treelike design, with branches occurring at each decision point. The inference engine browses this structure by performing question-style enquiries and using the answers it gains at each decision point to move systematically along the branches. For example, a program that mimics a dermatologist (skin disease expert) may begin with "Is all of the body affected?" and anticipate a YES/NO/DON'T KNOW response. With subsequent questions the expert system will move down the treelike structure of symptoms to identify the possible cause and suggest a line of treatment.

Robotics

A programmable machine capable of movement is called a "robot," a word that comes from a 1920 science fiction play by Czech playwright Karel Capek. In Czech *robota* means "forced labor." A robot may take any form, although humanoid robots tend to be called androids (*see* box p. 146). In the 20th century mass-production

Czech playwright Karel Capek first used the word "robot" in a science-fiction play in the 1920s. The word robota *means "forced labor" in Czech.*

> "*Domestic machines such as food processors, vacuum cleaners, and microwave ovens do not fill the void in families where all adults work outside the home . . . When will there be a robot to help around the house?*"
> — *Hans Moravec, 1988*

industries were the first to use robots to profitable ends, but they were far from intelligent. Such robots were computer controlled and lacked program flexibility, but were well suited to the endless, precise repetitions of simple assembly-line tasks. Some models did have "eyes," however, to help them correct mistakes.

Robots that attempt to behave in more complex and intelligent ways are restricted to public and private research programs, and form a crucial part of AI development. The main reason for this is that an AI robot that has a "body" and exists in a real world may be in a position to accumulate enough commonsense data to

solve the frame problem and to think meaningfully about its world, thus solving the intentionality problem.

For modeling purposes researchers must decide whether to build a robot physically or virtually. Physically means a

> "Because computers lack bodies and life experiences comparable to humans, intelligent systems will probably be inherently different."
> — David L. Waltz, 1988

robot that can walk or trundle around in the real world. Virtually means inside a computer. Arguably, physical robots are closer to the ultimate goal of AI—creating a humanlike machine. They can also be employed to carry out useful tasks, such as bomb disposal or microsurgery. However, such robots become more expensive as their complexity increases, and that limits their usefulness as AI research tools. By contrast, virtual robots are cheaper and

Robotic welders at a car plant. Each one performs 1,270 spot welds in less than four minutes. Mass-production assembly lines at the beginning of the 20th century were the first to use robots for commercial purposes. Although these machines may have some humanlike features such as hands, they lack intelligence because they do not have to think.

easier to manipulate. Researchers can create millions of them inside a computer, watch them evolve, alter the environment, and set them to solve various problems. Although the minds of these virtual robots are much less complex than those of people, they can still learn from experience. That makes these robots both practically useful and informative, enabling researchers to compare the workings of their virtual minds with those of a human mind.

The senses

People may argue over the intelligence, consciousness, and intentionality of computers, but fewer would dispute that artificial entities will never sense in the same way as humans, although they may be able to process sensory information. That is because, at a fundamental level, senses are just pieces of information.

Researchers have a reasonable idea of the type of information computers need to sense the world and have already built machines that can approximately simulate the human eyes, ears, mouth, nose, and

MORALITY IN ROBOTS

FOCUS ON

Born in Petrovichi, Russia, Isaac Asimov (1920–1992) moved to the United States as a boy. He was a gifted child and entered Columbia University at the age of 15 to study biochemistry. Two years later, following the publication of his first short story "Nightfall," he decided on two simultaneous career paths: scientist and author. Although he contributed prodigiously to popular science writing and science fiction, he also wrote books on the Bible and William Shakespeare.

In total Asimov produced more than 400 volumes, including some notable works on robots—which he believed should be completely predictable. As a former research chemist, he understood the utility of simple laws that always produce the same results. Consequently, he formulated three laws of robotics, which he often used to explain that apparently bizarre robot behavior was really a natural consequence of the application of these laws. The three laws are as follows:

• A robot may not injure a human or, through inaction, allow a human to come to harm.
• A robot must obey the orders given to it by humans except when such orders conflict with the first law.
• A robot must protect its own existence as long as such protection does not conflict with the first or second law.

These laws are both simple and practical, but how would a robot governed by these three rules behave, and what characteristics would it have? Asimov answered these questions through science fiction. In a series entitled *That Thou Art Mindful of Him* he described two robots left on a shelf. With nothing better to do, they begin to discuss the highs and lows of their existence, concluding that they embody the moral aspirations of humanity better than people. This is a recurrent theme throughout Asimov's work.

Other authors, such as Philip K. Dick and Eando Binder, make similar points about the moral nature of robots. They suggest that if ideal human moral behavior is selfless because of people's makeup, and ideal android behavior is selfless because of robots' makeup (designed by people), then this blurs the distinction between humanness and androidness. By discussing such concepts in their work, these science-fiction authors make people think about what it means to be human.

In his science-fiction writing, author and scientist Isaac Asimov defined three laws governing robot behavior. He also implied that the morality of robots is more human than that of people.

skin. They also have a good idea of the processing power required, thanks to Hans Moravec from Carnegie Mellon University. For vision alone—our primary sense—the system calculated that it takes one million instructions (each a single calculation, such as an addition or a subtraction) per second (MIPS) to track a white line or spot on a clear background. To follow complex gray-scale spots, 10 MIPS are required. To follow moderately unpredictable things, such as the course of a road, requires 100 MIPS, while accurate 3-D spatial awareness requires about 10,000 MIPS. In total the brain would need 100 million MIPS to carry out all its processing. So can a computer match this? On June 30, 2000, IBM unveiled its ASCI White computer (see p. 162), which has a reported speed of 3,000 million MIPS—comfortably faster than the human brain. Having the processing power is one thing, however; knowing how to use it is quite another, and researchers still do not fully understand how people's brains operate on the sensory information they receive.

Visual perception is so quick and effortless that many AI researchers in the 1960s believed they were close to creating

> *"What is the difference between today's computer and an intelligent being? The computer can be made to see but not to perceive."*
> — *Rudolf Arnheim, 1969*

robot vision. But by the 1970s it had become clear that vision was far more complex than they realized. Humans have evolved an efficient and intricate set of mechanisms that gradually transform light information into meaningful perception. Their visual system is structured in such a way that damage to specific areas of the brain can lead to specific impairments, indicating that separate areas of the brain are involved in processing movement, color, and even particular shapes such as human faces (*see* pp. 20–39).

If a robot is to move around, vision is obviously important. First, it must receive information through a video camera. Further visual processing then requires formal rules expressed as programs. One area studied by AI researchers is edge detection, which is crucial in perception because edges indicate where objects begin and end. Once edges have been detected, higher-level programs can start to operate on this information to identify an object's

ARTIFICIAL LIFE SYSTEMS

FOCUS ON

If it is so difficult to build complete humanlike robots, why make the task harder by attempting to build legions of them? The answer lies in the same mechanism that created people. According to the theory of evolution, all life on Earth originated in a kind of primordial soup of simple chemical arrangements. Nothing much happened until one day an arrangement appeared that was capable of reproducing itself: a highly improbable event, but it only had to happen once. Soon there were billions of these arrangements, all reproducing.

Due to natural mutation (change) and copying errors from one generation to the next, variants of these arrangements emerged. The stable characteristics of these variants were known as genes. Successful genes had a positive effect on an organism and thus became more common in the overall gene pool. Likewise, less successful genes became less common. The capacity to reproduce depended on many factors, particularly resources, and so variants that could make better use of these resources became more common.

Evolution is a powerful force responsible for people's most complex attributes, such as the brain. But can researchers harness that force for themselves? The reply is yes, but researchers need to begin with simple replicators (organisms) in a controlled environment (inside a computer). This evolution is virtual, not physical.

One example of virtual evolution is the Tierra system developed by Tom Ray at the University of Delaware and the ATR Human Information Processing Research Laboratories in Kyoto, Japan, in the 1990s. It is a virtual world in which the organisms are programs written in a popular computer language named C.

In real life the primary resources sought by plants and animals are generally oxygen (for energy-producing processes in the cell), water (as a required medium for these processes), and food (for energy, building, and repair). In the Tierra world an organism (program) needs a processor to carry out its instructions, so resources are represented by "attention" from the computer's processor. By interacting with each other, the programs evolve into better programs. The computer allows for several factors that may affect this virtual evolution: mutation rate (the degree of program change from one generation to the next), general disturbances, allocation of processor attention, size of the "world," and so on. Under these conditions the programs must compete for computer attention. Those that get more attention are more likely to reproduce.

Tierra is sufficiently complex to be useful for research into artificial life, but it remains to be seen whether computers will ever be powerful enough to simulate the richness of evolution—and creatures such as ourselves.

THE ETHICS OF ARTIFICIAL MINDS

Artificial organisms in the world at large, or at large in the world, pose an interesting ethical question for the future. They will have been built by humans for human use, just like airplanes, trains, and the Model T Ford. But if they are complex enough to act in a human way, or in a sentient, intelligent, or conscious way, will we have the right to control them in the way we control other machines?

One of the key debates of a future populated with artificial organisms may be about people's control of these organisms and the control that these organisms could have over people. Humans are slow to trust—and for good reason. Would you trust a car to drive you to school by itself, for example? Some vehicles (such as the van with an on-board computer from Carnegie Mellon University, which drove all but 52 of the 2,849 miles from Washington, DC, to San Diego) already drive themselves, although they can do little more at present because the technology is based on low-level visual processing. But what if you found an android at the wheel of your taxi? Issues abound when we consider what artificial organisms might do for people. They could be stronger, faster, live longer, and have more reliable memories.

Why employ a human to do a company's accounting when a robot could do it better and probably not expect to be paid? Why allow a coal miner to risk his or her life when a robot would risk only denting itself? Imagine the Superbowl with two teams of robots or a battle with the army's new Robotic Regiment. Damaged robots could immediately be fixed with replacement parts available at the shopping mall. Why not have them build bridges, space fleets, and more robots?

Not only might artificial organisms usher in a whole new era of human laziness, they could also pose problems if they were considered to be "alive." If a complex organism is alive, it automatically has certain rights. If it is conscious and humanlike, it has even more rights. To store it in the garage might be imprisonment, to call it "metal head" might be persecution, to ask it to do menial tasks might be torture, and to turn it off might be to commit murder.

features (*see* pp. 62–85). Any "seeing" computer must also deal with the problems that confront humans. For example, a piece of coal on a bright day will reflect more light than a snowball in twilight. Yet the coal still looks black and the snowball white. Evolution and experience have enabled humans to cope with processing such problems, but so far AI researchers have not managed to replicate this complexity. Instead, they have created an interesting number of spin-offs, such as self-driving vans, smart bombs, and cruise missiles.

Hearing is another process that has turned out to be more complicated than was first imagined. The ear (*see* pp. 62–85) is more than a microphone formed from cartilage, membranes, fluids, nerves, and bone—like all of the sense organs, it

Will computers ever match the processing power of the brain? The ASCI White computer is a nuclear war simulator that weighs the same as 17 elephants and occupies a space equivalent to two basketball courts. Its processing speed is 3,000 million MIPS (million instructions per second), and it can perform 12.3 trillion calculations per second—which is comfortably faster than the human brain.

actually processes some of the incoming data before the brain becomes involved. The brain then interprets the signals it receives so that a person can identify the location of sounds, detect musical notes, or hold a conversation in a noisy room. Trying to create artificial speech systems is particularly complex (*see* Vol. 1, pp. 118–125): Individual speech sounds (phonemes) must be identified, assembled into meaningful strings (morphemes), then into words, and finally into phrases.

Of course, sensing is more than computation. The sense of touch—of hot or cold, impact and pain—begins with free-ending nerve cells but culminates in a feeling, which may be pleasurable, painful, or neutral. Would a robot in a mountain breeze feel pleasure? Similarly, would a robot with taste and smell seek out peanut butter or take a moment to sniff a flower?

"Perhaps within the next few centuries, the universe will be full of intelligent life—silicon philosophers and planetary computers whose crude ancestors are evolving...now in our midst."
— *Margulis and Sagan, 1986*

CAN WE CREATE A SIXTH SENSE?

The question of whether a machine can be made fully "human" will not be answered easily or quickly, either philosophically or practically. The "sixth sense" that makes people human cannot be defined, but you will recognize it immediately: It is more than simply viewing a scene and detecting its edges and objects—it is da Vinci's Mona Lisa; more than segmenting speech sounds into words, phrases, and meaning, it is *Romeo and Juliet*; more than tactile sensation, it is summer rain; more than detecting chemicals, it is apple pie and ice cream. Critics of AI wonder if this sixth sense could ever be programmed. If a robot with pain receptors stubbed its toe

Cog was developed at MIT to study how humans learn by interacting with other people. Using visual and hearing systems, Cog can pinpoint a noise, track a moving object, and make eye contact. Cog's touch-sensitive hands enable "him" to classify objects, adjust his grip, and recognize when an object is slipping.

and emitted a shout from a speaker near its mouth, is it feeling pain? When asked, it will indignantly reply, "It certainly felt like it!" The robot has a mechanical brain based on the principles of your own; it has experienced a childhood of learning and interaction; it passes the Turing Test with flying colors. Do you believe it?

A few people think that human-level intelligence can be achieved by writing an adequate number of programs, but most researchers believe that fundamentally new ideas are required to replicate the brain, and that it cannot be predicted if or when artificial models of human-level intelligence will ever be achieved.

CONNECTIONS

- Computer Simulation: Volume 1, pp. 126–133
- The Biology of the Brain: pp. 20–39
- The Mind: pp. 40–61
- Perception: pp. 62–85
- Consciousness: pp. 110–139
- The Human Computer: Volume 3, pp. 6–23
- Intelligence: Volume 5, pp. 118–141

Set Glossary

abnormality Within abnormal psychology abnormality is the deviation from normal or expected behavior, generally involving maladaptive responses and personal distress both to the individuals with abnormal behavior and to those around them.

abnormal psychology The study and treatment of mental disorders.

acquisition The process by which something, such as a skill, habit, or language, is learned.

adaptation A change in behavior or structure that increases the survival chances of a species. Adjective: adaptive

addiction A state of dependence on a drug or a particular pattern of behavior.

adjustment disorder A mental disorder in which a patient is unable to adjust properly to a stressful life change.

affect A mood, emotion, or feeling. An affect is generally a shorter-lived and less-pronounced emotion than mood.

affective disorder A group of mental disorders, such as depression and bipolar 1 disorder, that are characterized by pronounced and often prolonged changes of mood.

agnosia A group of brain disorders involving impaired ability to recognize or interpret sensory information.

Alzheimer's disease A progressive and irreversible dementia in which the gradual destruction of brain tissue results in memory loss, impaired cognitive function, and personality change.

amnesia A partial or complete loss of memory.

amygdala An almond-shaped structure located in the front of the brain's temporal lobe that is part of the limbic system. Sometimes called the amygdaloid complex or the amygdaloid nucleus, the amygdala plays an important role in emotional behavior and motivation.

anorexia nervosa An eating disorder in which patients (usually young females) become obsessed with the idea that they are overweight and experience dramatic weight loss by not eating enough.

antidepressants A type of medication used to treat depression.

antianxiety drugs A type of medication used to treat anxiety disorders.

antipsychotic drugs A type of medication used to treat psychotic disorders such as schizophrenia. Sometimes known as neuroleptics.

anxiety disorder A group of mental disorders involving worry or distress.

anxiolytics *See* antianxiety drugs

aphasia A group of brain disorders that involve a partial or complete loss of language ability.

arousal A heightened state of awareness, behavior, or physiological function.

artificial intelligence (AI) A field of study that combines elements of cognitive psychology and computer science in an attempt to develop intelligent machines.

attachment theory A theory that describes how infants form emotional bonds with the adults they are close to.

attention The process by which someone can focus on particular sensory information by excluding other, less immediately relevant information.

attention deficit disorder (ADD) A mental disorder in which the patient (usually a child) is hyperactive, impulsive, and unable to concentrate properly.

autism A mental disorder, first apparent in childhood, in which patients are self-absorbed, socially withdrawn, and engage in repetitive patterns of behavior.

automatization The process by which complex behavior eventually becomes automatic. Such a process may be described as having automaticity or being automatized.

autonomic nervous system A part of the nervous system that controls many of the body's self-regulating (involuntary or automatic) functions.

aversion therapy A method of treating patients, especially those suffering from drink or drug addiction, by subjecting them to painful or unpleasant experiences.

axon Extension of the cell body of a neuron that transmits impulses away from the body of the neuron.

behavioral therapy A method of treating mental disorders that concentrates on modifying abnormal behavior rather than on the underlying causes of that behavior.

behaviorism A school of psychology in which easily observable and measurable behavior is considered to be the only proper subject of scientific study. Noun: behaviorist

bipolar I disorder A mental (affective) disorder involving periods of depression (depressed mood) and periods of mania (elevated mood).

body image The way in which a person perceives their own body or imagines it is perceived by other people.

body language The signals people send out to other people (usually unconsciously) through their gestures, posture, and other types of nonverbal communication.

Broca's area A region of the brain (usually located in the left hemisphere) that is involved with processing language.

bulimia nervosa An eating disorder in which patients consume large amounts of food in binges, then use laxatives or self-induced vomiting to prevent themselves putting on weight.

CAT scan *See* CT

causality The study of the causes of events or the connection between causes and effects.

central nervous system The part of the body's nervous system comprising the brain and spinal cord.

cerebellum A cauliflower-shaped structure at the back of the brain underneath the cerebral hemispheres that coordinates body movements.

cerebral cortex The highly convoluted outer surface of the brain's cerebrum.

cerebrum The largest part of the brain, consisting of the two cerebral hemispheres and their associated structures.

classical conditioning A method of associating a stimulus and a response that do not normally accompany one another. In Pavlov's well-known classical conditioning experiment dogs were trained so that they salivated (the conditioned response or CR) when Pavlov rang a bell (the conditioned stimulus or CS). Normally, dogs salivate

(an unconditioned response or UR) only when food is presented to them (an unconditioned stimulus or US).

clinical psychology An area of psychology concerned with the study and treatment of abnormal behavior.

cognition A mental process that involves thinking, reasoning, or some other type of mental information processing. Adjective: cognitive

cognitive behavioral therapy (CBT) An extension of behavioral therapy that involves treating patients by modifying their abnormal thought patterns as well as their behavior.

cognitive psychology An area of psychology that seeks to understand how the brain processes information.

competency In psycholinguistics the representation of the abstract rules of a language, such as its grammar.

conditioned stimulus/response (CS/CR) *See* classical conditioning

conditioning *See* classical conditioning; instrumental conditioning

connectionism A computer model of cognitive processes such as learning and memory. Connectionist models are based on a large network of "nodes" and the connections between them. Adjective: connectionist

consciousness A high-level mental process responsible for the state of self-awareness that people feel. Consciousness is thought by some researchers to direct human behavior and by others simply to be a byproduct of that behavior.

cortex *See* cerebral cortex

cross-cultural psychology The comparison of behavior, such as language

acquisition or nonverbal communication, between different peoples or cultures.

cross-sectional study An experimental method in which a large number of subjects are studied at a particular moment or period in time. Compare longitudinal study

CT (computed tomography) A method of producing an image of the brain's tissue using X-ray scanning, which is commonly used to detect brain damage. Also called CAT (computerized axial tomography).

culture-specific A behavior found only in certain cultures and not observed universally in all humankind.

declarative knowledge A collection of facts about the world and other things that people have learned. Compare procedural knowledge

declarative memory *See* explicit memory

defense mechanism A type of thinking or behavior that a person employs unconsciously to protect themselves from anxiety or unwelcome feelings.

deficit A missing cognitive function whose loss is caused by a brain disorder.

delusion A false belief that a person holds about themselves or the world around them. Delusions are characteristic features of psychotic mental illnesses such as schizophrenia.

dementia A general loss of cognitive functions usually caused by brain damage. Dementia is often, but not always, progressive (it becomes worse with time).

Dementia of the Alzheimer's type (DAT) See Alzheimer's disease

dendrite A treelike projection of a neuron's cell body that conducts nerve impulses toward the cell body.

dependency An excessive reliance on an addictive substance, such as a drug, or on the support of another person.

depression An affective mental disorder characterized by sadness, low self-esteem, inadequacy, and related symptoms.

desensitization A gradual reduction in the response to a stimulus when it is presented repeatedly over a period of time.

developmental psychology An area of psychology concerned with how people develop throughout their lives, but usually concentrating on how behavior and cognition develop during childhood.

discrimination In perception the ability to distinguish between two or more stimuli. In social psychology and sociology unequal treatment of people based on prejudice.

dysgraphia A brain disorder involving an ability to write properly.

dyslexia Brain disorders that disrupt a person's ability to read.

eating disorders A group of mental disorders that involve disturbed eating patterns or appetite.

echoic memory See sensory memory

ego The central part of a person's self. In Freudian psychology the ego manages the balance between a person's primitive, instinctive needs and the often conflicting demands of the world around them.

egocentric A person who is excessively preoccupied with themselves at the expense of the people and the world around them.

eidetic An accurate and persistent form of visual memory that is generally uncommon in adults (often misnamed "photographic memory").

electroconvulsive therapy (ECT) A treatment for severe depression that involves passing a brief and usually relatively weak electric shock through the front of a patient's skull.

electroencephalogram (EEG) A graph that records the changing electrical activity in a person's brain from electrodes attached to the scalp.

emotion A strong mood or feeling. Also a reaction to a stimulus that prepares the body for action.

episodic memory A type of memory that records well-defined events or episodes in a person's life. Compare semantic memory

ethnocentricity The use of a particular ethnic group to draw conclusions about wider society or humankind as a whole.

event-related potential (ERP) A pattern of electrical activity (the potential) produced by a particular stimulus (the event). EVPs are often recorded from the skull using electrodes.

evoked potential See event-related potential (ERP)

evolution A theory suggesting that existing organisms have developed from earlier ones by processes that include natural selection (dubbed "survival of the fittest") and genetic mutation.

evolutionary psychology An approach to psychology that uses the theory of evolution to explain the mind and human behavior.

explicit memory A type of memory containing information that is available to conscious recognition and recall.

flashbulb memory A very clear and evocative memory of a particular moment or event.

fMRI (functional magnetic resonance imaging) An MRI-based scanning technique that can produce images of the brain while it is engaged in cognitive activities.

functionalism An approach to psychology that concentrates on the functions played by parts of the mind and human behavior.

generalized anxiety disorder (GAD) A type of nonspecific anxiety disorder with symptoms that include worry, irritability, and tension.

genes A functional unit of the chromosome that determines how traits are passed on and expressed from generation to generation. Adjective: genetic

Gestalt psychology A psychology school that emphasizes the importance of appreciating phenomena as structured wholes in areas such as perception and learning, as opposed to breaking them down into their components. Most influential in the mid-1900s.

gray matter The parts of the nervous system that contain mainly nerve cell bodies.

habituation *See* desensitization

hallucination A vivid but imaginary perceptual experience that occurs purely in the mind, not in reality.

heritability The proportion of observed variation for a trait in a specific population that can be attributed to genetic factors rather than environmental ones. Generally expressed as a ratio of genetically caused variation to total variation.

hippocamus A part of the limbic system in the temporal lobe that is thought to play an important role in the formation of memories.

Humanism A philosophy that stresses the importance of human interests and values.

hypothalamus A small structure at the base of the brain that controls the autonomic nervous system.

hysteria A type of mental disturbance that may include symptoms such as hallucinations and emotional outbursts.

implicit memory A type of memory not normally available to conscious awareness. Sometimes also known as procedural or nondeclarative memory. Compare explicit memory

imprinting A type of learning that occurs in a critical period shortly after birth, such as when chicks learn to accept a human in place of their real mother.

individual psychology An approach to psychology that focuses on the differences between individuals. Also a theory advanced by Alfred Adler based on the idea of overcoming inferiority.

information processing In cognitive psychology the theory that the mind operates something like a computer, with sensory information processed either in a series of discrete stages or in parallel by something like a connectionist network.

ingroup A group whose members feel a strong sense of collective identity and act to exclude other people (the outgroup).

innate A genetically determined trait that is present at birth, as opposed to something that is acquired by learning.

instinct An innate and automatic response to a particular stimulus that usually involves no rational thought.

instrumental conditioning A type of conditioning in which reinforcement occurs only when an organism makes a certain, desired response. Instrumental

conditioning occurs, for example, when a pigeon is trained to peck a lever to receive a pellet of food.

internalize To make internal, personal, or subjective; to take in and make an integral part of one's attitudes or beliefs:

introspection A behaviorist technique of studying the mind by observing one's own thought processes.

language acquisition device (LAD) According to linguist Noam Chomsky, a part of the brain that is preprogrammed with a universal set of grammatical rules that can construct the rules of a specific language according to the environment it is exposed to.

libido The sexual drive.

limbic system A set of structures in the brain stem, including the hippocampus and the amygdala, that lie below the corpus callosum. It is involved in emotion, motivation, behavior, and various functions of the autonomic nervous system.

long-term memory A type of memory in which information is retained for long periods after being deeply processed. Generally used to store events and information from the past. Compare short-term memory

longitudinal study An experimental method that follows a small group of subjects over a long period of time. Compare cross-sectional study

maladaptive Behavior is considered maladapative or dysfunctional if it has a negative effect on society or on a person's ability to function in society.

medical model A theory that mental disorders, like diseases, have specific underlying medical causes, which must be addressed if treatment is to be effective.

mental disorder A psychiatric illness such as schizophrenia, anxiety, or depression.

metacognition The study by an individual of their own thought processes. *See also* introspection

mnemonic A technique that can be used to remember information or improve memory.

modeling The technique by which a person observes some ideal form of behavior (a role model) and then attempts to copy it. In artificial intelligence (AI) people attempt to build computers that model human cognition.

modularity A theory that the brain is composed of a number of modules that occupy relatively specific areas and that carry out relatively specific tasks.

morpheme The smallest unit of a language that carries meaning.

motor neuron *See* neuron.

MRI (magnetic resonance imaging) A noninvasive scanning technique that uses magnetic fields to produce detailed images of body tissue.

nature–nurture A long-running debate over whether genetic factors (nature) or environmental factors (nurture) are most important in different aspects of behavior.

neuron A nerve cell, consisting of a cell body (soma), an axon, and one or more dendrites. Motor (efferent) neurons produce movement when they fire by carrying information *from* the central nervous system *to* the muscles and glands; sensory (afferent) neurons carry information *from* the senses *to* the central nervous system.

neuropsychology An area of psychology that studies the connections between parts of the brain and neural processes, on one hand, and different cognitive processes and types of behavior, on the other.

neurotransmitter A substance that carries chemical "messages" across the synaptic gaps between the neurons of the brain.

nonverbal communication The way in which animals communicate without language (verbal communication), using such things as posture, tone of voice, and facial expressions.

operant conditioning *See* instrumental conditioning

outgroup The people who do not belong to an ingroup.

parallel processing A type of cognition in which information is processed in several different ways at once. In serial processing information passes through one stage of processing at a time.

peripheral nervous system All the nerves and nerve processes that connect the central nervous system with receptors, muscles, and glands.

personality The collection of character traits that makes one person different from another.

personality disorder A group of mental disorders in which aspects of someone's personality make it difficult for them to function properly in society.

PET (positron emission tomography) A noninvasive scanning technique that makes images of the brain according to levels of metabolic activity inside it.

phenomenology A philosophy based on the study of immediate experiences.

phobia A strong fear of a particular object (such as snakes) or social situation.

phoneme A basic unit of spoken language.

phrenology An early approach to psychology that studied the relationship between areas of the brain (based on skull shape) and mental functions. Phrenology has since been discredited.

physiology A type of biology concerned with the workings of cells, organs, and tissues.

positive punishment A type of conditioning in which incorrect responses are punished.

positive reinforcement A type of conditioning in which correct responses are rewarded.

primary memory *See* short-term memory

probability The likelihood of something happening.

procedural knowledge The practical knowledge of how to do things ("know-how"). Compare declarative knowledge

prosody A type of nonverbal communication in which language is altered by such things as the pitch of someone's voice and their intonation.

psyche The soul or mind of a person or a driving force behind their personality.

psychiatry The study, classification, and treatment of mental disorders.

psychoanalysis A theory of behavior and an approach to treating mental disorders pioneered by Austrian neurologist Sigmund Freud. Adjective: psychoanalytic

psychogenic A mental disorder that is psychological (as opposed to physical) in origin.

psycholinguistics The study of language-related behavior, including how the brain acquires and processes language.

psychosurgery A type of brain surgery designed to treat mental disorders.

psychotherapy A broad range of treatments for mental disorders based on different kinds of interaction between a patient and a therapist.

psychosis A mental state characterized by disordered personality and loss of contact with reality that affects normal social functioning. Psychosis is a feature of psychotic disorders, such as schizophrenia. Adjective: psychotic

reaction time The time taken for the subject in an experiment to respond to a stimulus.

recall The process by which items are recovered from memory. Compare recognition

recognition The process by which a person realizes they have previously encountered a particular object or event. Compare recall

reductionism A philosophy based on breaking complex things into their individual components. Also, an attempt to explain high-level sciences (such as psychology) in terms of lower-level sciences (such as chemistry or physics).

reflex An automatic response to a stimulus (a "knee-jerk" reaction).

reflex arc The neural circuit thought to be responsible for the control of a reflex.

rehearsing The process by which a person repeats information to improve its chances of being stored in memory.

representation A mental model based on perceptions of the world.

repression In psychoanalysis an unconscious mental process that keeps thoughts out of conscious awareness.

response The reaction to a stimulus.

reuptake The reabsorption of a neurotransmitter from the place where it was produced.

risk aversion A tendency not to take risks even when they may have beneficial results.

schema An abstract mental plan that serves as a guide to action or a more general mental representation.

schizophrenia A mental disorder characterized by hallucinations and disordered thought patterns in which a patient becomes divorced from reality. It is a type of psychotic disorder.

secondary memory *See* long-term memory

selective attention *See* attention

self-concept The ideas and feelings that people hold about themselves.

semantic memory A type of long-term memory that stores information based on its content or meaning. Compare episodic memory

senses The means by which people perceive things. The five senses are vision, hearing, smell, touch, and taste.

sensory memory An information store that records sensory impressions for a short period of time before they are processed more thoroughly.

sensory neuron *See* neuron

serotonin A neurotransmitter in the central nervous system that plays a key role in affective (mood) disorders, sleep, and the perception of pain. Serotonin is also known as 5-hydroxytryptamine (5-HT).

shaping A type of conditioning in which behavior is gradually refined toward some ideal form by successive approximations.

short-term memory A memory of very limited capacity in which sensory inputs are held before being processed more deeply and passing into long-term memory. Compare long-term memory

social cognition An area of psychology that combines elements of social and cognitive psychology in an attempt to understand how people think about themselves in relation to the other people around them.

social Darwinism A theory that society behaves according to Darwinian principles, with the most successful members thriving at the expense of the least successful ones.

social psychology An area of psychology that explores how individuals behave in relation to other people and to society as a whole.

sociobiology A theory that seeks to explain social behavior through biological approaches, notably the theory of evolution. *See also* evolutionary psychology

somatic Something that relates to the body as opposed to the mind; something physical as opposed to something mental.

stereopsis The process by which the brain assembles one 3-D image by combining a pair of 2-D images from the eyes.

stimulus A type of sensory input that provokes a response.

subject The person studied in a psychological experiment.

synapse The region across which nerve impulses are transmitted from one neuron to another. It includes the synaptic cleft (a gap) and the sections of the cell membranes on either side of the cleft. They are called the presynaptic and postsynaptic membranes.

synesthesia A process by which the stimulation of one sense (such as hearing a sound) produces a different kind of sensory impression (such as seeing a color).

thalamus A structure in the forebrain that passes sensory information on to the cerebral cortex.

theory of mind The realization by an individual (such as a growing child, for example) that other people have thoughts and mental processes of their own. It is universally accepted that humans have a theory of mind, and research has shown that some other animals, such as chimpanzees and dolphins, might also have a theory of mind, but this is still debated. Theory of mind is of interest to developmental psychologists since it is not something people are born with, but something that develops in infancy.

tranquilizers A type of medication with sedative, muscle-relaxant, or similar properties. Minor tranquilizers are also known as antianxiety or anxiolytic drugs; major tranquilizers are also known as antipsychotic drugs.

unconditioned stimulus/response (US/UR) *See* classical conditioning

unconscious In psychoanalytic and related theories the area of the mind that is outside conscious awareness and recall but that informs the contents of such things as dreams. In general usage *unconscious* simply refers to automatic cognitive processes that we are not aware of or the lack of consciousness (that is, "awareness") at times such as during sleep.

working memory *See* short-term memory

Resources

Further Reading

Altmann, G. T. M. *The Ascent of Babel: An Exploration of Language, Mind, and Understanding.* Cambridge, MA: Oxford University Press, 1999.

American Psychiatric Association. *Diagnostic and Statistical Manual of Mental Disorders, 4th edition, Text Revision.* Washington, DC: American Psychiatric Press, 2000.

Argyle, M. *The Psychology of Interpersonal Behaviour (5th edition).* London, UK: Penguin, 1994.

Asher, S. R. and Coie, J. D. (eds.). *Peer Rejection in Childhood.* Cambridge, UK: Cambridge University Press, 1990.

Atkinson, R. L. *et al. Hilgard's Introduction to Psychology (13th edition).* London, UK: International Thomson Publishing, 1999.

Barnouw, V. *Culture and Personality.* Chicago, IL: Dorsey Press, 1985.

Baron, J. *Thinking and Deciding.* Cambridge, UK: Cambridge University Press, 1994.

Barry, M. A. S. *Visual Intelligence: Perception, Image, and Manipulation in Visual Communication.* Albany, NY: State University of New York Press, 1997.

Beck, J. *Cognitive Therapy: Basics and Beyond.* London, UK: The Guildford Press, 1995.

Bickerton, D. *Language and Species.* Chicago, IL: The University of Chicago Press, 1990.

Blackburn, I. M. and Davison, K. *Cognitive Therapy for Depression and Anxiety: A Practitioner's Guide.* Oxford, UK: Blackwell, 1995.

Boden, M. A. *Piaget (2nd edition).* London, UK: Fontana Press, 1994.

Brehm, S. S., Kassin, S. M., and Fein, S. *Social Psychology (4th edition).* Boston, MA: Houghton Mifflin, 1999.

Brody, N. *Intelligence (2nd edition).* San Diego, CA: Academic Press, 1997.

Brown, D. S. *Learning a Living: A Guide to Planning Your Career and Finding a Job for People with Learning Disabilities, Attention Deficit Disorder, and Dyslexia.* Bethesda, MD: Woodbine House, 2000.

Bruhn, A. R. *Earliest Childhood Memories.* New York: Praeger, 1990.

Buunk, B. P. "Affiliation, Attraction and Close Relationships." *In* M. Hewstone and W. Stroebe (eds.), *Introduction to Social Psychology: A European Perspective.* Oxford, UK: Blackwell, 2001.

Cacioppo, J. T., Tassinary, L. G., and Berntson, G. G. (eds.). *Handbook of Psychophysiology (2nd edition).* New York: Cambridge University Press, 2000.

Cardwell, M. *Dictionary of Psychology.* Chicago, IL: Fitzroy Dearborn Publishers, 1999

Carson, R. C. and Butcher, J. N. *Abnormal Psychology and Modern Life (9th edition).* New York: HarperCollins Publishers, 1992.

Carter, R. *Mapping the Mind.* Berkeley, CA: University of California Press, 1998.

Cavan, S. *Recovery from Drug Addiction.* New York: Rosen Publishing Group, 2000.

Clarke-Stewart, A. *Daycare.* Cambridge, MA: Harvard University Press, 1993.

Cohen, G. *The Psychology of Cognition (2nd edition).* San Diego, CA: Academic Press, 1983.

Cramer, D. *Close Relationships: The Study of Love and Friendship.* New York: Arnold, 1998.

Daly, M. and Wilson, M. *Homicide.* New York: Aldine de Gruyter, 1988.

Davis, R. D., Braun, E. M., and Smith, J. M. *The Gift of Dyslexia: Why Some of the Smartest People Can't Read and How They Can Learn.* New York: Perigee, 1997.

Davison, G. C. and Neal, J. M. *Abnormal Psychology.* New York: John Wiley and Sons, Inc., 1994.

Dawkins, R. *The Selfish Gene.* New York: Oxford Universty Press, 1976.

Dennett, D. C. *Darwin's Dangerous Idea: Evolution and the Meanings of Life.* Carmichael, CA: Touchstone Books, 1996.

Dobson, C. *et al. Understanding Psychology.* London, UK: Weidenfeld and Nicolson, 1982.

Duck, S. *Meaningful Relationships: Talking, Sense, and Relating.* Thousand Oaks, CA: Sage Publications, 1994.

Durie, M. H. "Maori Psychiatric Admissions: Patterns, Explanations and Policy Implications." *In* J. Spicer, A. Trlin, and J. A. Walton (eds.), *Social Dimensions of Health and Disease: New Zealand Perspectives.* Palmerston North, NZ: Dunmore Press, 1994.

Eliot, L. *What's Going on in There? How the Brain and Mind Develop in the First Five Years of Life.* New York: Bantam Books, 1999.

Eysenck, M. (ed.). *The Blackwell Dictionary of Cognitive Psychology.* Cambridge, MA: Blackwell, 1991.

Faherty, C. and Mesibov, G. B. *Asperger's: What Does It Mean to Me?* Arlington, TX: Future Horizons, 2000.

Fernando, S. *Mental Health in a Multi-Ethnic Society: A Multi-Disciplinary Handbook.* New York: Routledge, 1995.

Fiske, S. T. and Taylor, S. E. *Social Cognition (2nd Edition).* New York: Mcgraw-Hill, 1991.

Franken, R. E. *Human Motivation (5th edition).* Belmont, CA: Wadsworth Thomson Learning, 2002.

Freud, S. and Brill, A. A. *The Basic Writings of Sigmund Freud.* New York: Modern Library, 1995.

Gardner, H. *The Mind's New Science: A History of the Cognitive Revolution.* New York: Basic Books, 1985.

Garnham, A. and Oakhill, J. *Thinking and Reasoning.* Cambridge, MA: Blackwell, 1994.

Gaw, A. C. *Culture, Ethnicity, and Mental Illness.* Washington, DC: American Psychiatric Press, 1992.

Giacobello, J. *Everything You Need to Know about Anxiety and Panic Attacks.* New York: Rosen Publishing Group, 2000.

Gazzaniga, M. S. *The Mind's Past.* Berkeley, CA: University of California Press, 1998.

Gazzaniga, M. S. (ed.). *The New Cognitive Neurosciences (2nd edition).* Cambridge, MA: MIT Press, 2000.

Gazzaniga, M. S., Ivry, R. B., and Mangun, G. R. *Cognitive Neuroscience: The Biology of the Mind (2nd edition).* New York: Norton, 2002.

Gernsbacher, M. A. (ed.). *Handbook of Psycholinguistics.* San Diego, CA: Academic Press, 1994.

Gigerenzer, G. *Adaptive Thinking: Rationality in the Real World.* New York: Oxford University Press, 2000.

Goodglass, H. *Understanding Aphasia.* San Diego, CA: Academic Press, 1993.

Gordon, M. *Jumpin' Johnny Get Back to Work! A Child's Guide to ADHD/Hyperactivity.* DeWitt, NY: GSI Publications Inc., 1991.

Gordon, M. A *I Would if I Could: A Teenager's Guide to ADHD/Hyperactivity.* DeWitt, NY: GSI Publications Inc., 1992.

Goswami, U. *Cognition in Children.* London, UK: Psychology Press, 1998.

Graham, H. *The Human Face of Psychology: Humanistic Psychology in Its Historical, Social, and Cultural Context.* Milton Keynes, UK: Open University Press, 1986.

Grandin, T. *Thinking in Pictures: And Other Reports from my Life with Autism.* New York: Vintage Books, 1996.

Greenberger, D. and Padesky, C. *Mind over Mood.* New York: Guilford Publications, 1995.

Groeger, J. A. *Memory and Remembering: Everyday Memory in Context.* New York: Longman, 1997.

Gross, R. and Humphreys, P. *Psychology: The Science of Mind and Behaviour.* London, UK: Hodder Arnold, 1993.

Halford, G. S. *Children's Understanding: The Development of Mental Models.* Hillsdale, NJ: Lawrence Erlbaum Associates, 1993.

Harley, T. A. *The Psychology of Language: From Data to Theory (2nd edition).* Hove, UK: Psychology Press, 2001.

Harris, G. G. *Casting out Anger: Religion among the Taita of Kenya.* New York: Cambridge University Press, 1978.

Hayes, N. *Psychology in Perspective (2nd edition).* New York: Palgrave, 2002.

Hearst, E. *The First Century of Experimental Psychology.* Hillsdale, NJ: Lawrence Erlbaum Associates, 1979.

Hecht, T. *At Home in the Street: Street Children of Northeast Brazil.* New York: Cambridge University Press, 1998.

Hetherington, E. M. *Coping with Divorce, Single Parenting, and Remarriage: A Risk and Resiliency Perspective.* Mawah, NJ: Lawrence Erlbaum Associates, 1999.

Higbee, K. L. *Your Memory: How It Works and How to Improve It (2nd edition).* New York: Paragon 1993.

Hinde, R. A. *Individuals, Relationships and Culture: Links between Ethology and the Social Sciences.* Cambridge, UK: Cambridge University Press, 1987.

Hogdon, L. A. *Solving Behavior Problems in Autism.* Troy, MI: Quirkroberts Publishing, 1999.

Hogg, M. A. (ed.). *Social Psychology.* Thousand Oaks, CA: Sage Publications, 2002.

Holden, G. W. *Parents and the Dynamics of Child Rearing.* Boulder, CO: Westview Press, 1997.

Holmes, J. *John Bowlby and Attachment Theory.* New York: Routledge, 1993.

Hughes, H. C. *Sensory Exotica: A World Beyond Human Experience.* Cambridge, MA: MIT Press, 1999.

Hyde, M. O. and Setano, J. F. *When the Brain Dies First.* New York: Franlin Watts Inc., 2000.

Ingersoll, B. D. *Distant Drums, Different Drummers: A Guide for Young People with ADHD.* Plantation, FL: A.D.D. WareHouse, 1995.

Jencks, C. and Phillips, M. *The Black-White Test Score Gap.* Washington, DC: Brookings Institution Press, 1998.

Johnson, M. J. *Developmental Cognitive Neuroscience.* Cambridge, MA: Blackwell, 1997.

Johnson, M. H. and Morton, J. *Biology and Cognitive Development. The Case of Face Recognition.* Cambridge, MA: Blackwell, 1991.

Johnson-Laird, P. N. *The Computer and the Mind: An Introduction to Cognitive Science.* Cambridge, MA: Harvard University Press, 1988.

Jusczyk, P. W. *The Discovery of Spoken Language.* Cambridge, MA: MIT Press, 1997.

Kalat, J. W. *Biological Psychology (7th edition).* Belmont, CA: Wadsworth Thomson Learning, 2001.

Kaplan, H. I. and Sadock, B. J. *Synopsis of Psychiatry: Behavioral Sciences, Clinical Psychiatry.* Philadelphia, PA: Lippincott, Williams and Wilkins, 1994.

Karen, R. *Becoming Attached: First Relationships and How They Shape Our Capacity to Love.* New York: Oxford University Press, 1998.

Kirk, S. A. and Kutchins, H. *The Selling of DSM: The Rhetoric of Science in Psychiatry.* New York: Aldine de Gruyter, 1992.

Kinney, J. *Clinical Manual of Substance Abuse.* St. Louis, MO: Mosby, 1995.

Kleinman, A. *Rethinking Psychiatry: From Cultural Category to Personal Experience.* New York: Free Press, 1988.

Kosslyn, S. M. and Koenig, O. *Wet Mind: The New Cognitive Neuroscience.* New York: Free Press, 1992.

Kutchins, H. and Kirk, S. A. *Making Us Crazy: DSM: The Psychiatric Bible and the Creation of Mental Disorders.* New York: Free Press, 1997.

LaBruzza, A. L. *Using DSM-IV; A Clinician's Guide to Psychiatric Diagnosis.* St. Northvale, NJ: Jason Aronson Inc., 1994.

Leahey, T. A. *A History of Psychology: Main Currents in Psychological Thought (5th edition).* Upper Saddle River, NJ: Prentice Hall, 2000.

LeDoux, J. *The Emotional Brain.* New York: Simon and Schuster, 1996.

Levelt, W. J. M. *Speaking: From Intention to Articulation.* Cambridge, MA: MIT Press, 1989.

Lewis, M. and Haviland-Jones, J. M. (eds.). *Handbook of Emotions (2nd edition).* New York: Guilford Press, 2000.

Lowisohn, J. H. *et al. Substance Abuse: A Comprehensive Textbook (3rd edition).* Baltimore, MD: Williams & Wilkins, 1997.

McCabe, D. *To Teach a Dyslexic.* Clio, MI: AVKO Educational Research, 1997.

McCorduck, P. *Machines Who Think: A Personal Inquiry into the History and Prospects of Artificial Intelligence.* San Francisco: W. H. Freeman, 1979.

McIlveen, R. and Gross, R. *Biopsychology (5th edition).* Boston, MA: Allyn and Bacon, 2002.

McLachlan, J. *Medical Embryology.* Reading, MA: Addison-Wesley Publishing Co., 1994.

Manstead, A. S. R. and Hewstone M. (eds.). *The Blackwell Encyclopaedia of Social Psychology.* Oxford, UK: Blackwell, 1996.

Marsella, A. J., DeVos, G., and Hsu, F. L. K. (eds.). *Culture and Self: Asian and Western Perspectives.* New York: Routledge, 1988.

Matlin, M. W. *The Psychology of Women.* New York: Harcourt College Publishers, 2000.

Matsumoto, D. R. *People: Psychology from a Cultural Perspective.* Pacific Grove, CA: Brooks/Cole Publishing, 1994.

Matsumoto, D. R. *Culture and Modern Life.* Pacific

Grove, CA: Brooks/Cole Publishing, 1997.

Mazziotta, J .C., Toga, A. W., and Frackowiak, R. S. J. (eds.). *Brain Mapping: The Disorders.* San Diego, CA: Academic Press, 2000.

Nadeau, K. G., Littman, E., and Quinn, P. O. *Understanding Girls with ADHD.* Niagara Falls, NY: Advantage Books, 2000.

Nadel, J. and Camioni, L. (eds.). *New Perspectives in Early Communicative Development.* New York: Routledge, 1993.

Nobus, D. *Jacques Lacan and the Freudian Practice of Psychoanalysis.* Philadelphia, PA: Routledge, 2000.

Oakley, D. A. "The Plurality of Consciousness." *In* D. A. Oakley (ed.), *Brain and Mind*, New York: Methuen, 1985.

Obler, L. K. and Gjerlow, K. *Language and the Brain.* New York: Cambridge University Press, 1999.

Ogden, J. A. *Fractured Minds: A Case-study Approach to Clinical Neuropsychology.* New York: Oxford University Press, 1996.

Owusu-Bempah, K. and Howitt, D. *Psychology beyond Western Perspectives.* Leicester, UK: British Psychological Society Books, 2000.

Paranjpe, A. C. and Bhatt, G. S. "Emotion: A Perspective from the Indian Tradition." *In* H. S. R. Kao and D. Sinha (eds.), *Asian Perspectives on Psychology.* New Delhi, India: Sage Publications, 1997.

Peacock, J. *Depression.* New York: Lifematters Press, 2000.

Pfeiffer, W. M. "Culture-Bound Syndromes." *In* I. Al-Issa (ed.), *Culture and Psychopathology.* Baltimore, MD: University Park Press, 1982.

Pillemer, D. B. *Momentous Events, Vivid Memories.* Cambridge, MA: Harvard University Press, 1998.

Pinel, J. P. J. *Biopsychology (5th edition).* Boston, MA: Allyn and Bacon, 2002.

Pinker, S. *The Language Instinct.* New York: HarperPerennial, 1995.

Pinker, S. *How the Mind Works.* New York: Norton, 1997.

Porter, R. *Medicine: A History of Healing: Ancient Traditions to Modern Practices.* New York: Barnes and Noble, 1997.

Ramachandran, V. S. and Blakeslee, S. *Phantoms in the Brain: Probing the Mysteries of the Human Mind.* New York: William Morrow, 1998.

Ridley, M. *Genome: The Autobiography of a Species in 23 Chapters.* New York: HarperCollins, 1999.

Robins, L. N. and Regier, D. A. *Psychiatric Disorders in America.* New York: Free Press, 1991.

Robinson, D. N. *Toward a Science of Human Nature: Essays on the Psychologies of Mill, Hegel, Wundt, and James.* New York: Columbia University Press, 1982.

Rugg, M. D. and Coles, M. G. H. (eds.). *Electrophysiology of the Mind: Event-Related Brain Potentials and Cognition.* Oxford, UK: Oxford University Press, 1995.

Rutter, M. "The Interplay of Nature and Nurture: Redirecting the Inquiry." *In* R. Plomin and G. E. McClearn (eds.), *Nature, Nurture, and Psychology.* Washington, DC: American Psychological Association, 1993.

Sarason, I. G. and Sarason B. R. *Abnormal Psychology: The Problem of Maladaptive Behavior (9th edition).* Upper Saddle River, NJ: Prentice Hall, 1998.

Savage-Rumbaugh, S., Shanker, S. G., and Taylor, T. J. *Apes, Language, and the Human Mind.* New York: Oxford University Press, 1998.

Schab, F. R., & Crowder, R. G. (eds.). *Memory for Odors.* Mahwah, NJ: Lawrence Erlbaum Associates, 1995.

Segal, N. L. *Entwined Lives: Twins and What They Tell Us about Human Behavior.* New York: Plume, 2000.

Seeman, M. V. *Gender and Psychopathology.* Washington, DC: American Psychiatric Press, 1995.

Seligman, M. E. P. *Helplessness: On Depression, Development, and Death.* San Francisco, CA: W. H. Freeman and Co., 1992.

Shorter, E. *A History of Psychiatry: From the Era of Asylum to the Age of Prozac.* New York: John Wiley and Sons, Inc., 1997.

Siegler, R. S. *Children's Thinking (3rd edition).* Englewood Cliffs, NJ: Prentice Hall, 1998.

Simpson, E. M. *Reversals: A Personal Account of Victory over Dyslexia.* New York: Noonday Press, 1992.

Singer, D. G. and Singer, J. L. (eds.). *Handbook of Children and the Media.* Thousand Oaks, CA: Sage Publications, 2001.

Skinner, B. F. *Science and Human Behavior.* New York: Free Press, 1965.

Slavney, P. R. *Psychiatric Dimensions of Medical Practice: What Primary-Care Physicians Should Know about Delirium, Demoralization, Suicidal Thinking, and Competence to Refuse Medical Advice.* Baltimore, MD: The Johns Hopkins University Press, 1998.

Smith McLaughlin, M., Peyser Hazouri, S., and Peyser Hazouri, S. *Addiction: The "High" That Brings You Down.* Springfield, NJ: Enslow publishers, 1997.

Sommers, M. A. *Everything You Need to Know about Bipolar Disorder and Depressive Illness.* New York: Rosen Publishing Group, 2000.

Stanovich, K. E. *Who Is Rational? Studies of Individual Differences in Reasoning.* Mahwah, NJ: Lawrence Erlbaum Associates, 1999.

Symons, D. *The Evolution of Human Sexuality.* New York: Oxford University Press, 1979.

Symons, D. "Beauty is in the Adaptations of the Beholder: The Evolutionary Psychology of Human Female Sexual Attractiveness." *In* P. R. Abramson and S. D. Pinkerton (eds.), *Sexual Nature, Sexual Culture.* Chicago, IL: University of Chicago Press, 1995.

Tavris, C. *The Mismeasure of Women.* New York: Simon and Schuster, 1992.

Triandis, H. C. *Culture and Social Behavior.* New York: McGraw-Hill, 1994.

Tulving, E and Craik, F. I. M. *The Oxford Handbook of Memory.* Oxford, UK: Oxford University Press, 2000.

Vygotsky, L. S. *Mind in Society: The Development of Higher Psychological Processes.* Cambridge, MA: Harvard University Press, 1978.

Weiten, W. *Psychology: Themes and Variations.* Monterey, CA: Brooks/Cole Publishing, 1998.

Werner, E. E. and Smith, R. S. *Overcoming the Odds: High-Risk Children from Birth to Adulthood.* Ithaca, NY: Cornell University Press, 1992.

White, R. W. and Watt, N. F. *The Abnormal Personality (5th edition).* Chichester, UK: John Wiley and Sons, Inc., 1981.

Wickens, A. *Foundations of Biopsychology.* Harlow, UK: Prentice Hall, 2000.

Wilson, E. O. *Sociobiology: A New Synthesis.* Cambridge, MA: Harvard University Press, 1975.

Winkler, K. *Teens, Depression, and the Blues: A Hot Issue.* Springfield, NJ: Enslow publishers, 2000.

Wolman, B. (ed.). *Historical Roots of Contemporary Psychology.* New York: Harper and Row, 1968.

Wrightsman, L. S. and Sanford, F. H. *Psychology: A Scientific Study of Human Behavior.* Monterey, CA: Brooks/Cole Publishing, 1975.

Yap, P. M. *Comparative Psychiatry: A Theoretical Framework.* Toronto, Canada: University of Toronto Press, 1974.

Zarit, S. H. and Knight, B. G. *A Guide to Psychotherapy and Aging.* Washington, DC: American Psychological Association, 1997.

Useful Websites

Amazing Optical Illusions
http://www.optillusions.com
See your favorite optical illusions at this fun site.

American Psychological Association
http://www.apa.org
Here you can read a peer-reviewed e-journal published by the APA, follow the development of new ethical guidelines for pscychologists, and find a wealth of other information.

Association for Advancement of Behavior Therapy
http://www.aabt.org
An interdisciplinary organization concerned with the application of behavioral and cognitive sciences to the understanding of human behavior.

Association for Cross-Cultural Psychology
http://www.fit.edu/CampusLife/clubs-org/iaccp
Including a full-text downloadable version of their journal.

Bedlam
http://www.museum-london.org.uk/MOLsite/exhibits/bedlam/f_bed.htm
The Museum of London's online exhibition about Bedlam, the notorious mental institution.

Bipolar Disorders Information Center
http://www.mhsource.com/bipolar
Articles and information about bipolar 1 disorder.

Brain and Mind
http://www.epub.org.br/cm/home_i.htm
An online magazine with articles devoted to neuroscience, linguisitics, imprinting, and many other related topics.

Exploratorium
http://www.exploratorium.edu/exhibits/nf_exhibits.html
Click on "seeing" or "hearing" to check out visual and auditory illusions and other secrets of the mind.

Freud and Culture

http://www.loc.gov/exhibits/freud

An online Library of Congress exhibition that examines Sigmund Freud's life and key ideas and his effect on 20th-century thinking.

Jigsaw Classroom

http://www.jigsaw.org

The official web site of the Jigsaw Classroom, a cooperative learning technique that reduces racial conflict between schoolchildren. Learn about its history and how to implement the techniques.

Kidspsych

http://www.kidspsych.org/index1.html

American Psychological Association's childrens' site, with games and exercises for kids. Also useful for students of developmental psychology. Follow the "about this activity" links to find out the theories behind the fun and games.

Kismet

http://www.ai.mit.edu/projects/humanoid-robotics-group/kismet/kismet.html

Kismet is the MIT's expressive robot, which has perceptual and motor functions tailored to natural human communication channels.

Museum of Psychological Instrumentation

http://chss.montclair.edu/psychology/museum/museum.html

Look at images of early psychological laboratory research apparatus, such as Wilhelm Wundt's eye motion demonstrator.

National Academy of Neuropsychology

http://nanonline.org/content/pages/research/acn.shtm

A site where you can download the archives of Clinical Neuropsychology, a journal that focuses on disorders of the central nervous system.

Neuroscience for Kids

http://faculty.washington.edu/chudler/neurok.html

A useful website for students and teachers who want to learn about the nervous system. Enjoy activities and experiments on your way to learning all about the brain and spinal cord.

National Eating Disorders Society

http://www.nationaleatingdisorders.org

Information on eating disorders, their precursors, how to help a friend, and the importance of treatment.

Neuroscience Tutorial

http://thalamus.wustl.edu/course

The Washington University School of Medicine's online tutorial offers an illustrated guide to the basics of clinical neuroscience, with useful artworks and user-friendly text.

Online Dictionary of Mental Health

http://www.shef.ac.uk/~psysc/psychotherapy

The Centre for Psychotherapeutic Studies at Sheffield University, UK, runs this online dictionary. There are links to many sites offering different viewpoints on major mental health issues.

Personality Theories

http://www.ship.edu/~cgboeree/perscontents.html

An electronic textbook covering personality theories for undergraduate and graduate courses.

Psychology Central

http://emerson.thomsonlearning.com/psych

Links to many useful articles grouped by subject as well as cool, animated figures that improve your understanding of psychological principles.

Schizophrenia.com

http://www.schizophrenia.com

Information and resources on this mental disorder provided by a charitable organization.

Seeing, Hearing, and Smelling the World

http://www.hhmi.org/senses/

A downloadable illustrated book dealing with perception from the Howard Hughes Medical Institute.

Sigmund Freud Museum

http://freud.t0.or.at/freud/

The online Sigmund Freud Museum has videos and audio recordings of the famous psychoanalyst—there are even images of Freud's famous couch.

Social Psychology Network

http://www.socialpsychology.org

The largest social psychology database on the Internet. Within these pages you will find more than 5,000 links to psychology-related resources and research groups, and there is also a useful section on general psychology.

Stanford Prison Experiment

http://www.prisonexp.org/

A fascinating look at the Stanford Prison Experiment, which saw subjects placed in a prison to see what happens to "good people in a bad environment." Learn why the experiment had to be abandoned after six days due to the unforeseen severity of the effects on participants.

Stroop effect

http://www.dcity.org/braingames/stroop/index.htm

Take part in an online psychological experiment to see the Stroop effect in action.

Quote Attributions

opening quote

> **Abnormal Psychology**
>
> ## What Is Abnormality?
>
> — Investigating an indefinite concept —
>
> The scientific study of psychological disorders, or "psychopathology," is sometimes referred to as the field of abnormal psychology. One of the first major issues students of abnormal psychology encounter is that the answers to questions like "What is abnormal?" and "What is a mental disorder?" are constantly evolving. Guidelines have been established, however, that help psychologists and others diagnose and treat people suffering from mental disorders, which can cause distress, fear, and sometimes even physical pain in sufferers or those around them.
>
> A young man in his first year at college feels sad and lonely as he tries to adjust to living away from home for the first time. A woman begins to panic when she drives over a bridge. A little boy has difficulty learning to speak. A grandmother feels disoriented and can't remember how to get home. Are these people having abnormal experiences? Do they have a mental disorder? The answers to these questions are complex and depend on who is answering them. That is because terms like "abnormal" and "mental disorder" are in part defined by social and cultural beliefs, which differ from culture to culture and change over time. This is not to say that some mental disorders might not have physical causes. Many are firmly based in biology, but it is not possible to diagnose or identify mental disorders with simple medical procedures, such as blood tests. In many cases (for example, phobias) there may be no biological cause to detect. Even if there is a biological cause, it is often difficult for a psychologist to determine whether or not a person needs treatment, and what sort of treatment that should be. In such cases a clinician's definitions of abnormality and mental disorders and their severity are crucial.
>
> *Whether or not someone is diagnosed as having a mental, or psychological, disorder has many important implications. For example, during a trial (below), if defendants are found to be mentally disordered, they might receive a different sentence than if they were considered psychologically healthy.*
>
> *"nearly half of all Americans will experience a mental or emotional problem at least once during their lifetime that, if diagnosed, would be classified as a mental disorder."*
> —R. C. Kessler and others, 1994
>
> Although there is no one definitive definition of psychological abnormality, a variety of definitions have been proposed and accepted. In the United States one official definition of mental disorders that is accepted by a large number of mental health professionals, despite some critics, can be found in the *Diagnostic and Statistical Manual of Mental Disorders*—or the DSM (see box p. 9). The DSM is published by the American Psychiatric Association (APA) to help psychologists, psychiatrists, and other medical professionals identify and diagnose psychological problems.
>
> 6

quote

Each chapter in *Psychology* contains quotes that relate to the topics covered. These quotes appear both within the main text and at the start of the chapters, and their attributions are detailed here. Quotes are listed in the order that they appear in the chapter, and the page numbers at the end of each attribution refer to the pages in this volume where the quote appears.

History of the Brain

Aristotle. *De Motu Animalium. c.* 350 B.C., p.6.

Horax, G. *Neurosurgery: An Historical Sketch.* Springfield, IL: Thomas, 1952, p. 7.

Penfield, W. and Roberts, L. *Speech and Brain Mechanisms.* Princeton, NJ: Princeton University Press, 1959, p. 13.

Biology of the Brain

Maugham, W. S. *The Summing Up.* Toronto, Canada: Heinemann, 1938, p. 29.

Sherrington, C. S. *The Integrative Action of the Nervous System.* New York: Scribner's Sons, 1906, p. 32.

Noordenbos, W. *Pain: Problems Pertaining to the Transmission of Nerve Impulses Which Give Rise to Pain.* Amsterdam, Nederlands: Elsevier, 1959, p. 37.

The Mind

Aristotle. *De Anima, c.* 350 B.C, p. 40

Descartes, R. *Discourse on the Method of Rightly Conducting the Reason, and Seeking Truth in the Sciences.* 1637, p. 41.

Locke, J. *An Essay Concerning Human Understanding.* 1690, p. 42.

Kant, I. *Critique of Pure Reason.* 1787, p. 44.

Churchland, P. "Can Neurobiology Teach Us Anything About Consciousness?" Presentation at the University of California, San Diego. 1995, p. 48.

Searle, J. R. *The Rediscovery of the Mind.* Cambridge, MA: MIT Press, 1992, p. 49.

Sacks, O. W. *Awakenings.* London: Duckworth, 1973, p. 51

Jackson, J. H. Cited in J. Taylor, *Selected Writings of John Hughlings Jackson.* London, U.K: Hodder and Stoughton, 1931, p. 55.

Perception

Swift, J. (1667–1745). Unpublished quote, p. 62.

Abram, D. "The Perceptual Implications of Gaia." *Ecologist,* **15**, 1985, p.62.

Barry, M. A. S. *Visual Intelligence: Perception, Image, and Manipulation in Visual Communication.* Albany, NY: State University of New York Press, 1997, p.65.

Hubel, D. "The Brain." *Scientific American,* **241**, 1979, p. 70.

Carroll, L. *Through the Looking Glass and What Alice Found There.* 1871, p. 74.

Clarke, A. C. *Report on Planet Three and Other Speculations.* New York: Harper and Row, 1972, p. 78.

Bagehat, W. *Physics and Politics.* 1869, p. 81.

Keller, H. *The Story of My Life.* 1903, p. 83.

Emotion and Motivation

Darwin, C. R. *The Expression of Emotions in Man and Animals.* 1872, p. 87.

Ekman, P. *et al.* "Workshop on Facial Expression Understanding." *At* http://mambo.ucsu.edu/psl/nsf.txt, 1992, p. 88.

Malik, K. "An Expression of the Facts." *Independent on Sunday,* February 1, 1998, p. 90.

James, W. *The Varieties of Religious Experience.* 1902, p. 92.

Greenberg, L. S. and Safran, J. D. *Emotion in Psychotherapy: Affect, Cognition, and the Process of Change.* New York: Guilford Press, 1987, p. 94.

Hippocrates. *On the Sacred Disease. c.* 400 B.C., p. 100.

Maclean, P. *The Triune Brain in Evolution.* New York: Plenum Press, 1990, p. 104.

Consciousness

Mumford, L. *The Conduct of Life*. New York: Harcourt, Brace, 1951, p. 111.

Nagel, T., "What Is It Like to Be a Bat?" *Philosophical Review*, **83**, 1974, p. 112.

Chalmers, D. *The Conscious Mind: In Search of a Fundamental Theory*. New York: Oxford University Press, 1996, p. 113.

Swami Sivananda, S. *Symbolisms in the Ramatana*. Rishikesh, India: Divine Life Society, 1947, p. 124.

Rolling Stone. Cited in J. Morgan and L. Zimmer, *New Public Health Policies and Programs for the Reduction of Drug-related Harm*. Toronto, Canada: University of Toronto Press, 1989, p. 126.

U.S. Department of Justice. *At* http://www.usdoj.gov/dea/concern/heroin.htm, 2002, p. 127.

Franklin, B. *The Way to Wealth*. 1757, p. 130.

Palahniuk, C. *Fight Club*. New York: Henry Holt, 1999, p. 131.

Crick, F. and Mitchison, G. "The Function of Dream Sleep." *Nature*, **304**, 1983, p. 133.

Freud, S. *The Interpretation of Dreams*. London, UK: Butler and Tanner, 1900, p. 134.

Jung, C. G. *Memories, Dreams, and Reflections*. New York: Vintage Books, 1957, p. 135.

The Bible. *Genesis* ch. 1. vr. 3, p. 139.

Artificial Minds

Champandard, A. J. "Intelligence Is a Long-term Objective." *The Field of Artificial Intelligence*, **16**, 2001, p. 140.

Mead, C. *Analog VLSI and Neural Systems*. Reading, MA: Addison-Wesley, 1989, p. 142.

Aristotle. *De Anima*, *c.* 350 B.C, p. 147.

Hofstadter, D. R. *Metamagical Themas: Questing for the Essence of the Mind and Pattern*. New York: Basic Books, p. 148.

McCarthy, J. "Mathematical Logic in Artificial Intelligence." *In* S. R. Graubard (ed.), *The Artificial Intelligence Debate: False Starts, Real Foundations*. Cambridge, MA: MIT Press, 1990, p. 149.

Waltz, D. "The Prospects for Building Truly Intelligent Machines." *In* S. R. Graubard (ed.), *The Artificial Intelligence Debate: False Starts, Real Foundations.* Cambridge, MA: MIT Press, 1990, p. 151.

Penrose, R. *The Emperor's New Mind*. Oxford, UK: Oxford University Press, 1990, p. 152.

Moravec, H. P. *Mind Children: The Future of Robot and Human Intelligence*. Cambridge, MA: Harvard University Press, 1988, p. 154.

Newell, A. "Fairy Tales." *AI Magazine*, **13**, 1992, p. 160.

Margulis, L. and Sagan, D. *Microcosmos: Four Billion Years of Microbial Evolution*. Berkeley, CA: University of California Press, 1997, p. 163.

Arnheim, R. *Visual Thinking*. Berkeley, CA: University of California Press, 1969, p. 161.

Every effort has been made to attribute the quotes throughout *Psychology* correctly. Any errors or omissions brought to the attention of the publisher are regretted and will be credited in subsequent editions.

Set Index